Orion Books Ltd
Orion House
5 Upper St Martin's Lane
London WC2H 9EA

First published by Orion in 2004

Drawings by Michael Martin

Cover illustrations by Alex Graham

© Associated Newspapers plc 2004

ISBN 0 75285 930 7

Printed and bound in Great Britain by
Butler & Tanner Ltd, Frome and London

www.orionbooks.co.uk

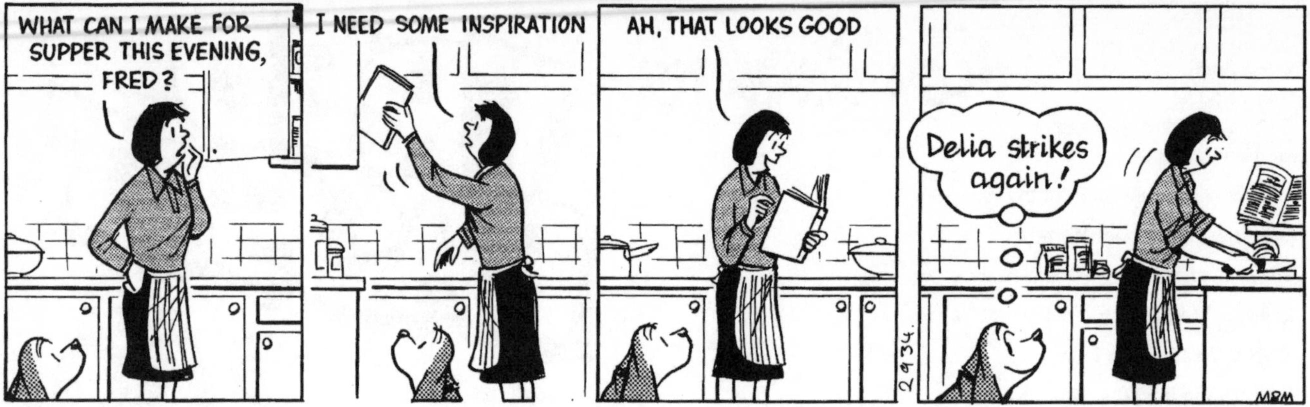
WHAT CAN I MAKE FOR SUPPER THIS EVENING, FRED?
I NEED SOME INSPIRATION
AH, THAT LOOKS GOOD
2934.
Delia strikes again!
M&M

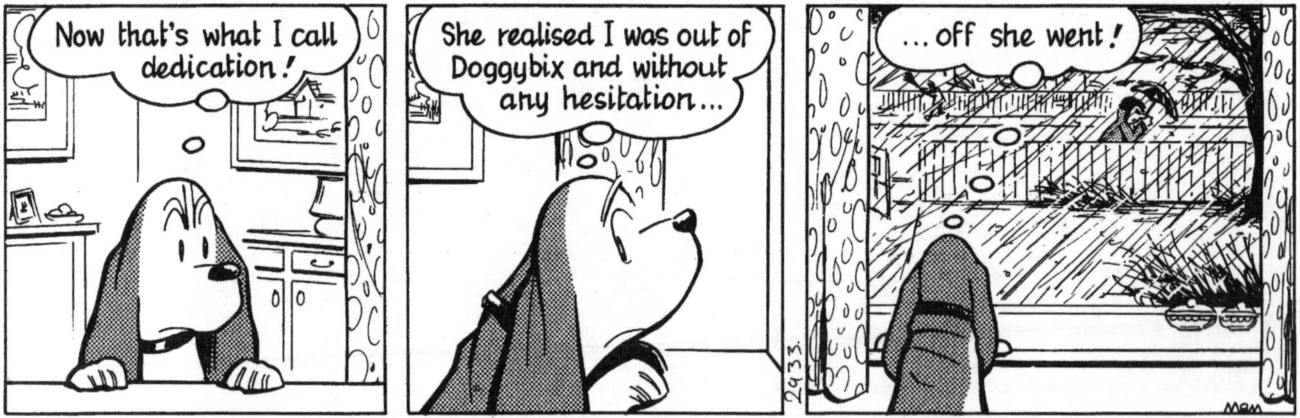
Now that's what I call dedication!
She realised I was out of Doggybix and without any hesitation...
2933.
...off she went!
M&M

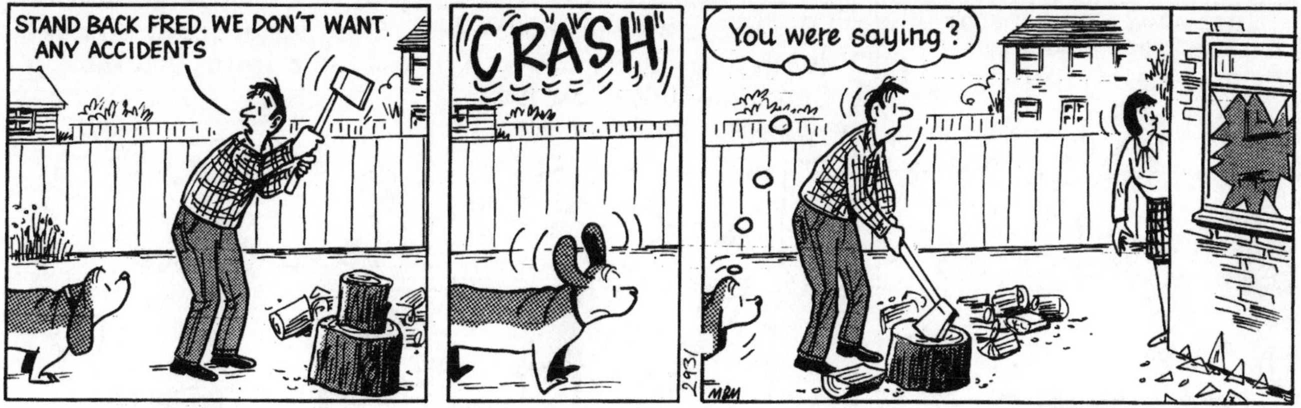
STAND BACK FRED. WE DON'T WANT ANY ACCIDENTS
CRASH
You were saying?
2931
MBM

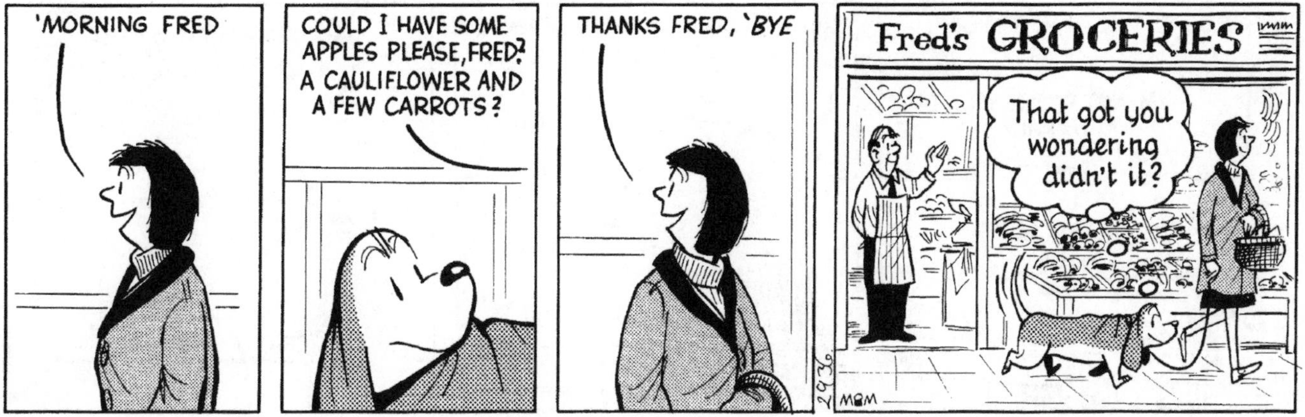
'MORNING FRED
COULD I HAVE SOME APPLES PLEASE, FRED? A CAULIFLOWER AND A FEW CARROTS?
THANKS FRED, 'BYE
Fred's GROCERIES
That got you wondering didn't it?
2936
MBM

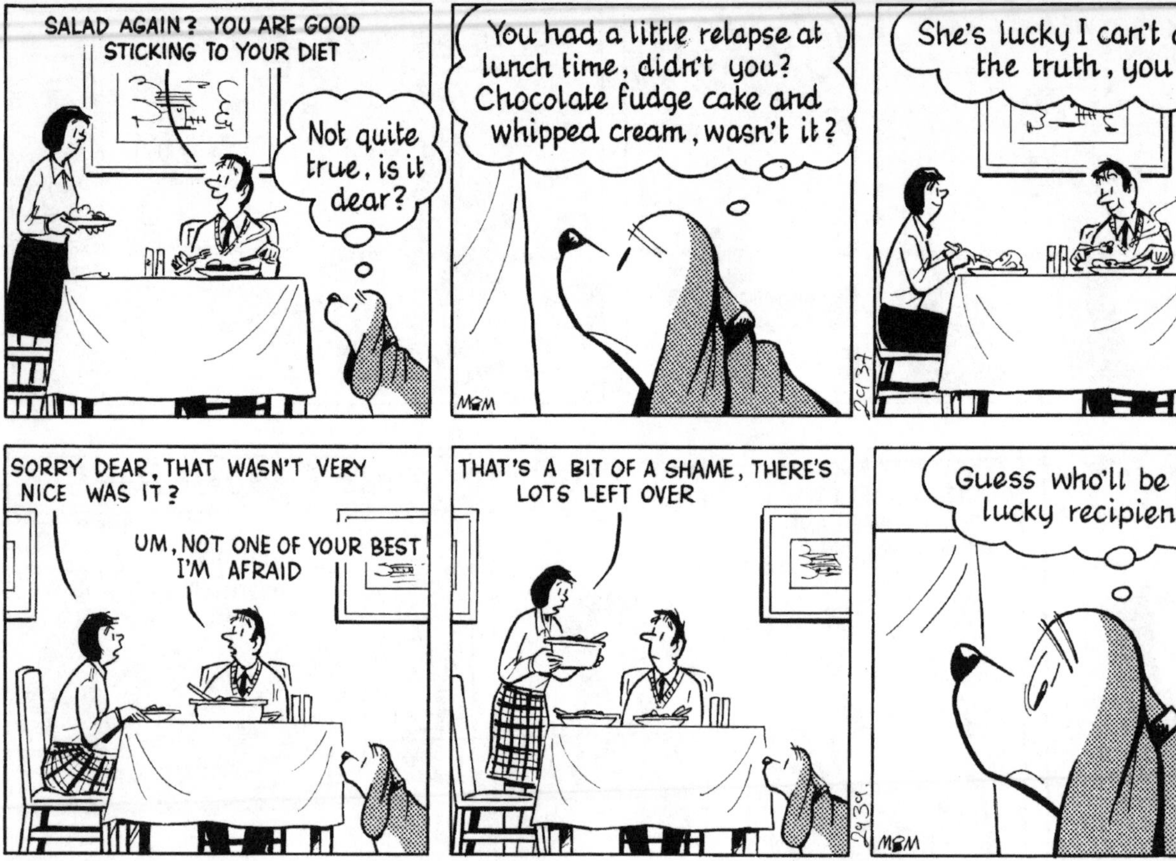
SALAD AGAIN? YOU ARE GOOD STICKING TO YOUR DIET
Not quite true, is it dear?
You had a little relapse at lunch time, didn't you? Chocolate fudge cake and whipped cream, wasn't it?
She's lucky I can't divulge the truth, you know!
SORRY DEAR, THAT WASN'T VERY NICE WAS IT?
UM, NOT ONE OF YOUR BEST I'M AFRAID
THAT'S A BIT OF A SHAME, THERE'S LOTS LEFT OVER
Guess who'll be the lucky recipient?

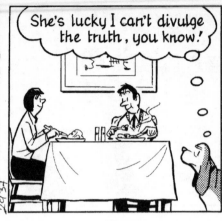

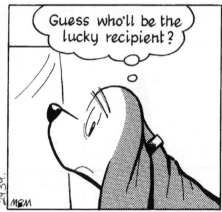

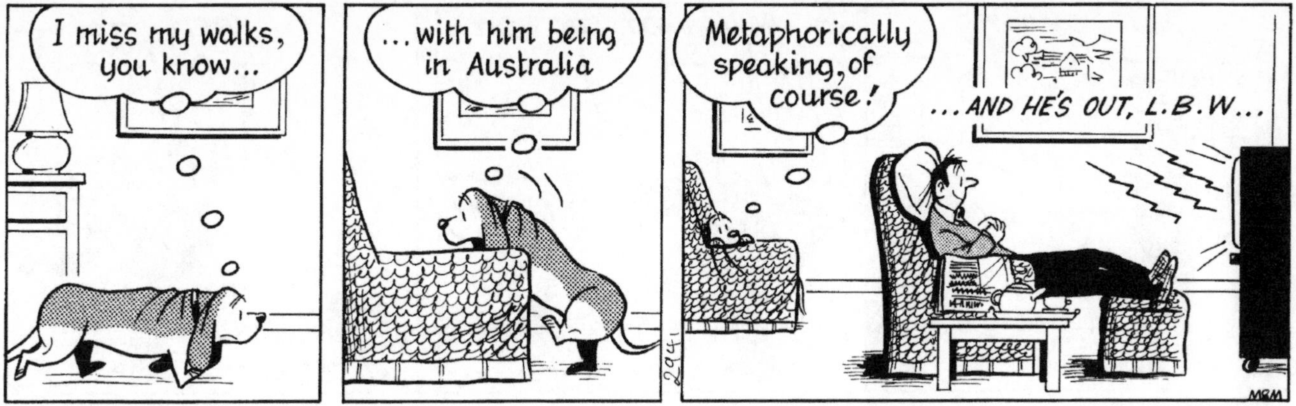
I miss my walks, you know...
...with him being in Australia
Metaphorically speaking, of course!
...AND HE'S OUT, L.B.W...
2944
MBM

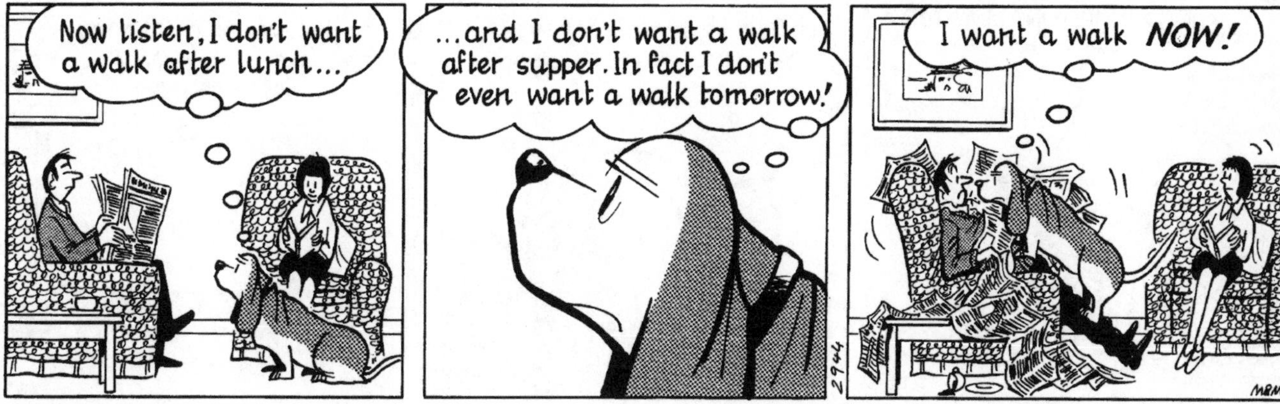
Now listen, I don't want a walk after lunch...
...and I don't want a walk after supper. In fact I don't even want a walk tomorrow!
I want a walk **NOW!**
2944
MBM

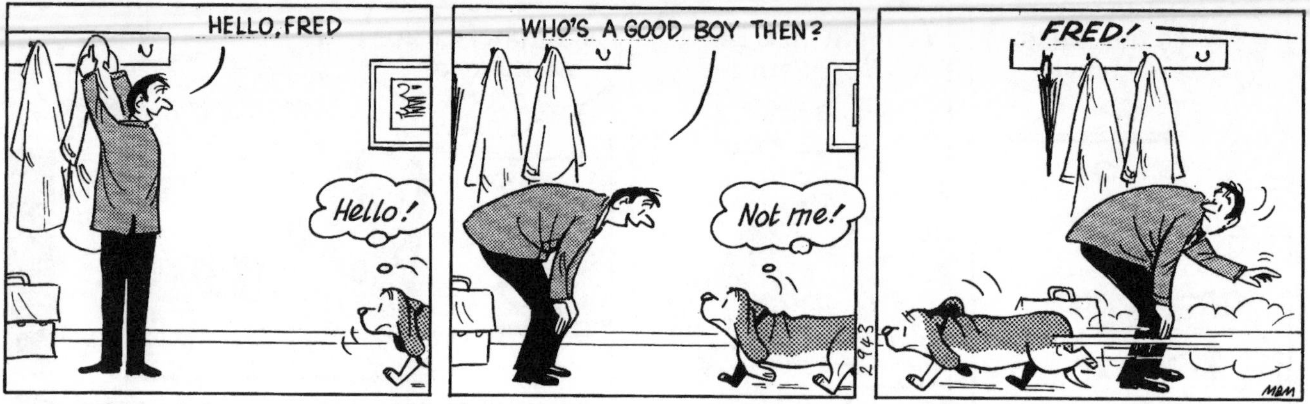
HELLO, FRED
Hello!
WHO'S A GOOD BOY THEN?
Not me!
FRED!

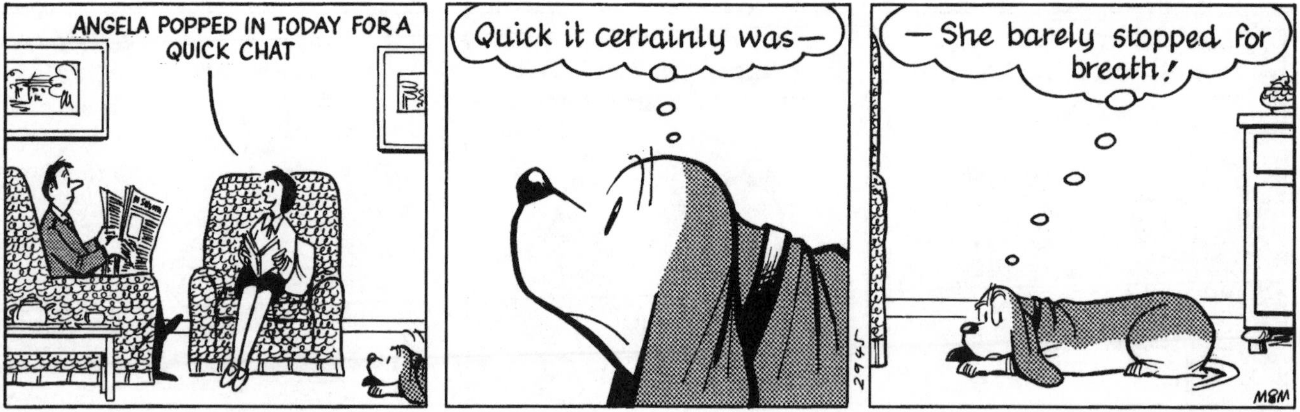
ANGELA POPPED IN TODAY FOR A QUICK CHAT
Quick it certainly was—
—She barely stopped for breath!

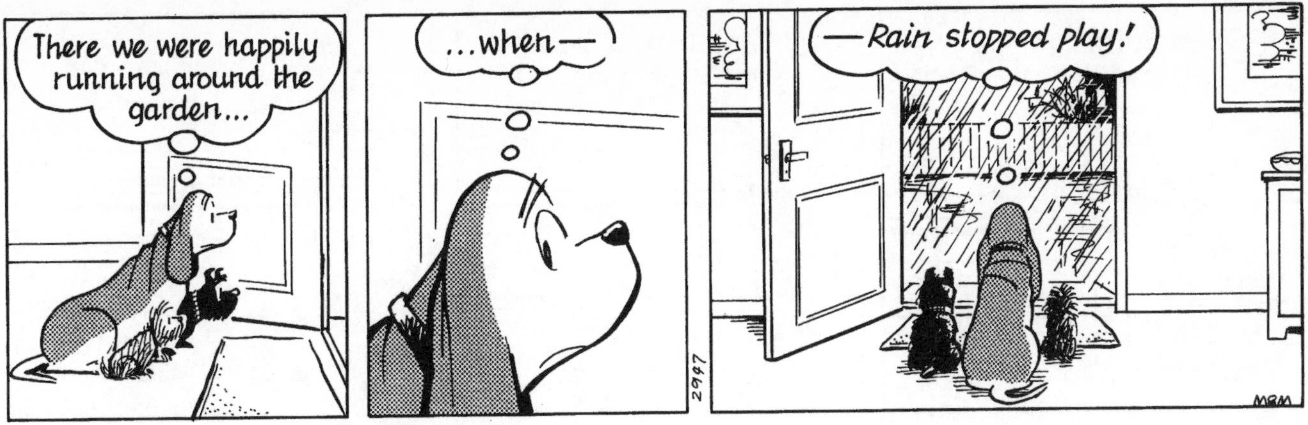
There we were happily running around the garden...
...when—
—Rain stopped play!
2947
MGM

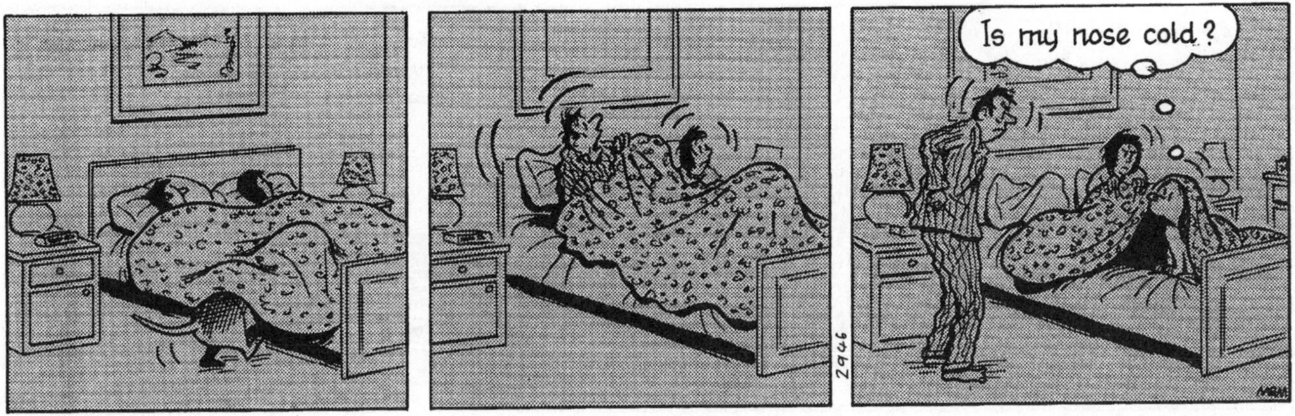
Is my nose cold?
2946
MGM

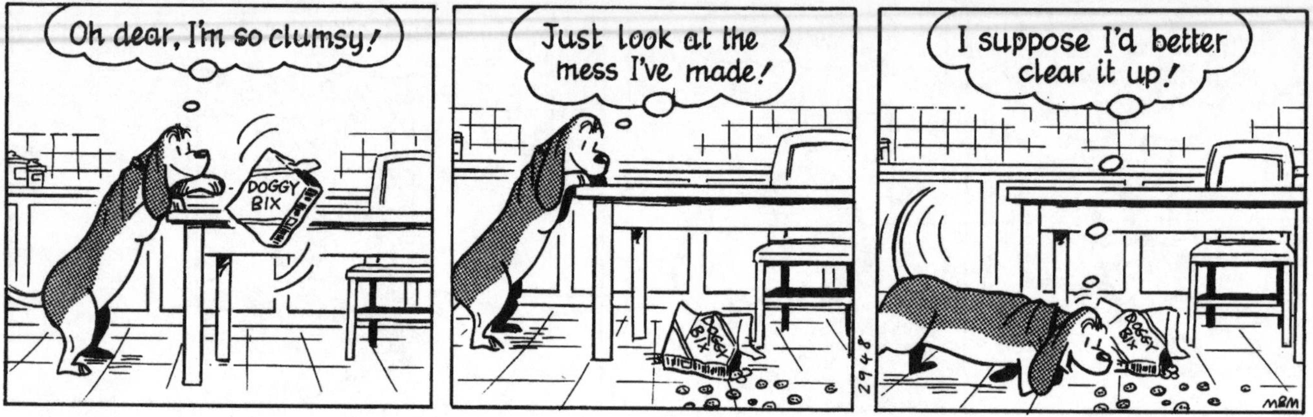
Oh dear, I'm so clumsy!
DOGGY BIX
Just look at the mess I've made!
I suppose I'd better clear it up!
2948
MBM

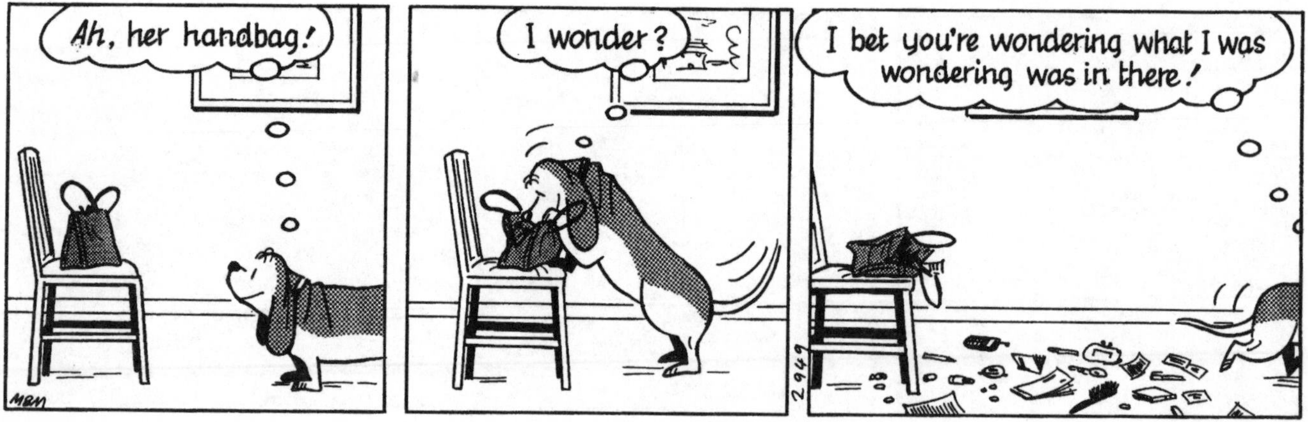
Ah, her handbag!
MBM
I wonder?
I bet you're wondering what I was wondering was in there!
2949

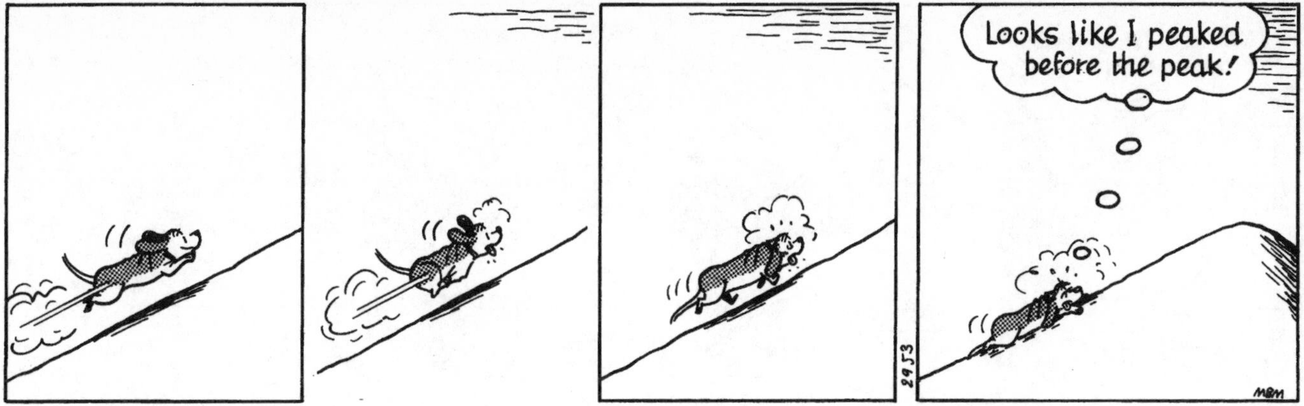
Looks like I peaked before the peak!
2953
MBM

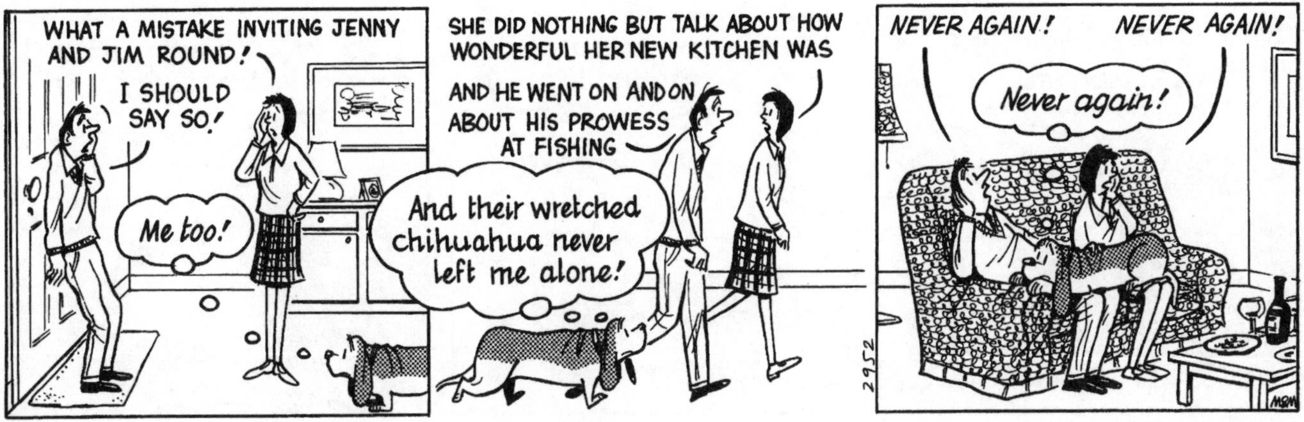
WHAT A MISTAKE INVITING JENNY AND JIM ROUND!
I SHOULD SAY SO!
Me too!
SHE DID NOTHING BUT TALK ABOUT HOW WONDERFUL HER NEW KITCHEN WAS
AND HE WENT ON AND ON ABOUT HIS PROWESS AT FISHING
And their wretched chihuahua never left me alone!
NEVER AGAIN!
NEVER AGAIN!
Never again!
2952
MBM

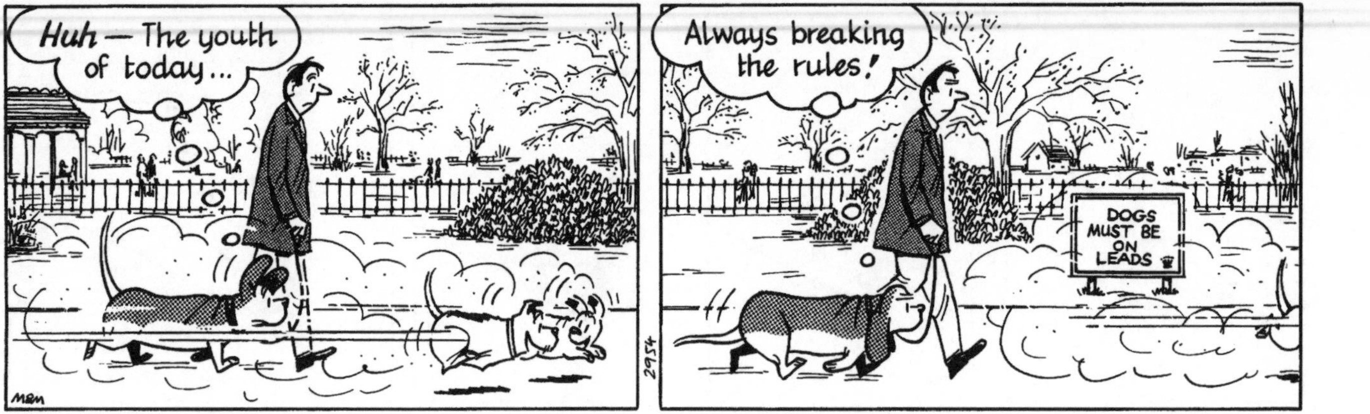
Huh — The youth of today...
Always breaking the rules!
DOGS MUST BE ON LEADS
2954

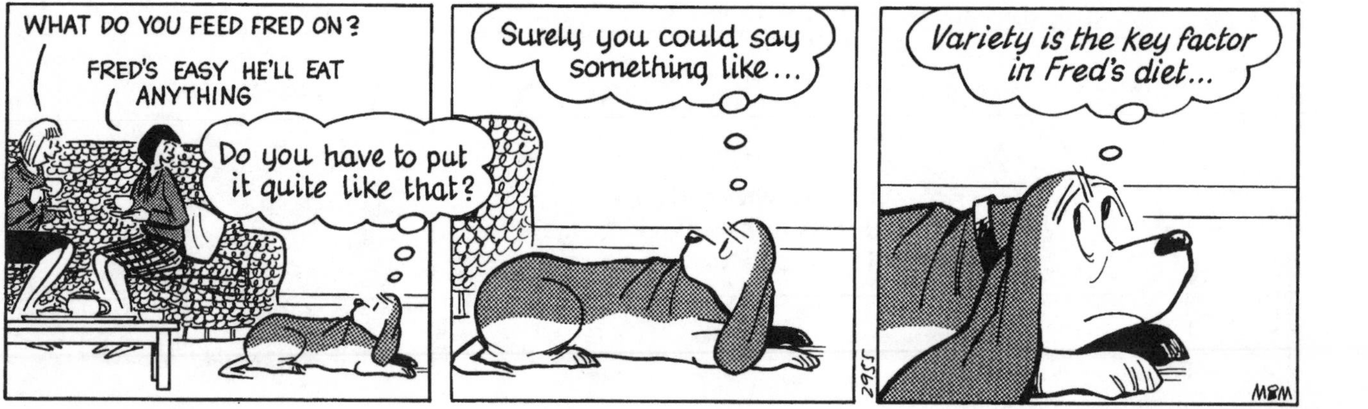
WHAT DO YOU FEED FRED ON?
FRED'S EASY HE'LL EAT ANYTHING
Do you have to put it quite like that?
Surely you could say something like...
Variety is the key factor in Fred's diet...
2955

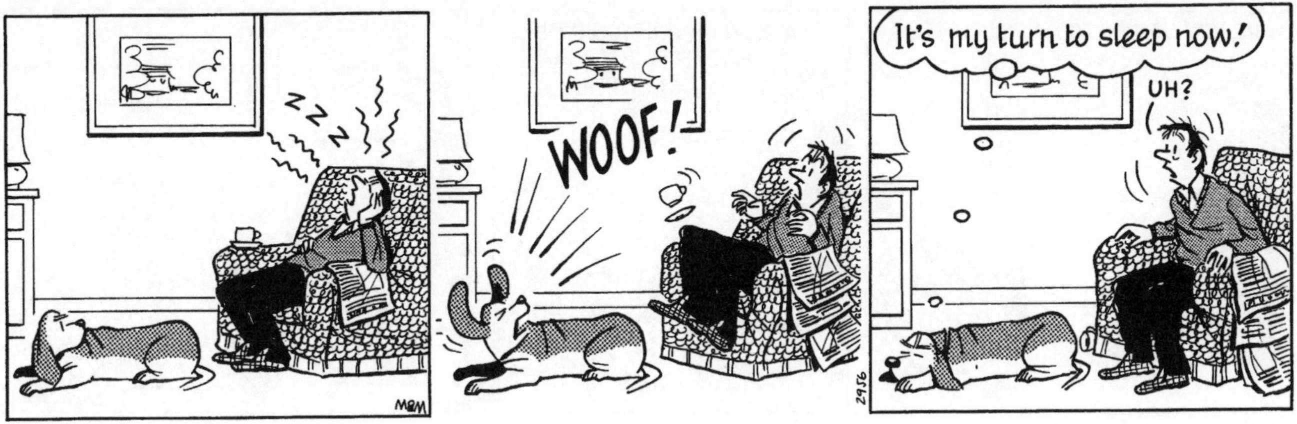
Z Z Z
WOOF!
It's my turn to sleep now!
UH?

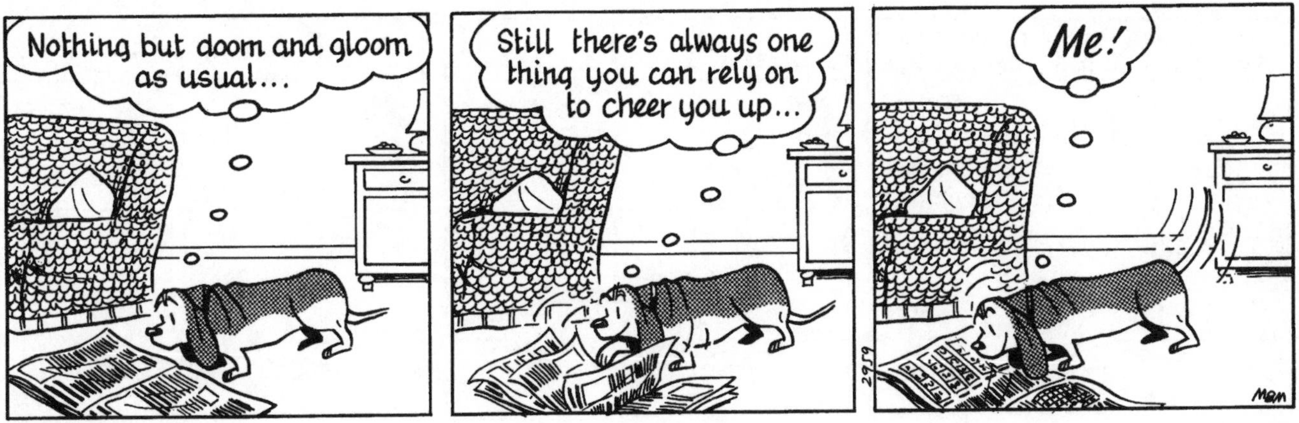
Nothing but doom and gloom as usual...
Still there's always one thing you can rely on to cheer you up...
Me!

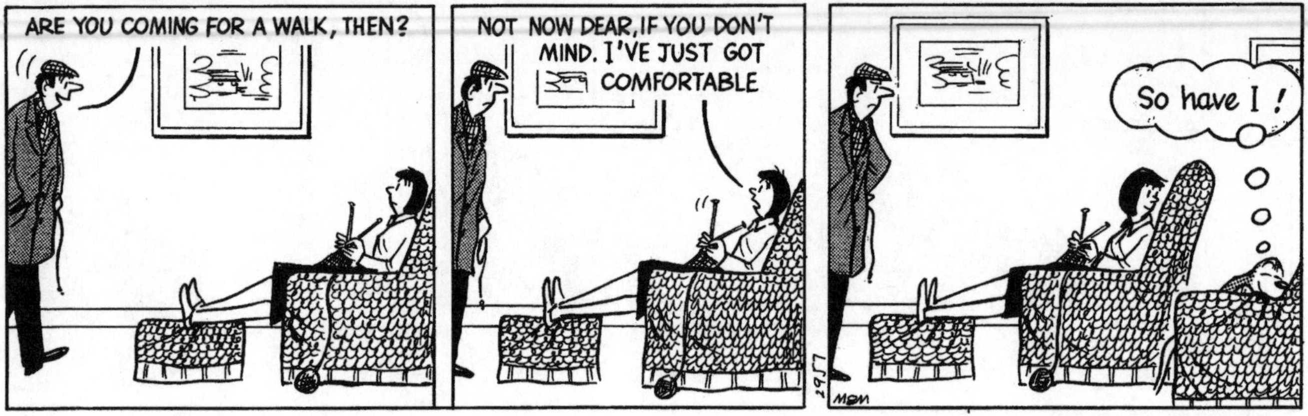
ARE YOU COMING FOR A WALK, THEN?
NOT NOW DEAR, IF YOU DON'T MIND. I'VE JUST GOT COMFORTABLE
So have I !
2957

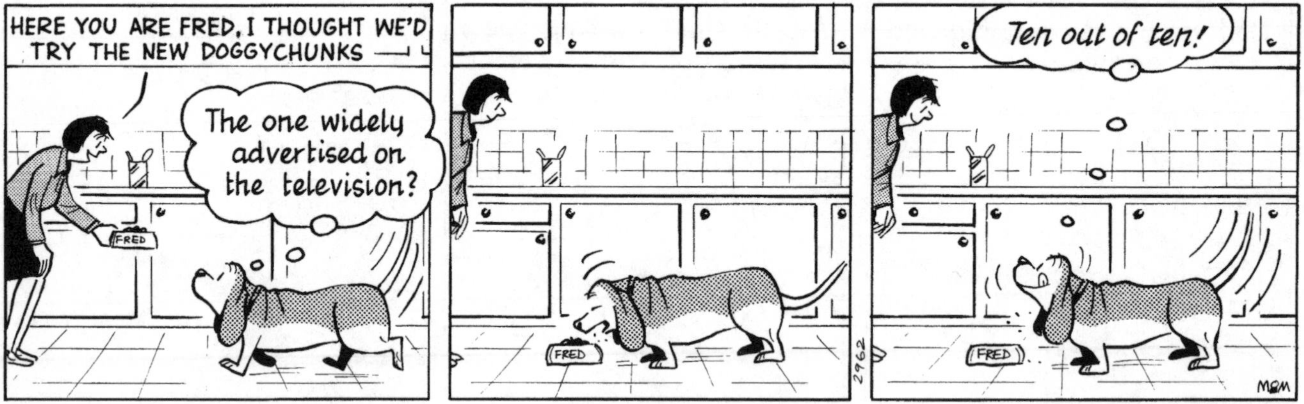
HERE YOU ARE FRED, I THOUGHT WE'D TRY THE NEW DOGGYCHUNKS
The one widely advertised on the television?
FRED
FRED
2962
Ten out of ten!
FRED

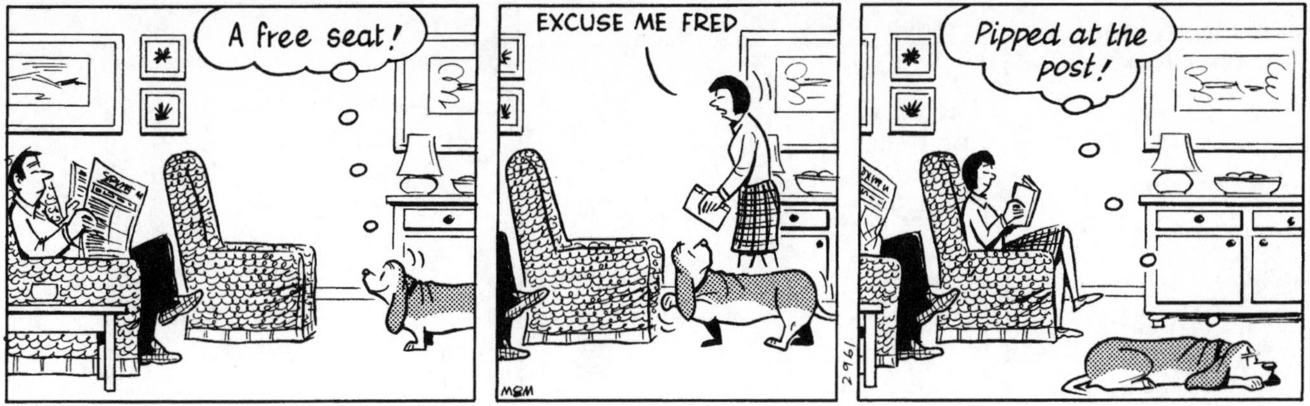
A free seat!
EXCUSE ME FRED
MSM
2961
Pipped at the post!

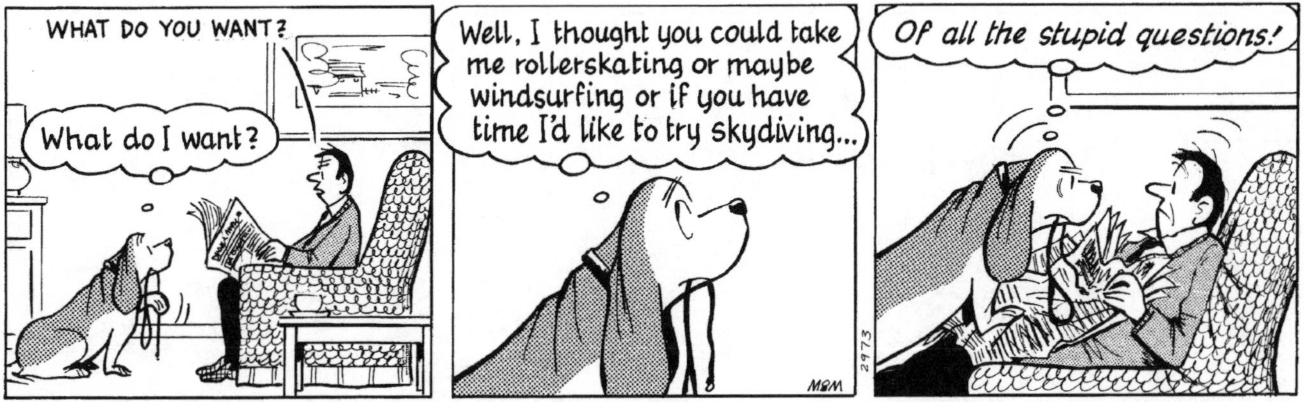
WHAT DO YOU WANT?
What do I want?
Well, I thought you could take me rollerskating or maybe windsurfing or if you have time I'd like to try skydiving...
MSM
2973
Of all the stupid questions!

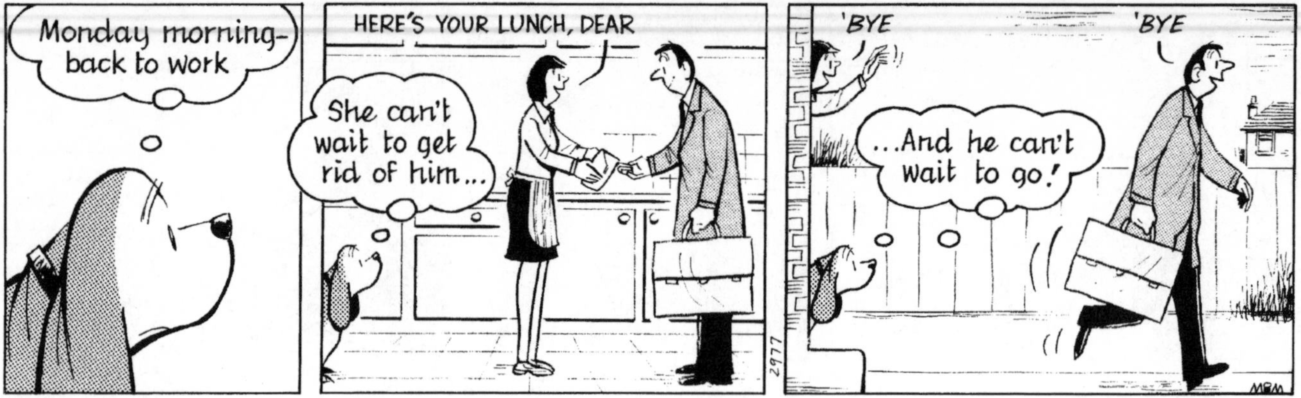
Monday morning-
back to work
HERE'S YOUR LUNCH, DEAR
She can't
wait to get
rid of him...
'BYE
'BYE
...And he can't
wait to go!
2977

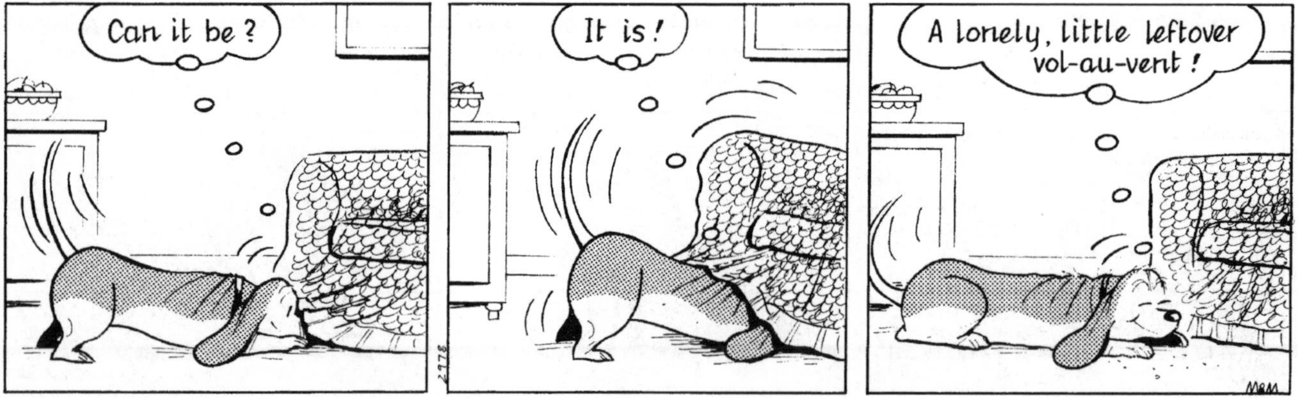
Can it be?
It is!
A lonely, little leftover
vol-au-vent!
2978

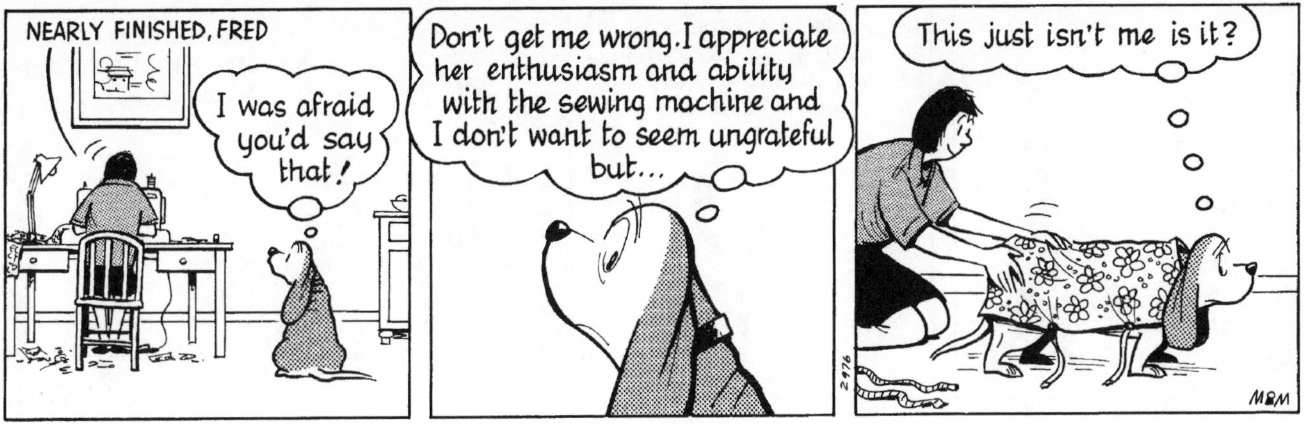
NEARLY FINISHED, FRED
I was afraid you'd say that!
Don't get me wrong. I appreciate her enthusiasm and ability with the sewing machine and I don't want to seem ungrateful but...
This just isn't me is it?

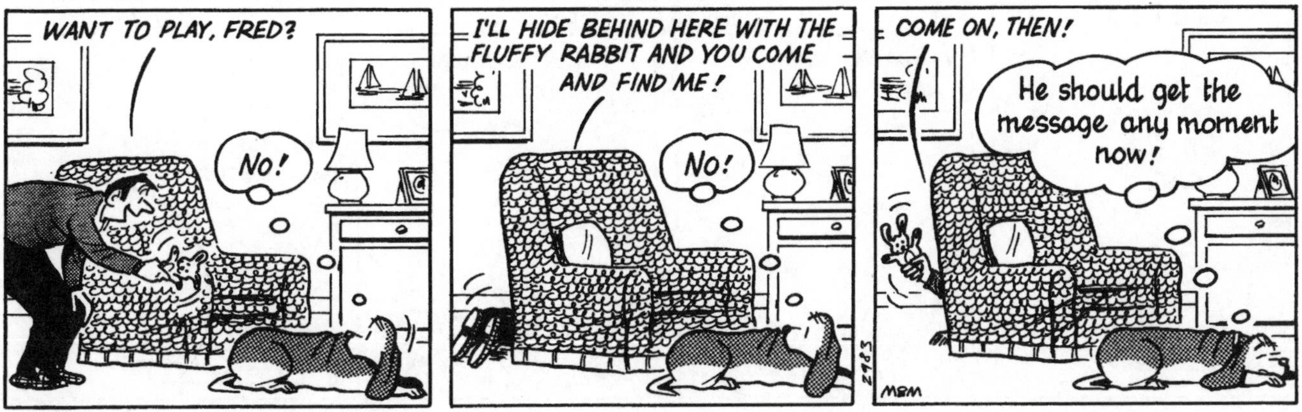
WANT TO PLAY, FRED?
No!
I'LL HIDE BEHIND HERE WITH THE FLUFFY RABBIT AND YOU COME AND FIND ME!
No!
COME ON, THEN!
He should get the message any moment now!

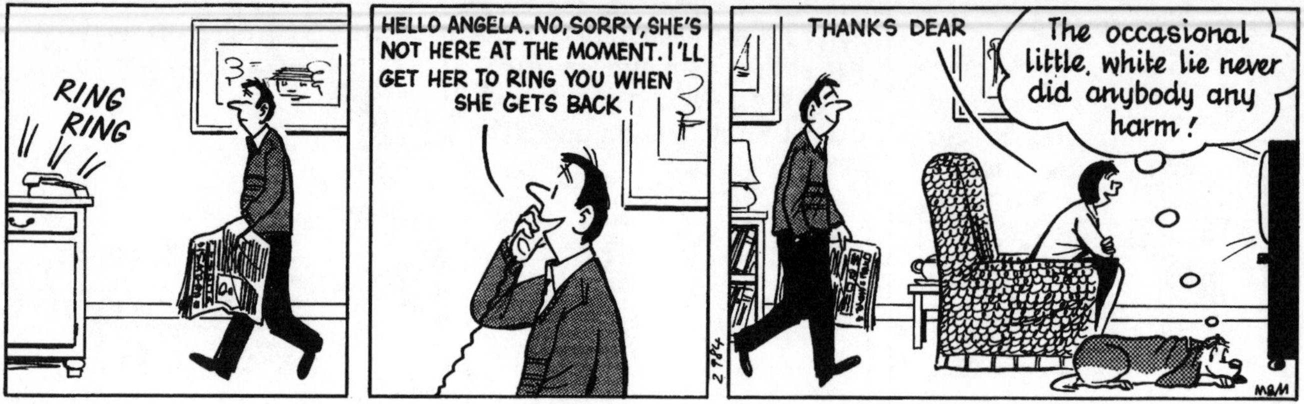
RING RING
HELLO ANGELA. NO, SORRY, SHE'S NOT HERE AT THE MOMENT. I'LL GET HER TO RING YOU WHEN SHE GETS BACK
THANKS DEAR
The occasional little, white lie never did anybody any harm!

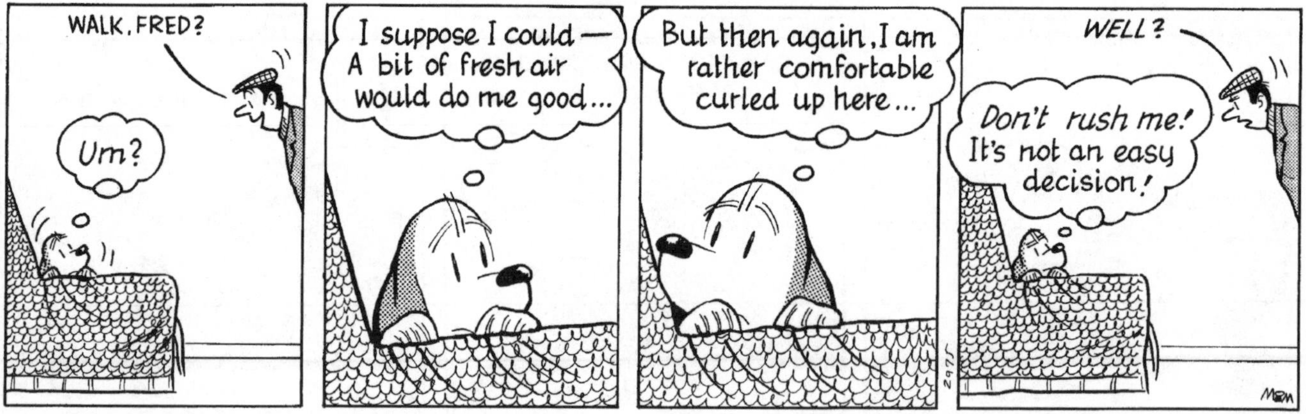
WALK, FRED?
Um?
I suppose I could — A bit of fresh air would do me good...
But then again, I am rather comfortable curled up here...
WELL?
Don't rush me! It's not an easy decision!

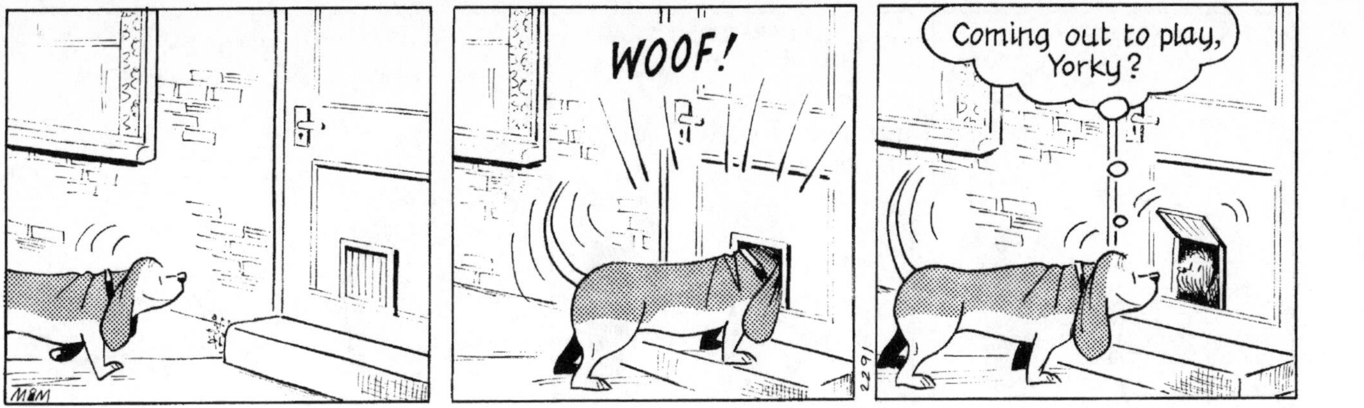
M&M
WOOF!
Coming out to play, Yorky?
2291

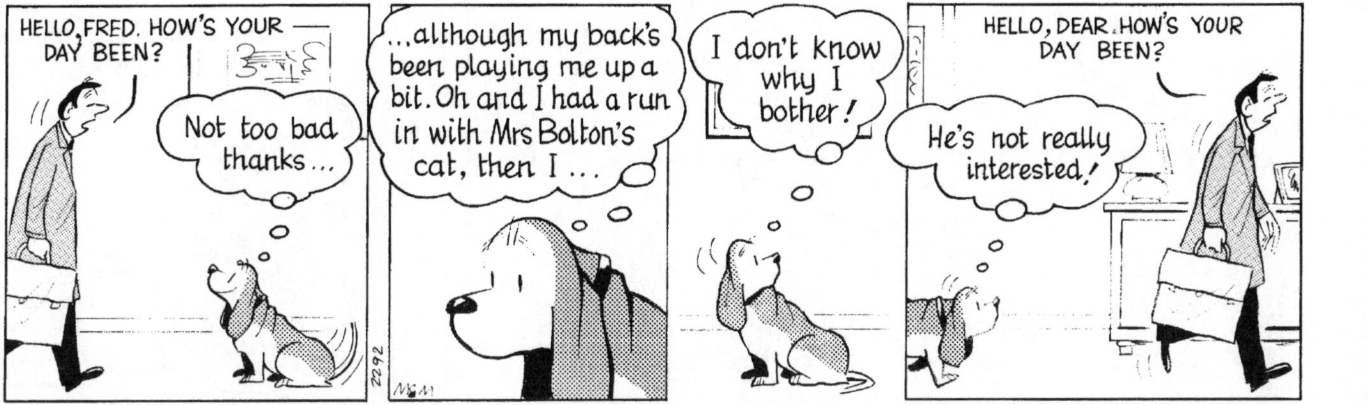
HELLO, FRED. HOW'S YOUR DAY BEEN?
Not too bad thanks...
2292
...although my back's been playing me up a bit. Oh and I had a run in with Mrs Bolton's cat, then I...
M&M
I don't know why I bother!
HELLO, DEAR. HOW'S YOUR DAY BEEN?
He's not really interested!

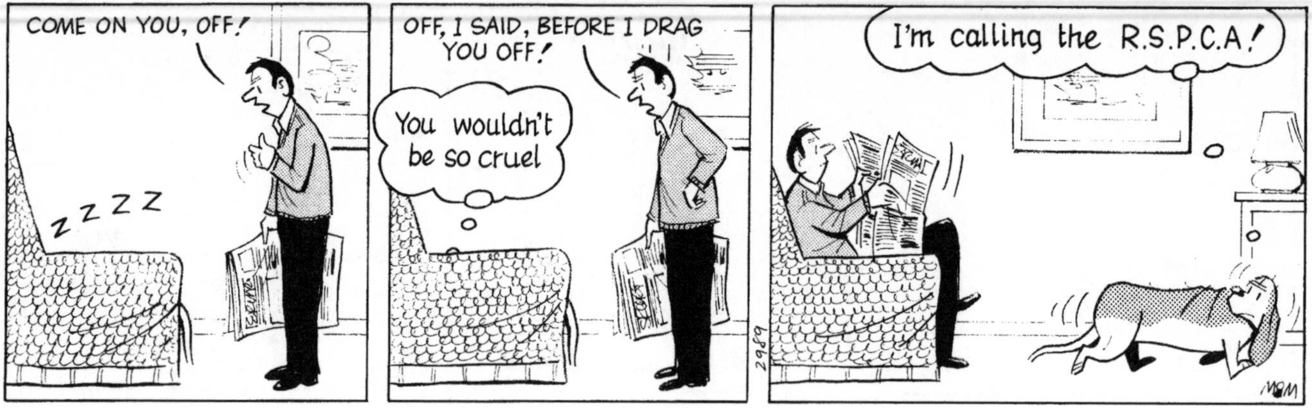
COME ON YOU, OFF!
Z Z Z Z
OFF, I SAID, BEFORE I DRAG YOU OFF!
You wouldn't be so cruel
2989
I'm calling the R.S.P.C.A!

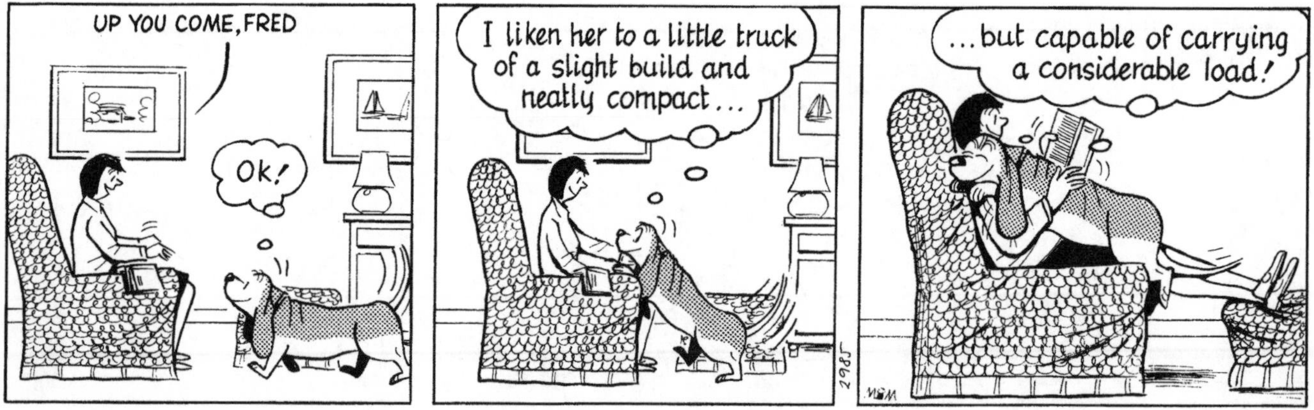
UP YOU COME, FRED
Ok!
I liken her to a little truck of a slight build and neatly compact ...
2985
... but capable of carrying a considerable load!

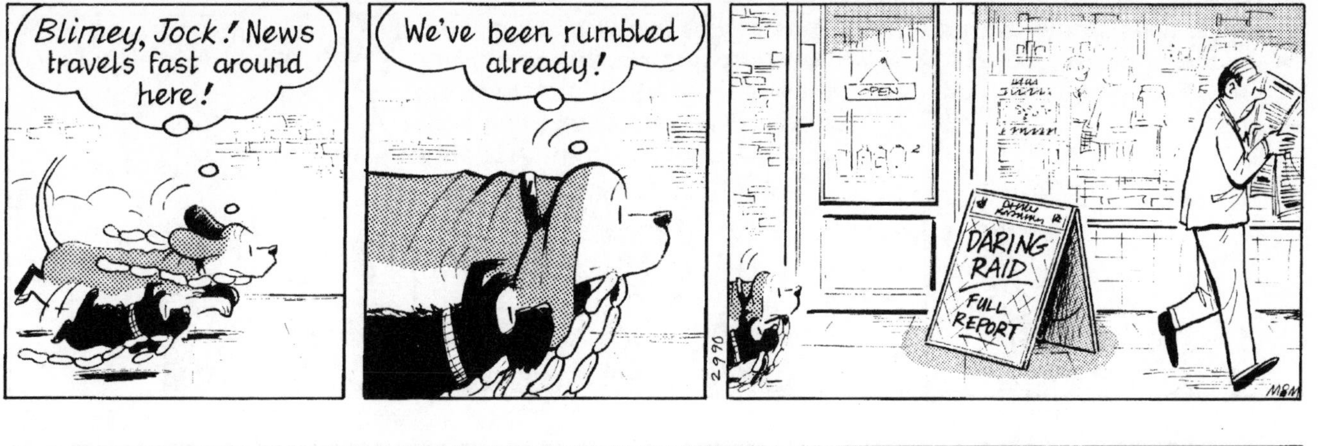
Blimey, Jock! News travels fast around here!
We've been rumbled already!
OPEN
DARING RAID
FULL REPORT
2990
MGM

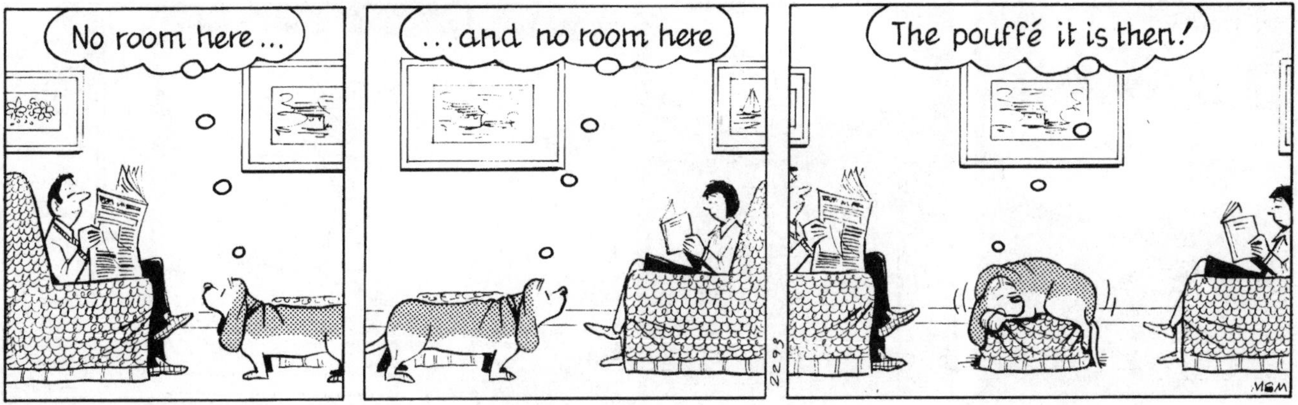
No room here ...
... and no room here
The pouffé it is then!
2293
MGM

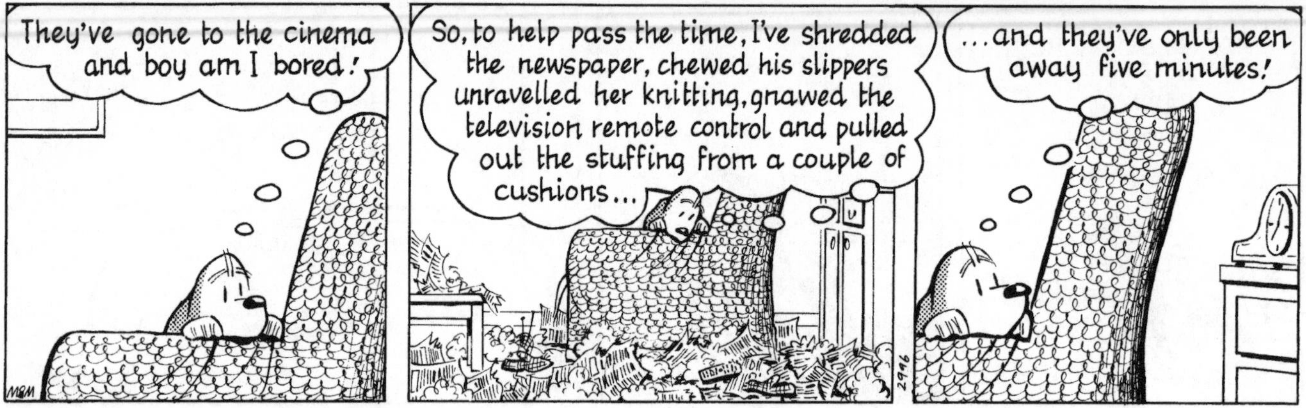
They've gone to the cinema and boy am I bored!
So, to help pass the time, I've shredded the newspaper, chewed his slippers unravelled her knitting, gnawed the television remote control and pulled out the stuffing from a couple of cushions...
...and they've only been away five minutes!

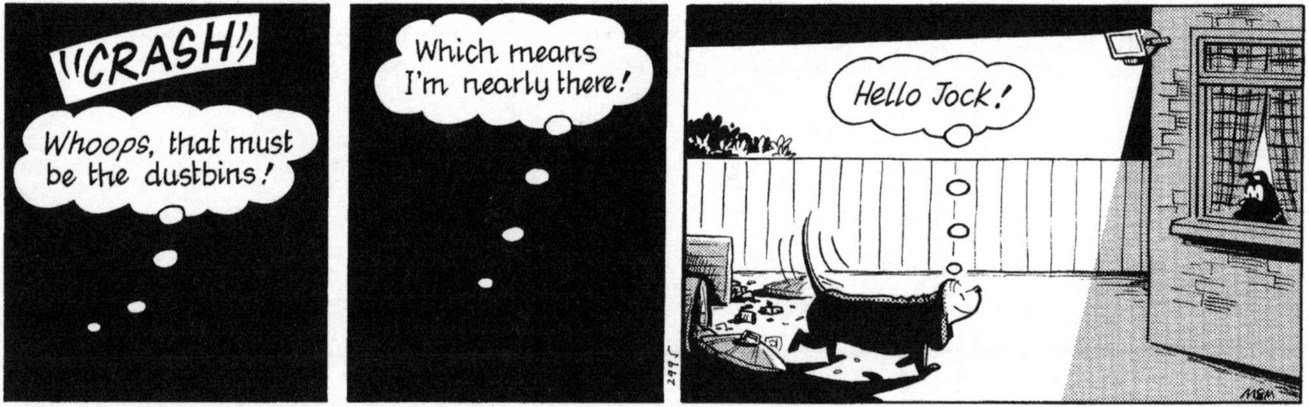
"CRASH"
Whoops, that must be the dustbins!
Which means I'm nearly there!
Hello Jock!

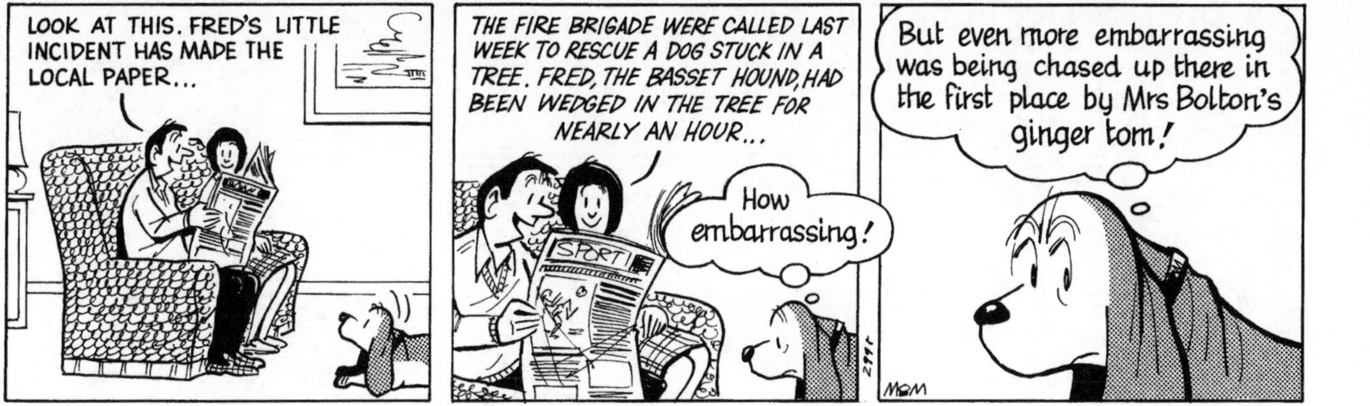
LOOK AT THIS. FRED'S LITTLE INCIDENT HAS MADE THE LOCAL PAPER...
SPORT
THE FIRE BRIGADE WERE CALLED LAST WEEK TO RESCUE A DOG STUCK IN A TREE. FRED, THE BASSET HOUND, HAD BEEN WEDGED IN THE TREE FOR NEARLY AN HOUR...
How embarrassing!
But even more embarrassing was being chased up there in the first place by Mrs Bolton's ginger tom!

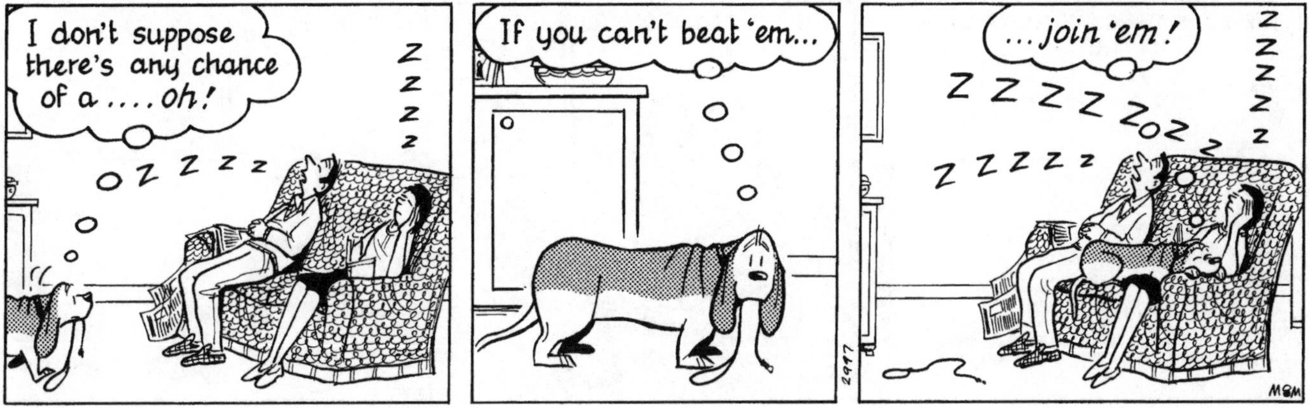
I don't suppose there's any chance of a .... oh!
Z Z Z Z
O Z Z Z Z
If you can't beat 'em...
... join 'em!
Z Z Z Z Z ZOZ Z Z
Z Z Z Z Z
Z Z Z Z Z Z

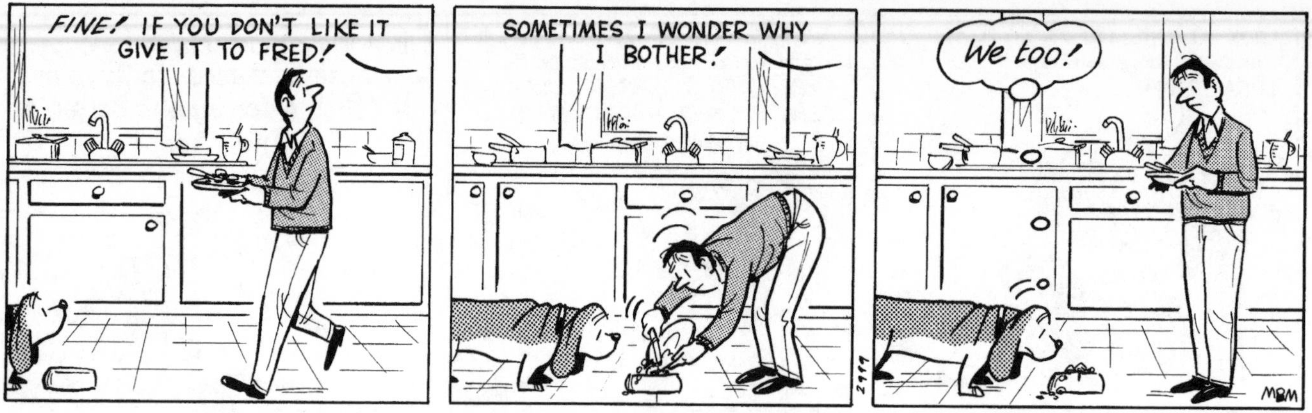
FINE! IF YOU DON'T LIKE IT GIVE IT TO FRED!
SOMETIMES I WONDER WHY I BOTHER!
We too!

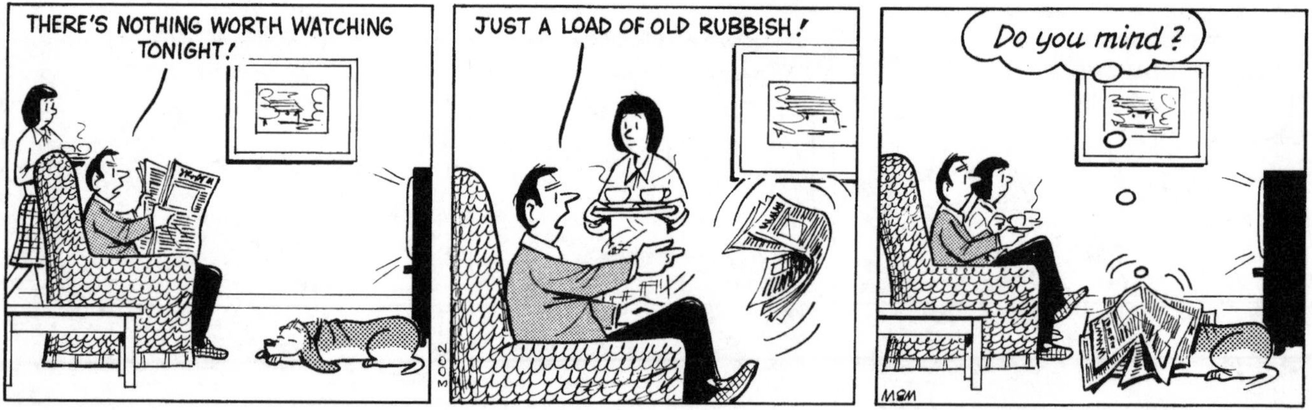
THERE'S NOTHING WORTH WATCHING TONIGHT!
JUST A LOAD OF OLD RUBBISH!
Do you mind?

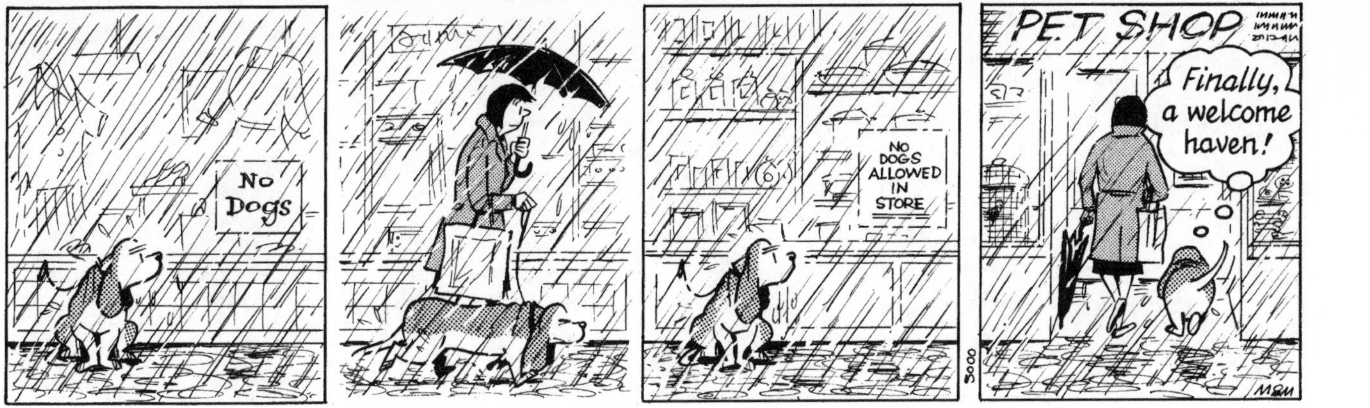
No Dogs
NO DOGS ALLOWED IN STORE
PET SHOP
Finally, a welcome haven!
3000

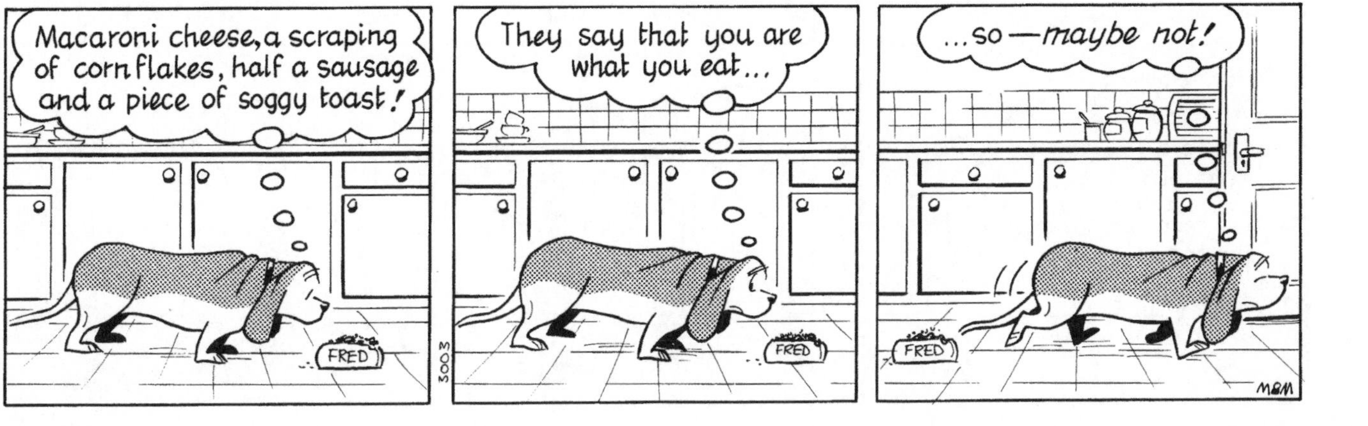
Macaroni cheese, a scraping of corn flakes, half a sausage and a piece of soggy toast!
FRED
3003
They say that you are what you eat...
FRED
...so—maybe not!
FRED

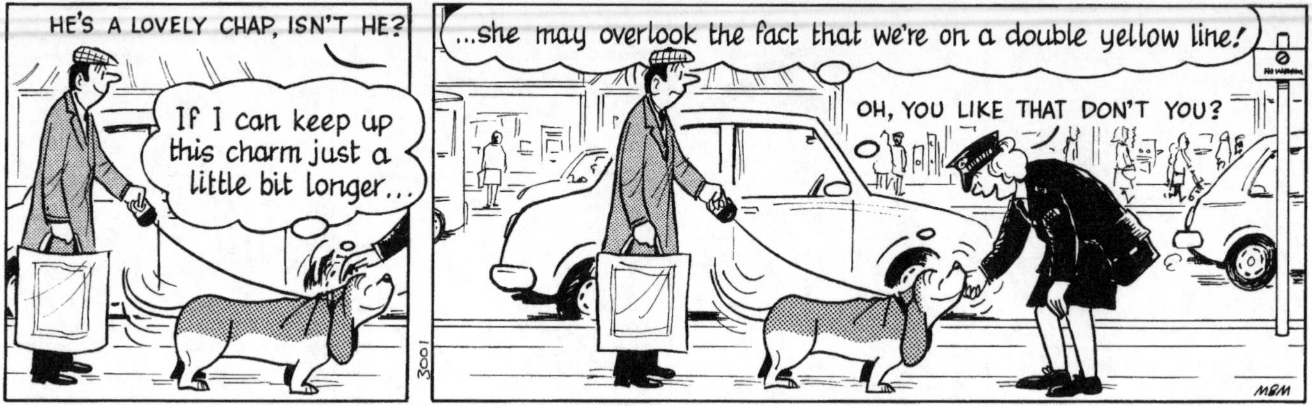
HE'S A LOVELY CHAP, ISN'T HE?
If I can keep up this charm just a little bit longer...
...she may overlook the fact that we're on a double yellow line!
OH, YOU LIKE THAT DON'T YOU?
3001
MBM

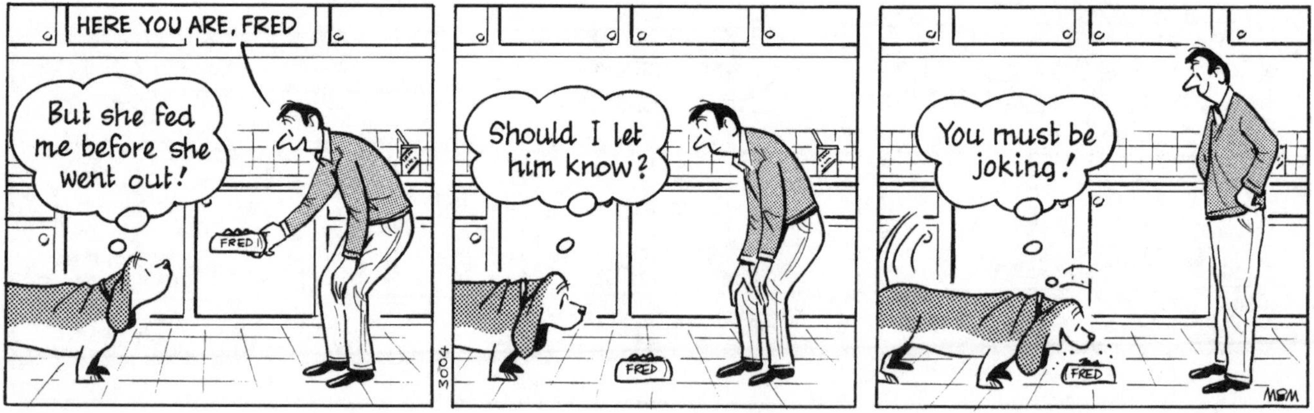
HERE YOU ARE, FRED
But she fed me before she went out!
FRED
Should I let him know?
FRED
You must be joking!
FRED
3004
MBM

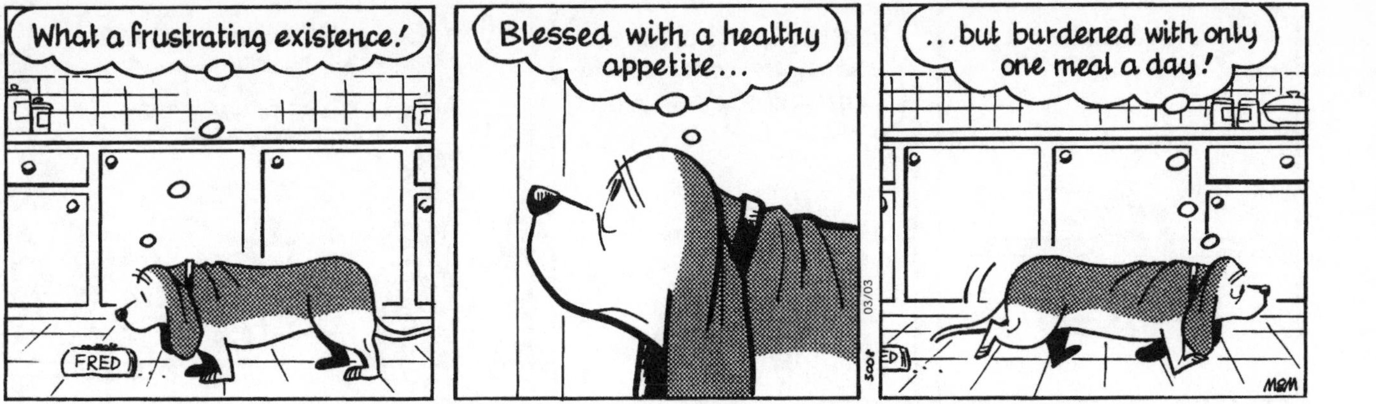
What a frustrating existence!
FRED
Blessed with a healthy appetite...
...but burdened with only one meal a day!

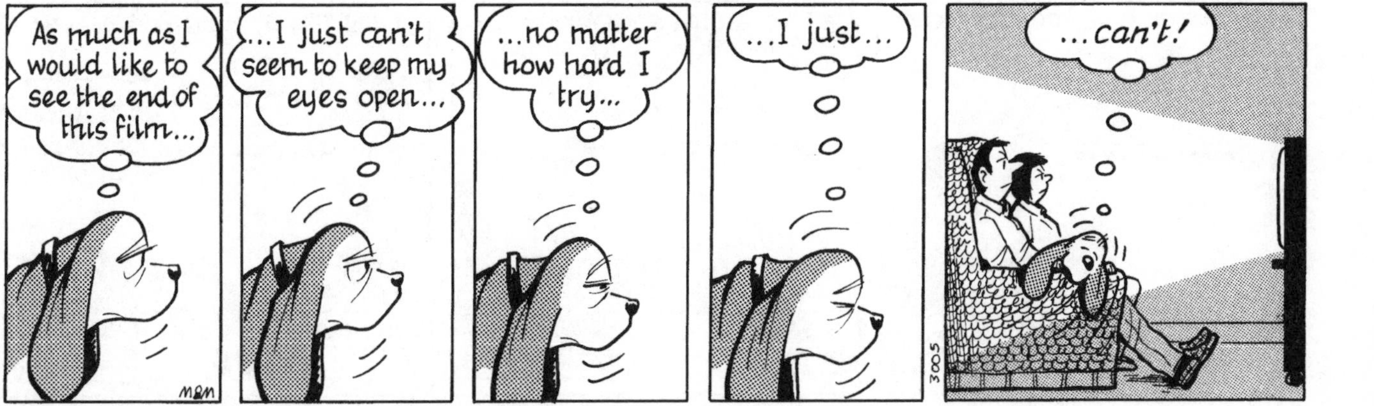
As much as I would like to see the end of this film...
...I just can't seem to keep my eyes open...
...no matter how hard I try...
...I just...
...can't!

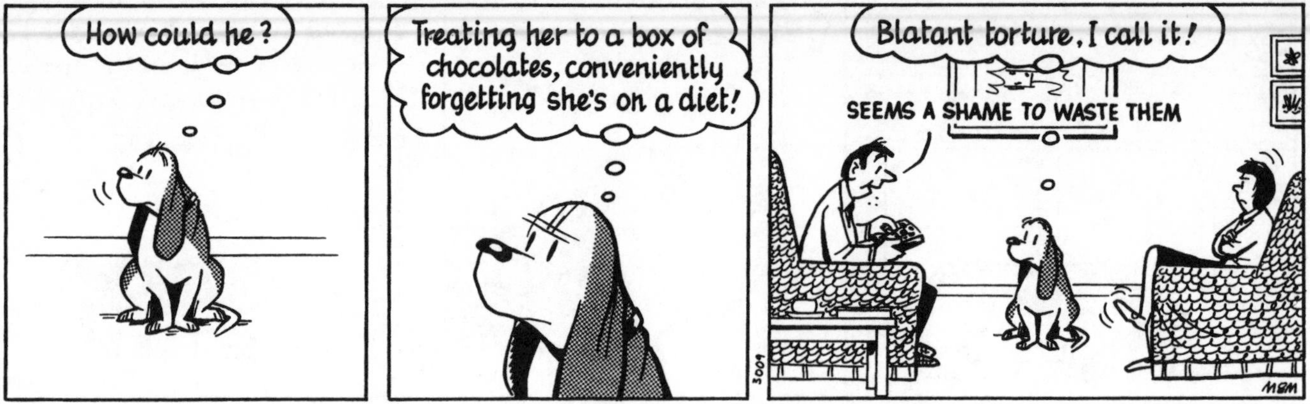
How could he?
Treating her to a box of chocolates, conveniently forgetting she's on a diet!
3009
Blatant torture, I call it!
SEEMS A SHAME TO WASTE THEM
MBM

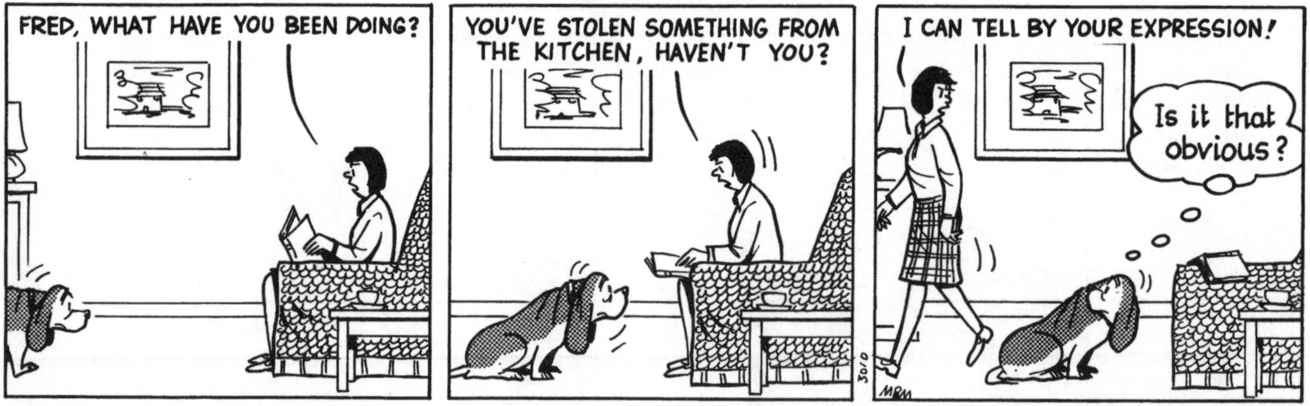
FRED, WHAT HAVE YOU BEEN DOING?
YOU'VE STOLEN SOMETHING FROM THE KITCHEN, HAVEN'T YOU?
3010
I CAN TELL BY YOUR EXPRESSION!
Is it that obvious?
MBM

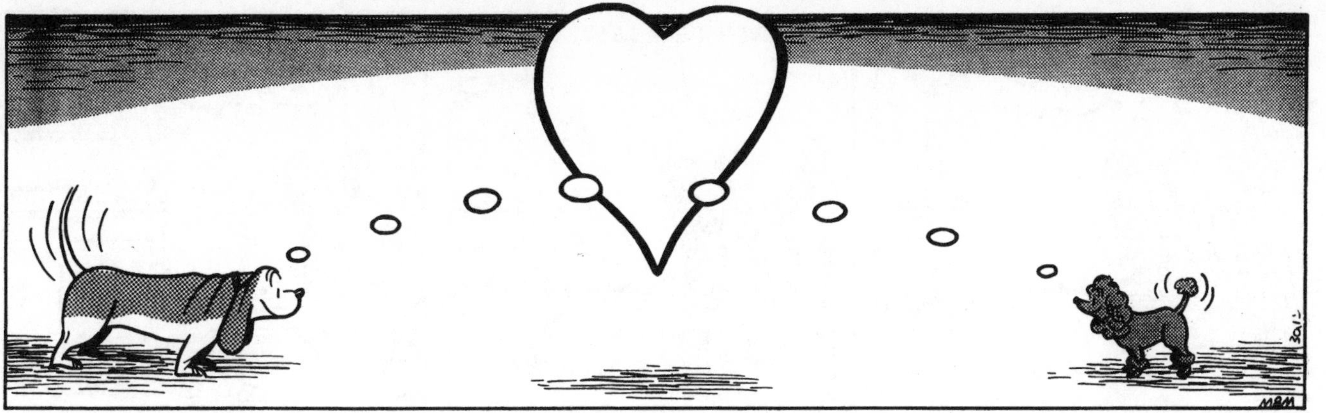

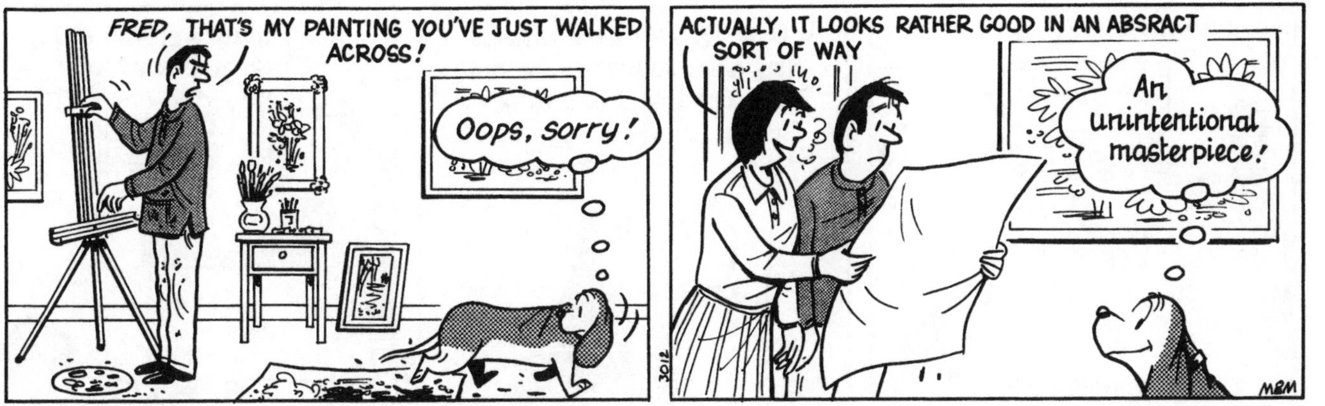
FRED, THAT'S MY PAINTING YOU'VE JUST WALKED ACROSS!
Oops, sorry!
ACTUALLY, IT LOOKS RATHER GOOD IN AN ABSRACT SORT OF WAY
An unintentional masterpiece!

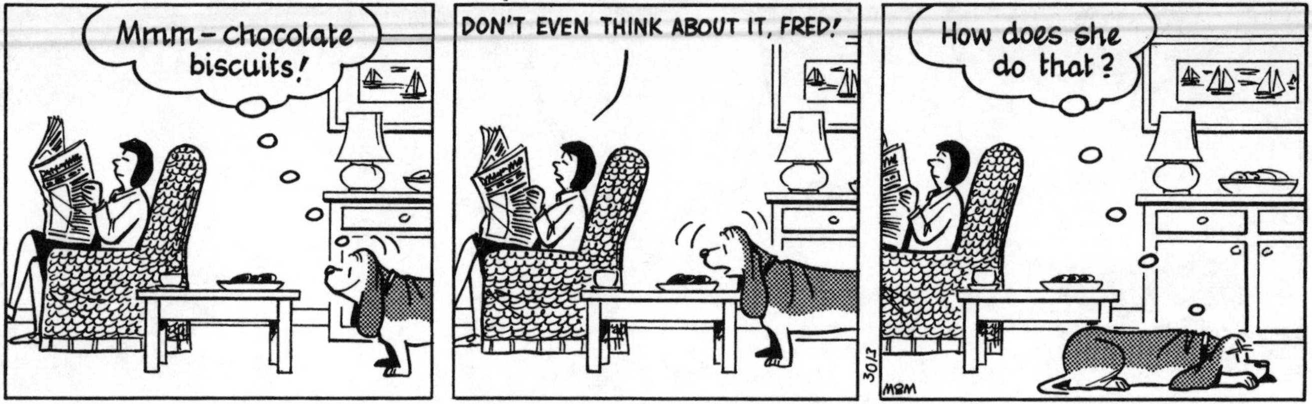
Mmm - chocolate biscuits!
DON'T EVEN THINK ABOUT IT, FRED!
How does she do that?

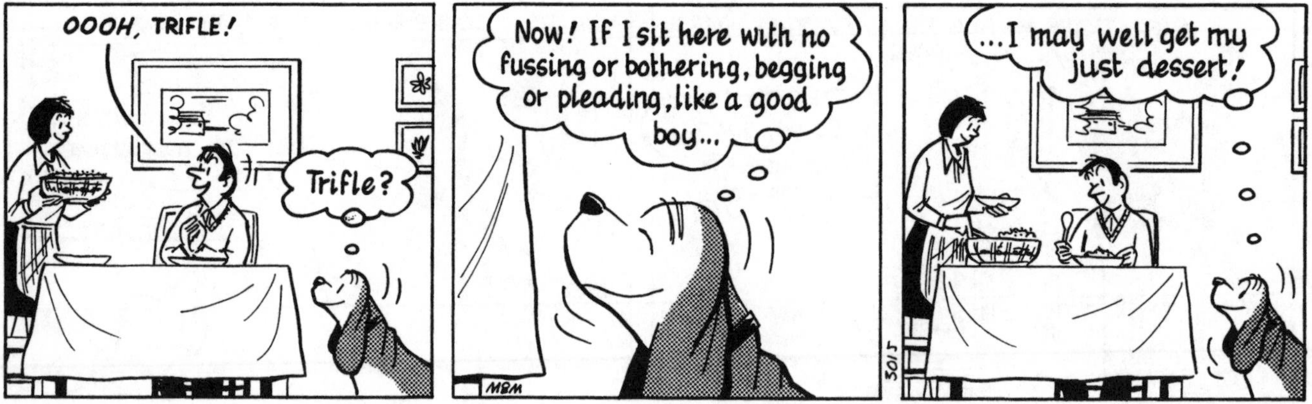
OOOH, TRIFLE!
Trifle?
Now! If I sit here with no fussing or bothering, begging or pleading, like a good boy...
...I may well get my just dessert!

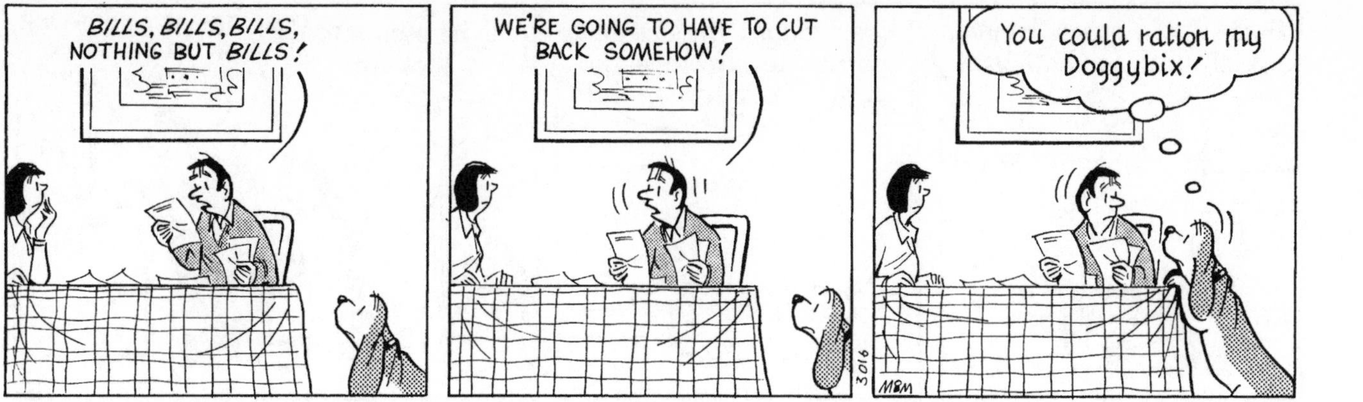
BILLS, BILLS, BILLS, NOTHING BUT BILLS!
WE'RE GOING TO HAVE TO CUT BACK SOMEHOW!
3016
You could ration my Doggybix!
MBM

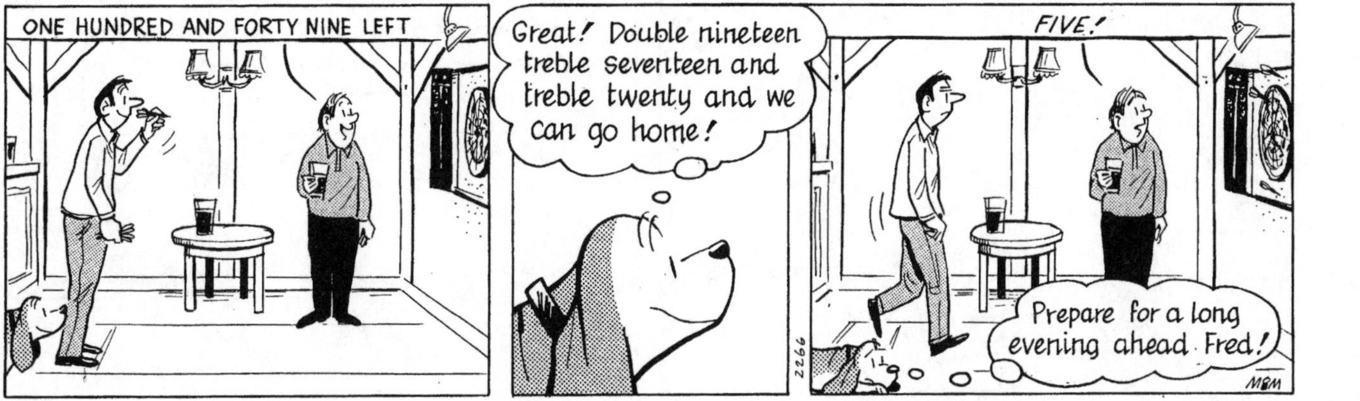
ONE HUNDRED AND FORTY NINE LEFT
Great! Double nineteen treble seventeen and treble twenty and we can go home!
2266
FIVE!
Prepare for a long evening ahead Fred!
MBM

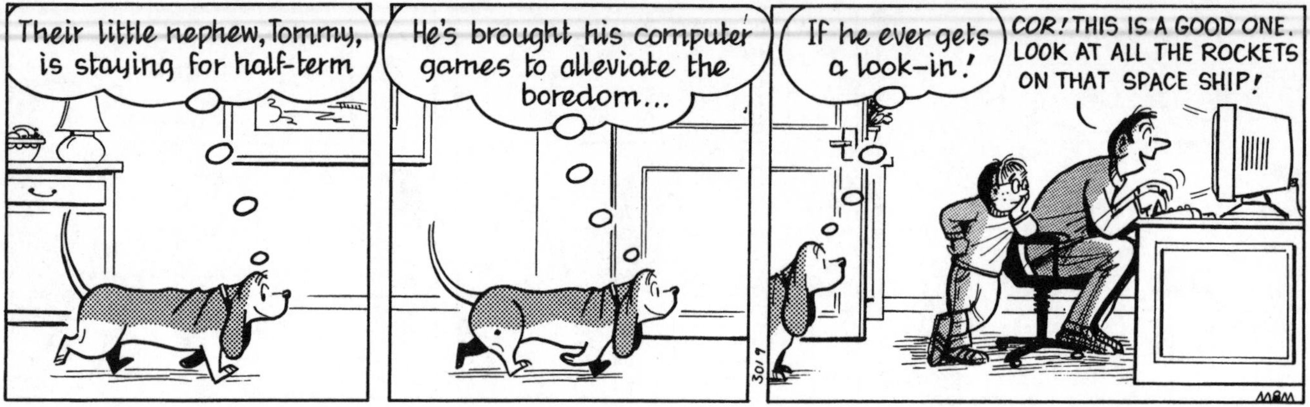
Their little nephew, Tommy, is staying for half-term
He's brought his computer games to alleviate the boredom...
If he ever gets a look-in!
COR! THIS IS A GOOD ONE. LOOK AT ALL THE ROCKETS ON THAT SPACE SHIP!

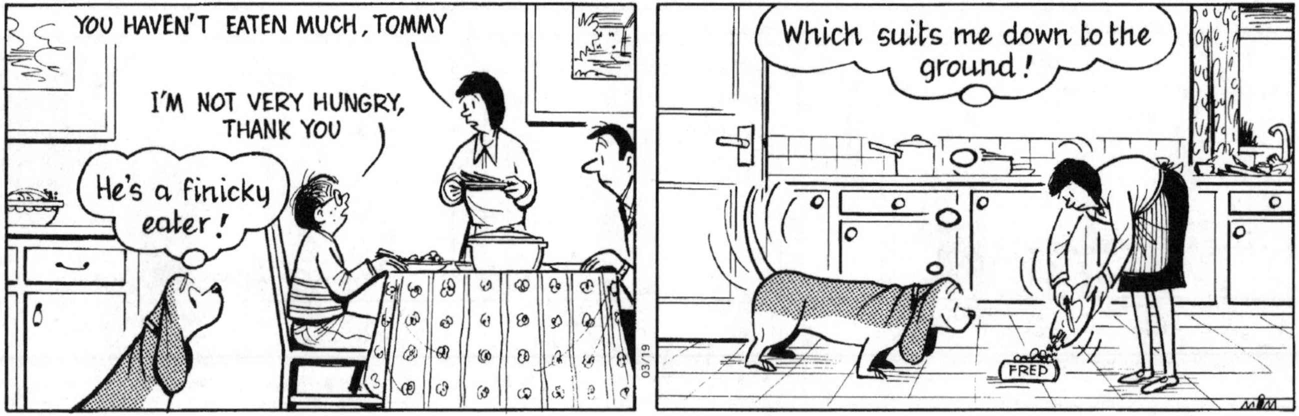
YOU HAVEN'T EATEN MUCH, TOMMY
I'M NOT VERY HUNGRY, THANK YOU
He's a finicky eater!
Which suits me down to the ground!
FRED

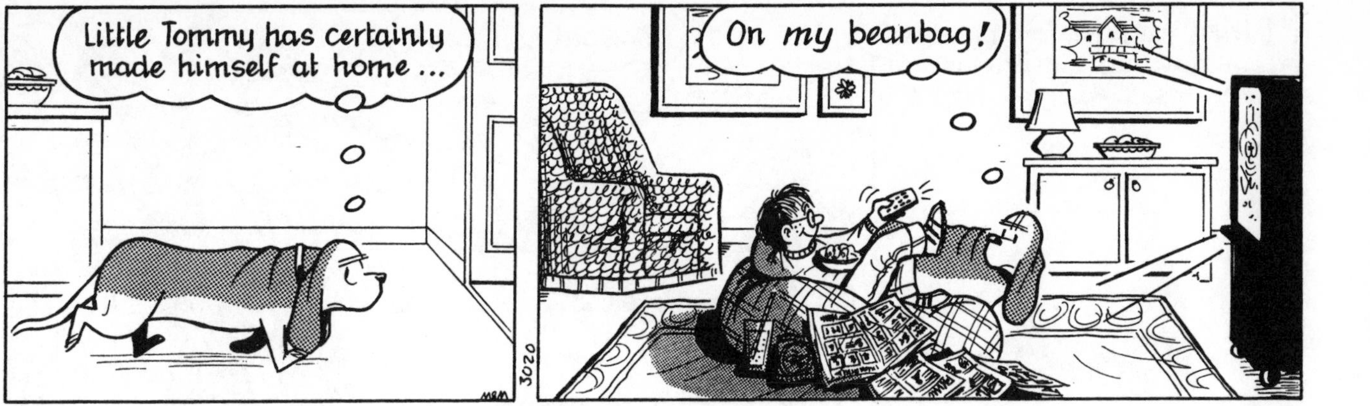
Little Tommy has certainly made himself at home ...
On my beanbag!
3020

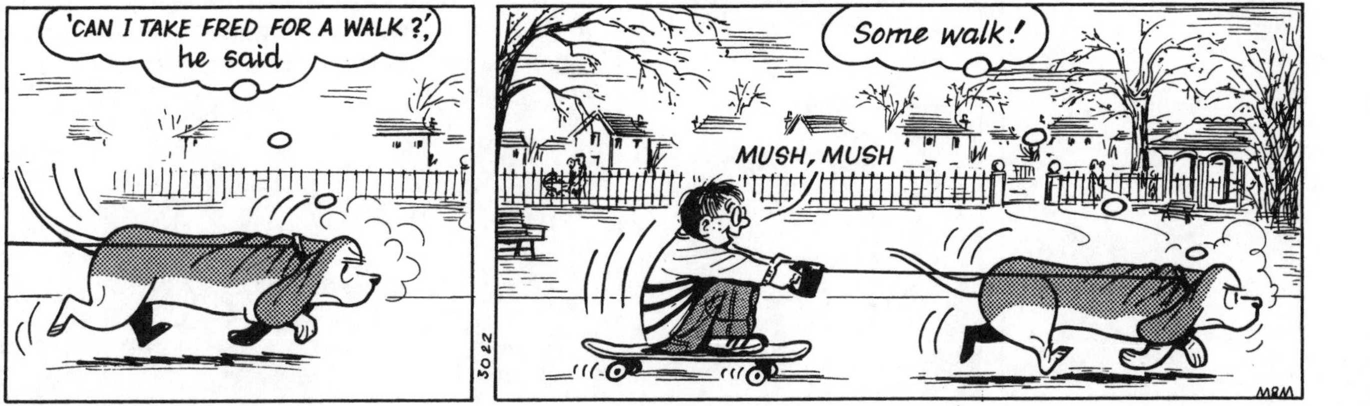
'CAN I TAKE FRED FOR A WALK?', he said
3022
MUSH, MUSH
Some walk!

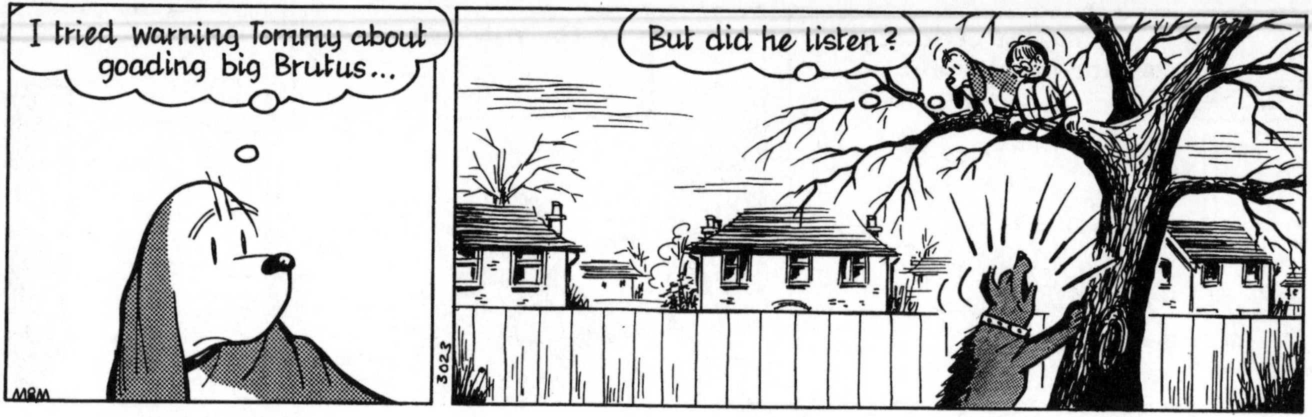
I tried warning Tommy about goading big Brutus...
But did he listen?

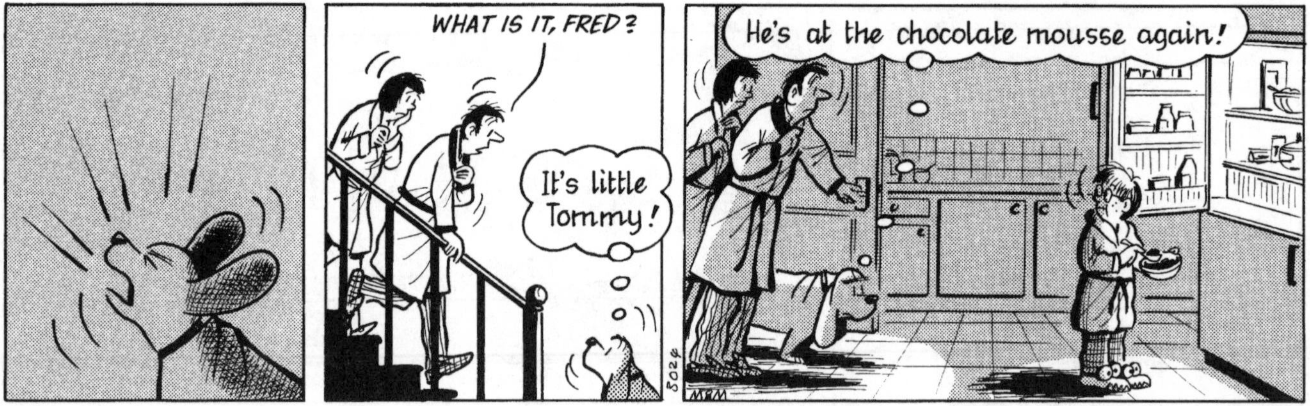
WHAT IS IT, FRED?
It's little Tommy!
He's at the chocolate mousse again!

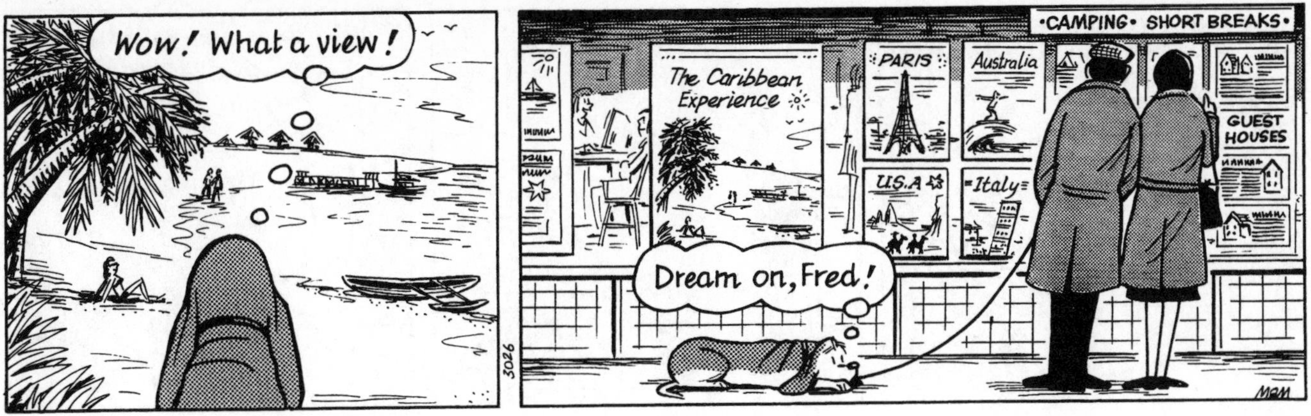
Wow! What a view!
•CAMPING• SHORT BREAKS•
The Caribbean Experience
PARIS
Australia
U.S.A
Italy
GUEST HOUSES
Dream on, Fred!
3026

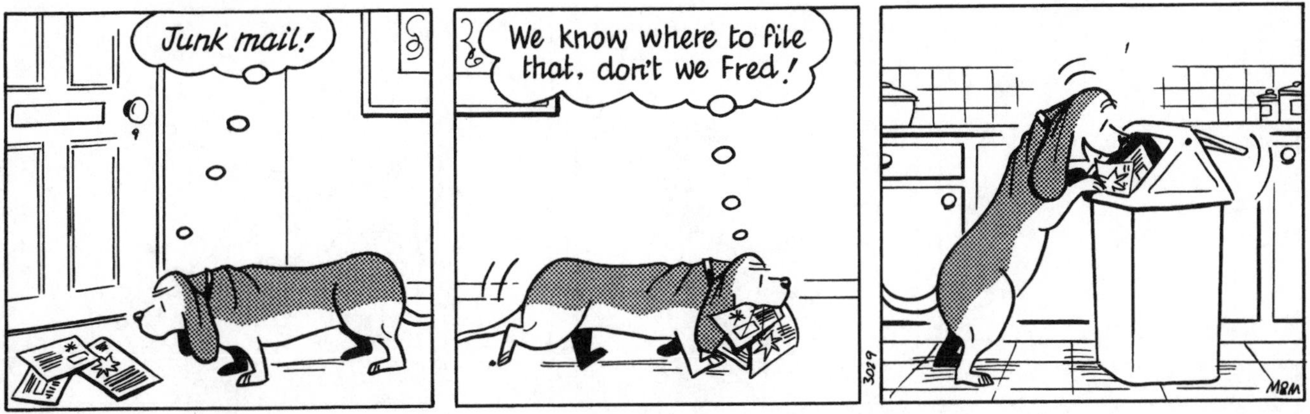
Junk mail!
We know where to file that, don't we Fred!
3029

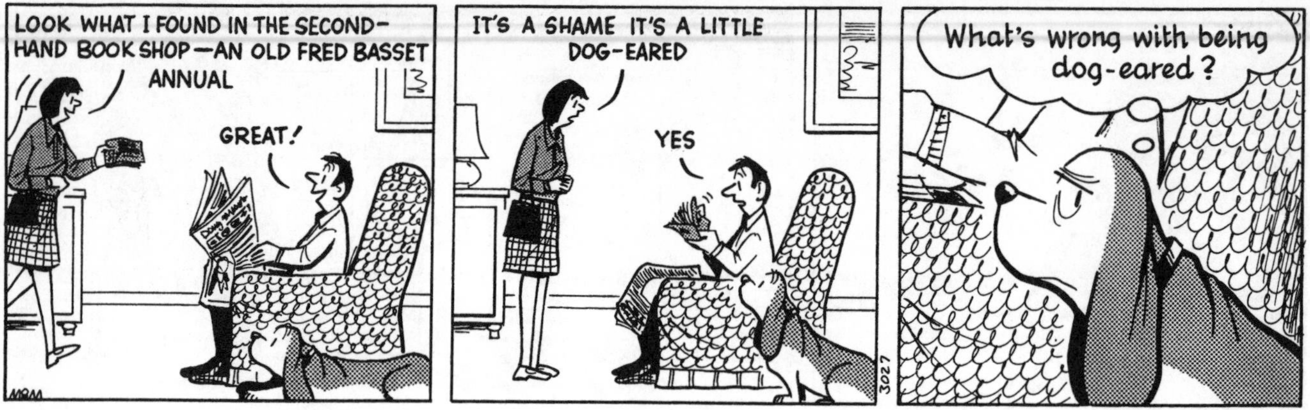
LOOK WHAT I FOUND IN THE SECOND-HAND BOOK SHOP—AN OLD FRED BASSET ANNUAL
GREAT!
IT'S A SHAME IT'S A LITTLE DOG-EARED
YES
What's wrong with being dog-eared?
3027

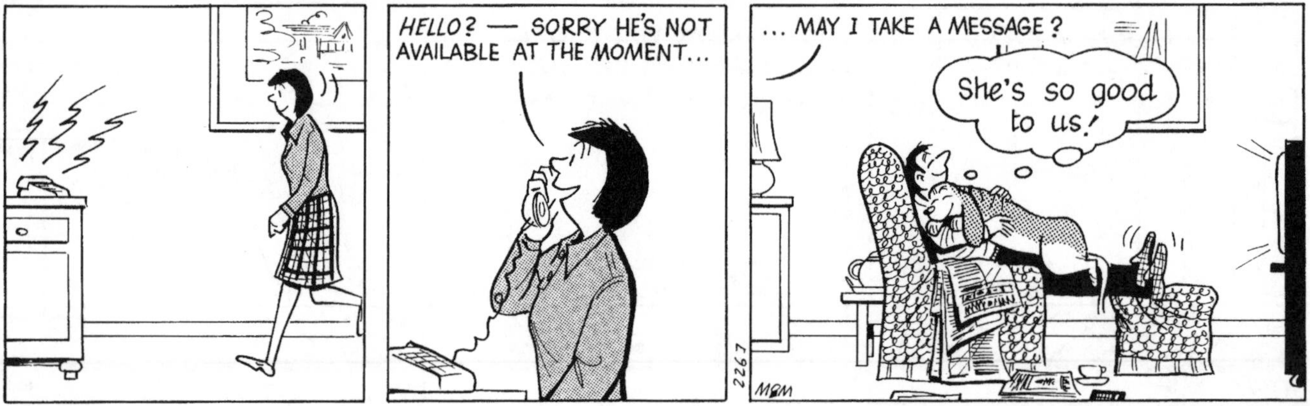
HELLO? — SORRY HE'S NOT AVAILABLE AT THE MOMENT...
... MAY I TAKE A MESSAGE?
She's so good to us!
2267

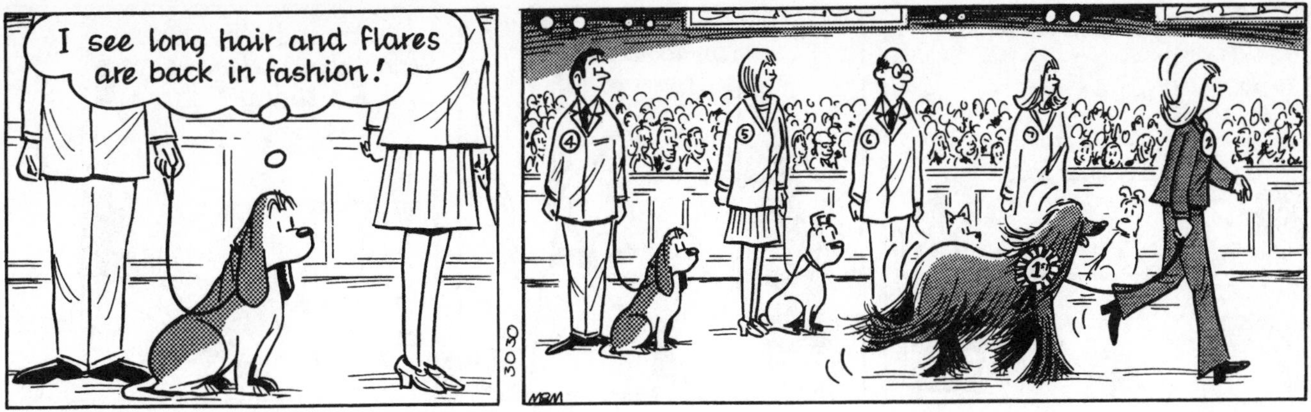
I see long hair and flares are back in fashion!
3030
MBM

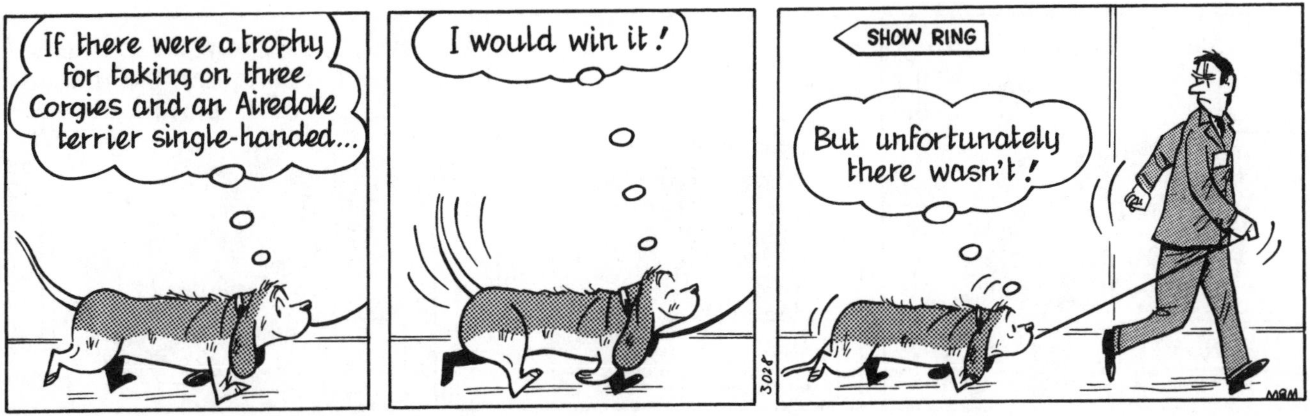
If there were a trophy for taking on three Corgies and an Airedale terrier single-handed...
I would win it!
3028
SHOW RING
But unfortunately there wasn't!
MBM

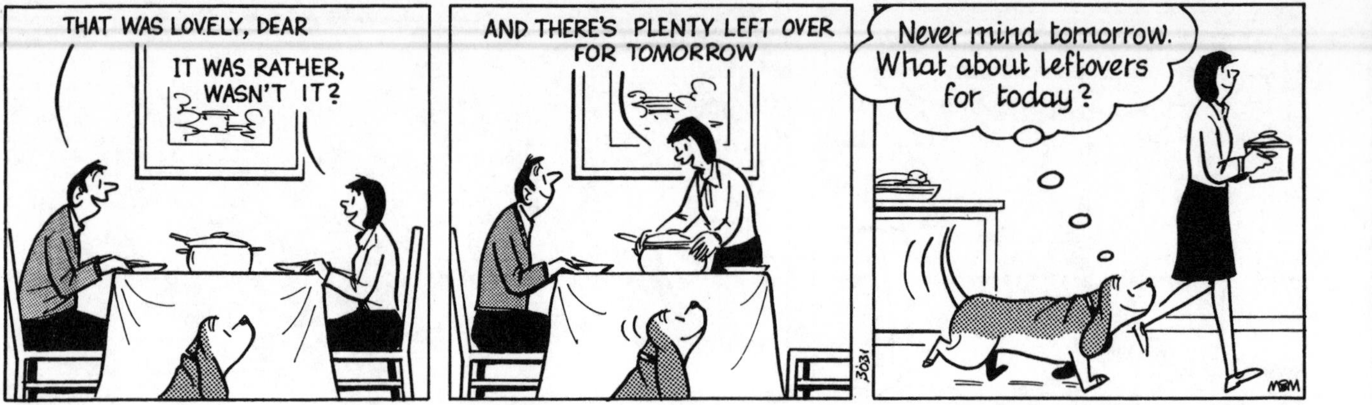
THAT WAS LOVELY, DEAR
IT WAS RATHER, WASN'T IT?
AND THERE'S PLENTY LEFT OVER FOR TOMORROW
3031
Never mind tomorrow. What about leftovers for today?
MBM

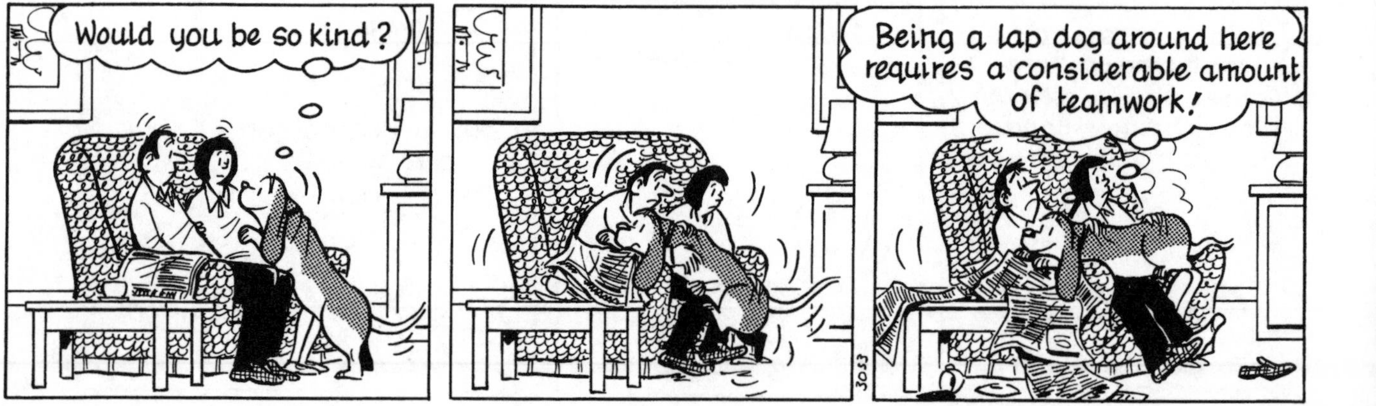
Would you be so kind?
3033
Being a lap dog around here requires a considerable amount of teamwork!

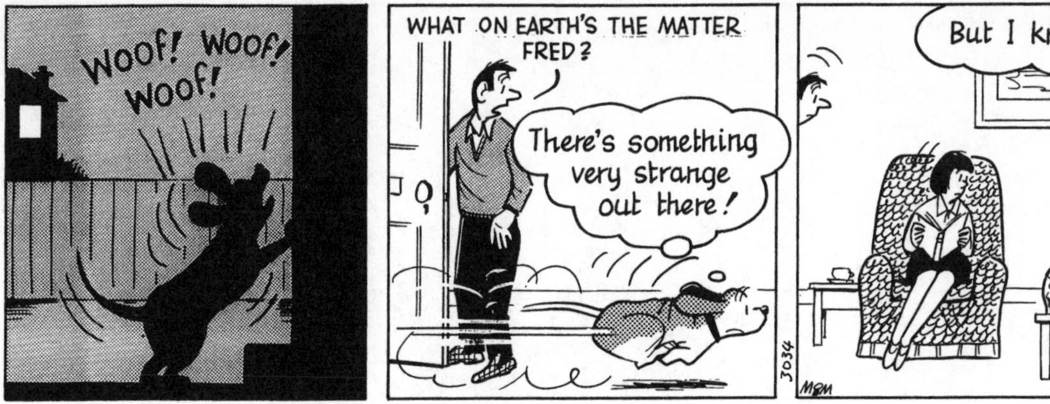
WOOF! WOOF! WOOF!
WHAT ON EARTH'S THE MATTER FRED?
There's something very strange out there!
3034
But I know not what!

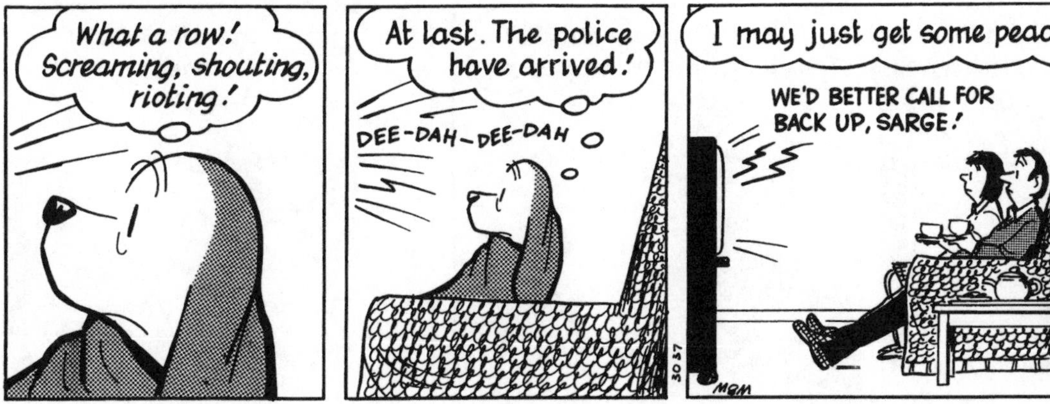
What a row! Screaming, shouting, rioting!
At last. The police have arrived!
DEE-DAH-DEE-DAH
3037
I may just get some peace and quiet now!
WE'D BETTER CALL FOR BACK UP, SARGE!

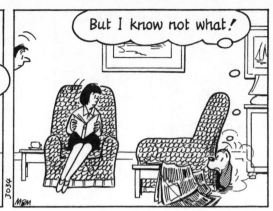

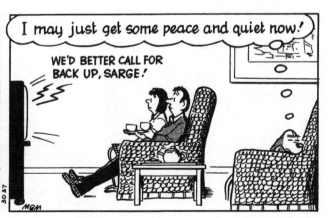

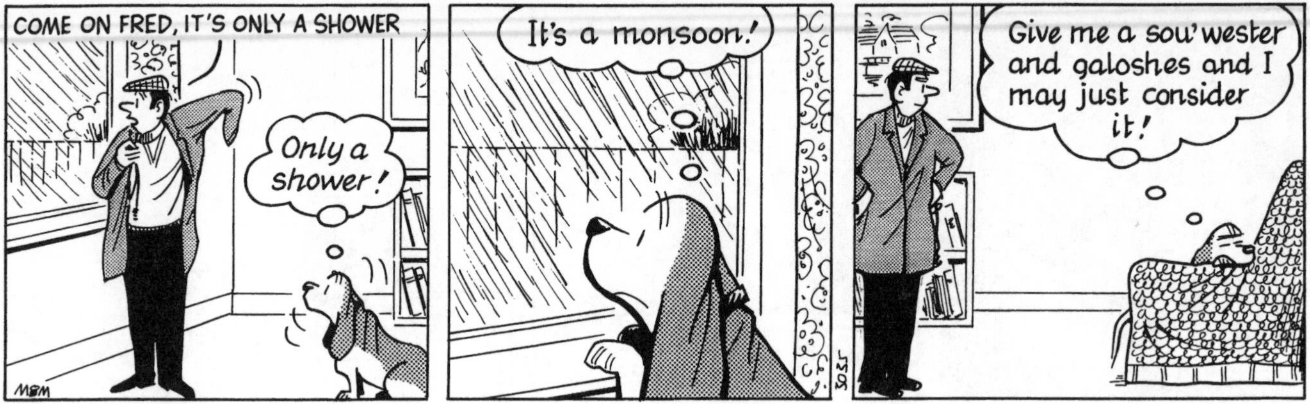
COME ON FRED, IT'S ONLY A SHOWER
Only a shower!
It's a monsoon!
Give me a sou'wester and galoshes and I may just consider it!

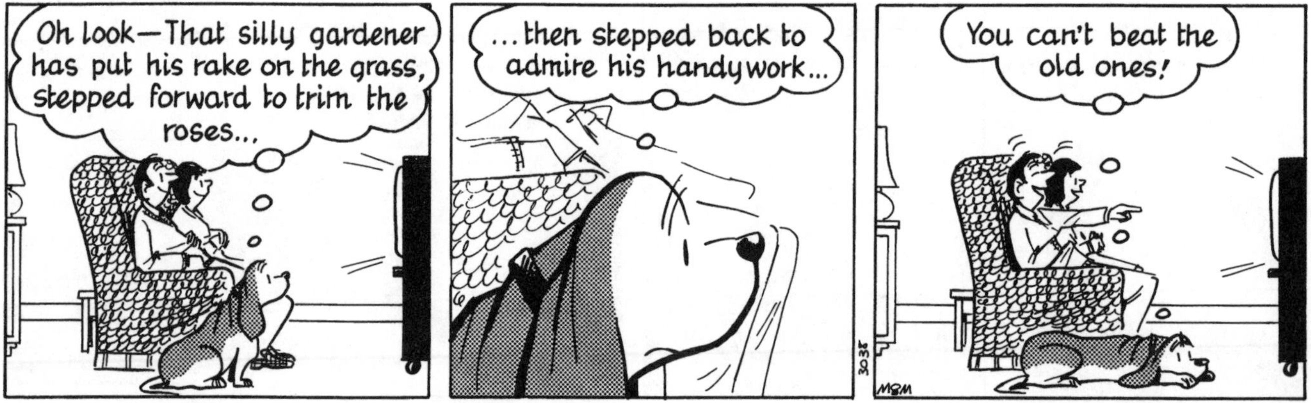
Oh look—That silly gardener has put his rake on the grass, stepped forward to trim the roses...
...then stepped back to admire his handywork...
You can't beat the old ones!

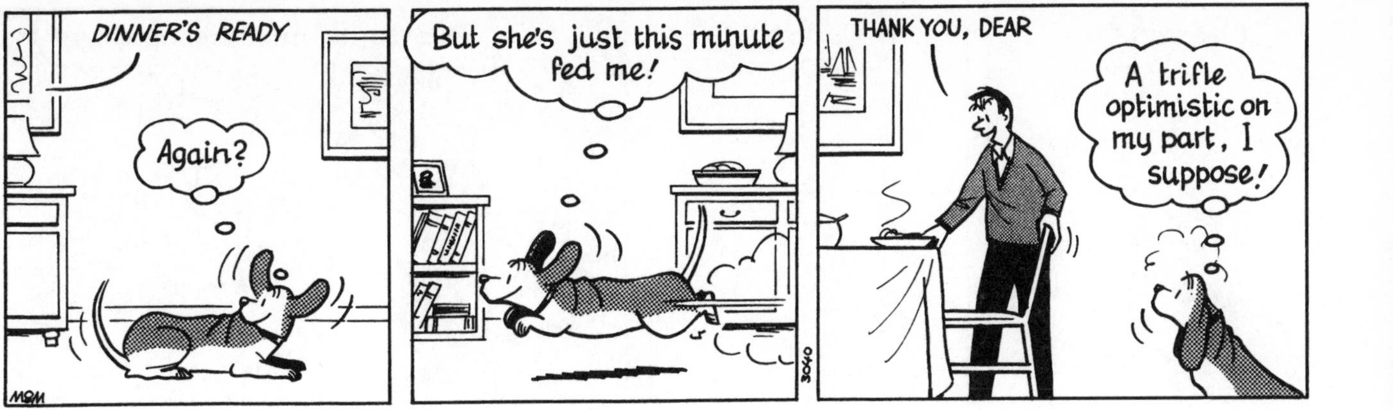
DINNER'S READY
Again?
But she's just this minute fed me!
THANK YOU, DEAR
A trifle optimistic on my part, I suppose!

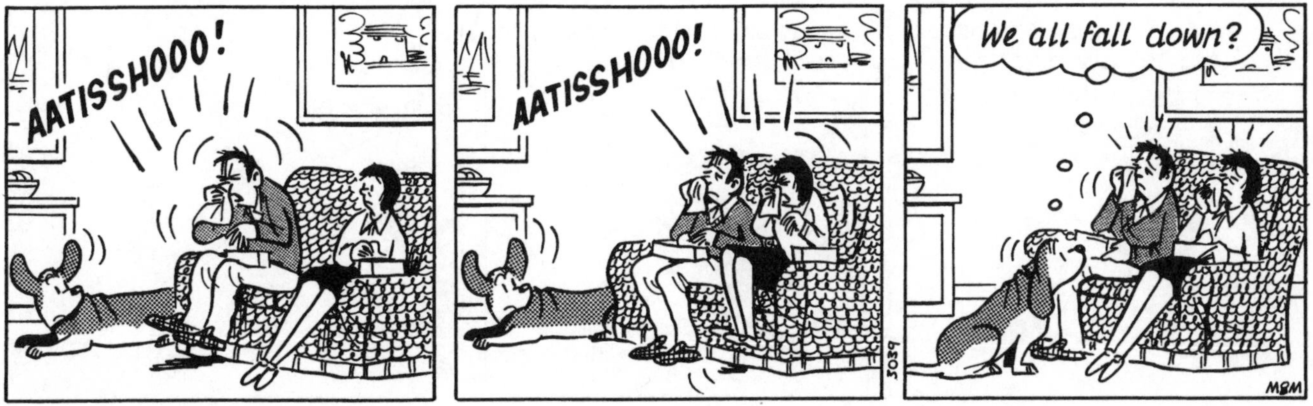
AATISSHOOO!
AATISSHOOO!
We all fall down?

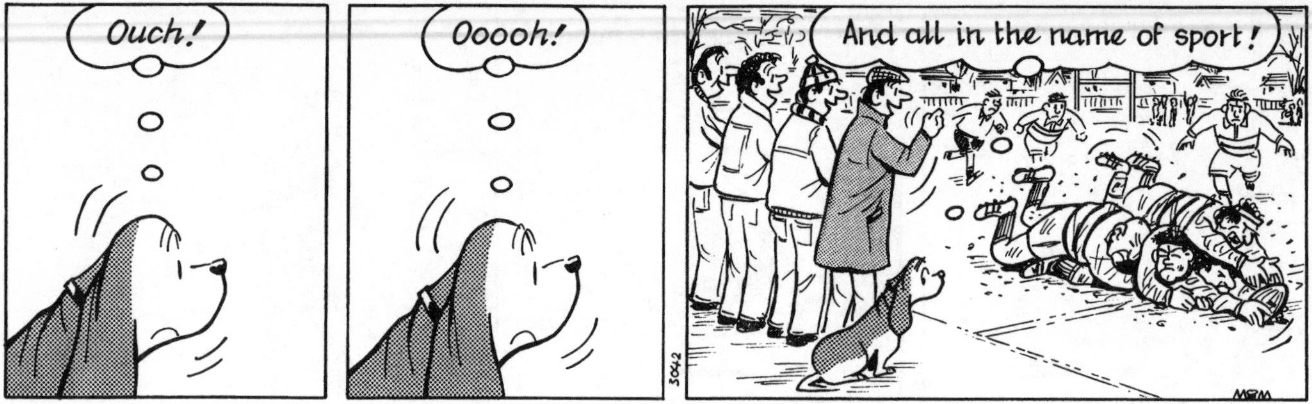
Ouch!
Ooooh!
And all in the name of sport!

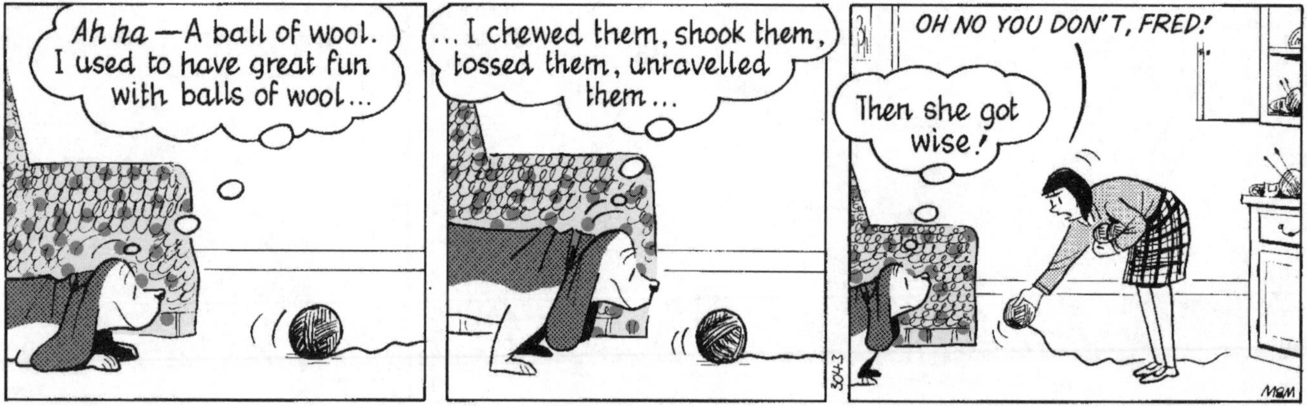
Ah ha—A ball of wool. I used to have great fun with balls of wool...
...I chewed them, shook them, tossed them, unravelled them...
OH NO YOU DON'T, FRED!
Then she got wise!

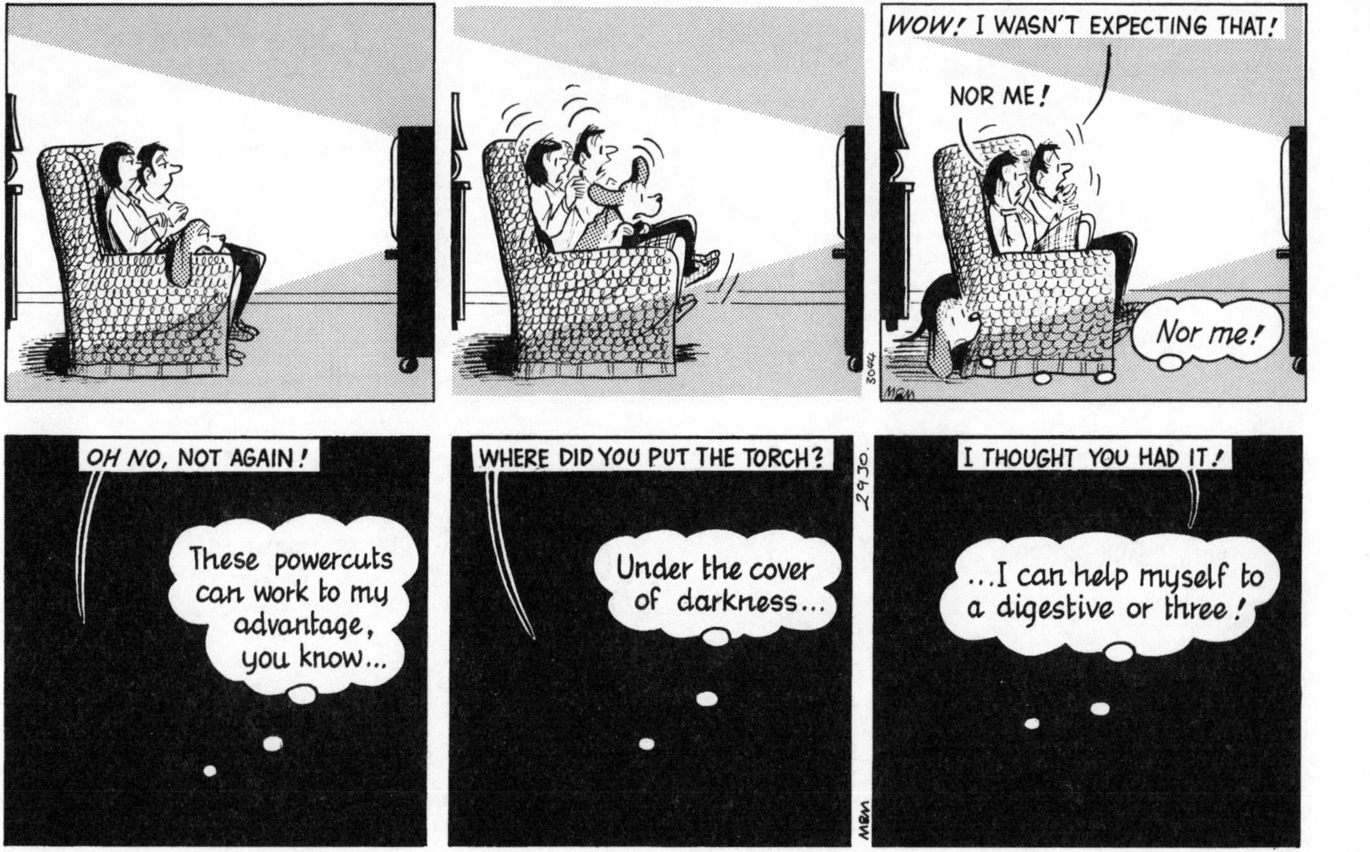
WOW! I WASN'T EXPECTING THAT!
NOR ME!
Nor me!
OH NO, NOT AGAIN!
These powercuts can work to my advantage, you know...
WHERE DID YOU PUT THE TORCH?
Under the cover of darkness...
I THOUGHT YOU HAD IT!
...I can help myself to a digestive or three!

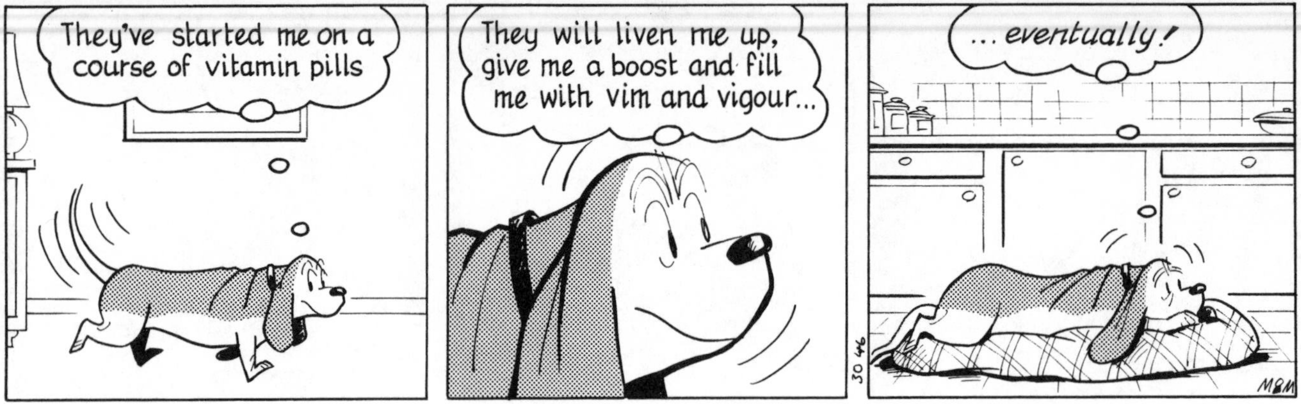
They've started me on a course of vitamin pills
They will liven me up, give me a boost and fill me with vim and vigour...
... *eventually!*

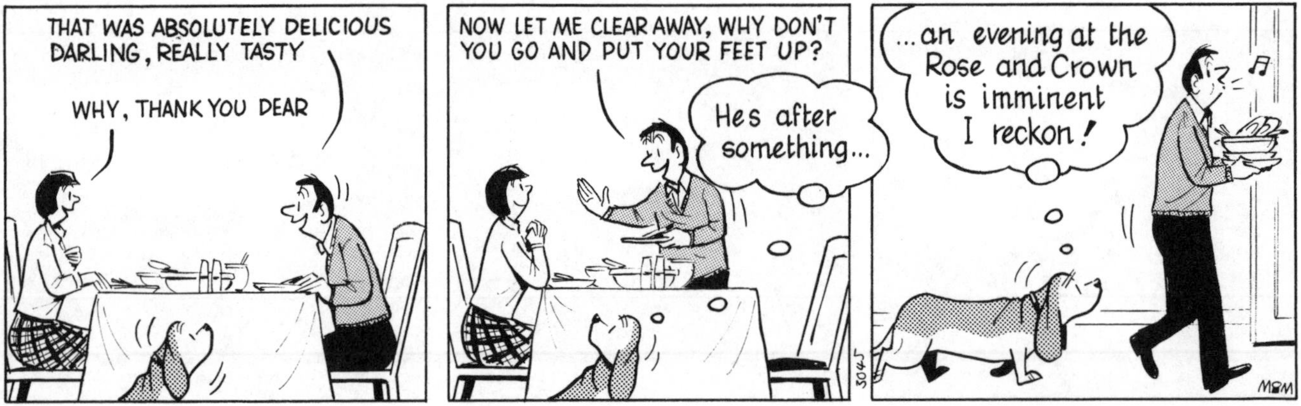
THAT WAS ABSOLUTELY DELICIOUS DARLING, REALLY TASTY
WHY, THANK YOU DEAR
NOW LET ME CLEAR AWAY, WHY DON'T YOU GO AND PUT YOUR FEET UP?
He's after something...
... an evening at the Rose and Crown is imminent I reckon!

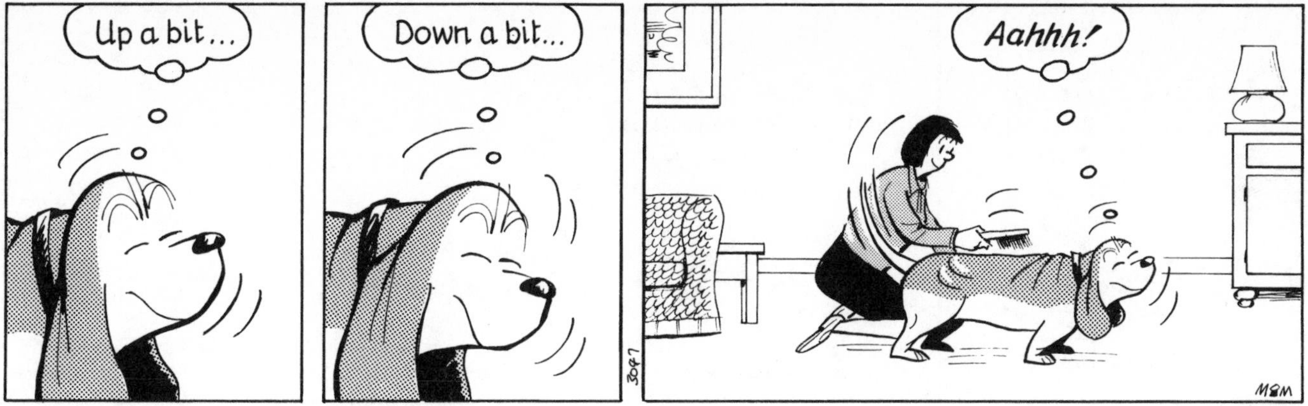
Up a bit...
Down a bit...
3047
Aahhh!

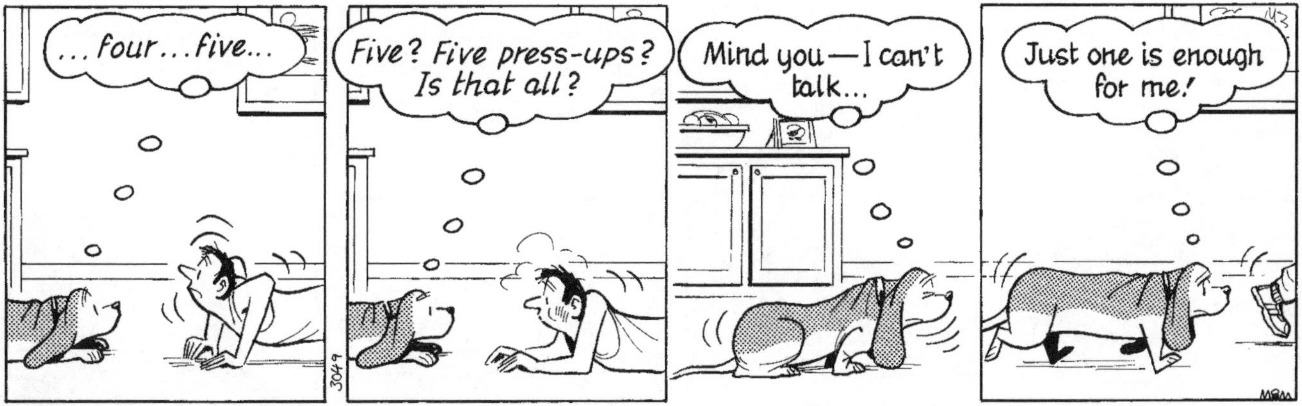
...four...five...
3049
Five? Five press-ups? Is that all?
Mind you—I can't talk...
Just one is enough for me!

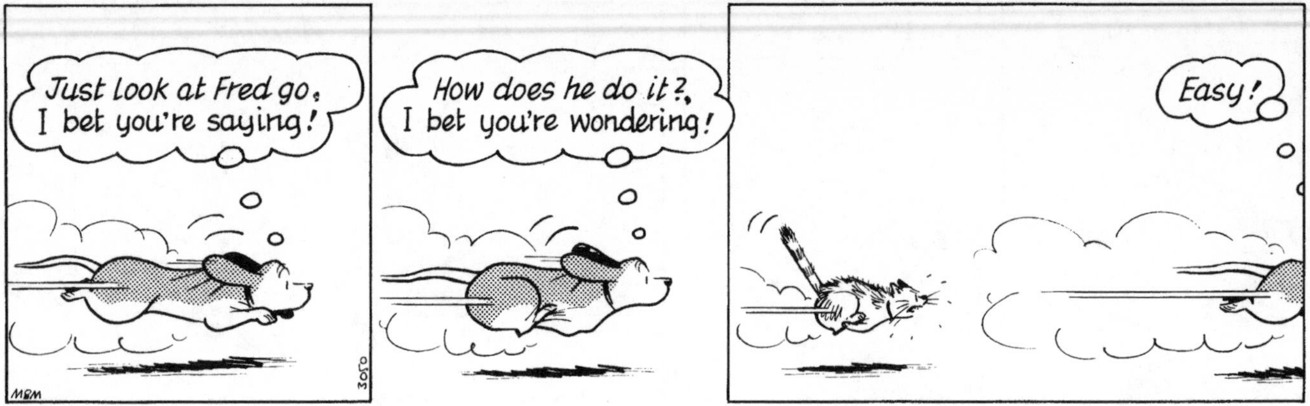
Just look at Fred go, I bet you're saying!
How does he do it?, I bet you're wondering!
Easy!
MBM
3050

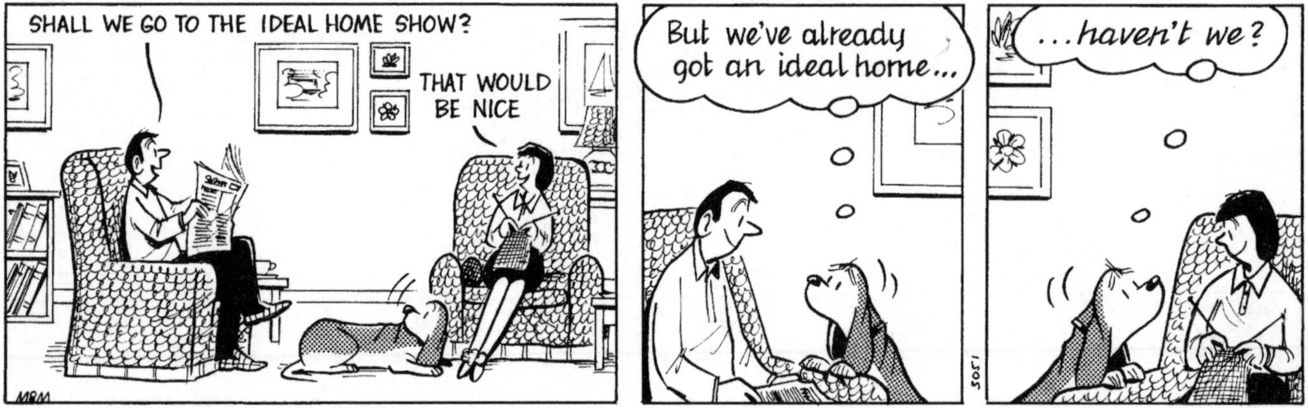
SHALL WE GO TO THE IDEAL HOME SHOW?
THAT WOULD BE NICE
But we've already got an ideal home...
...haven't we?
MBM
3051

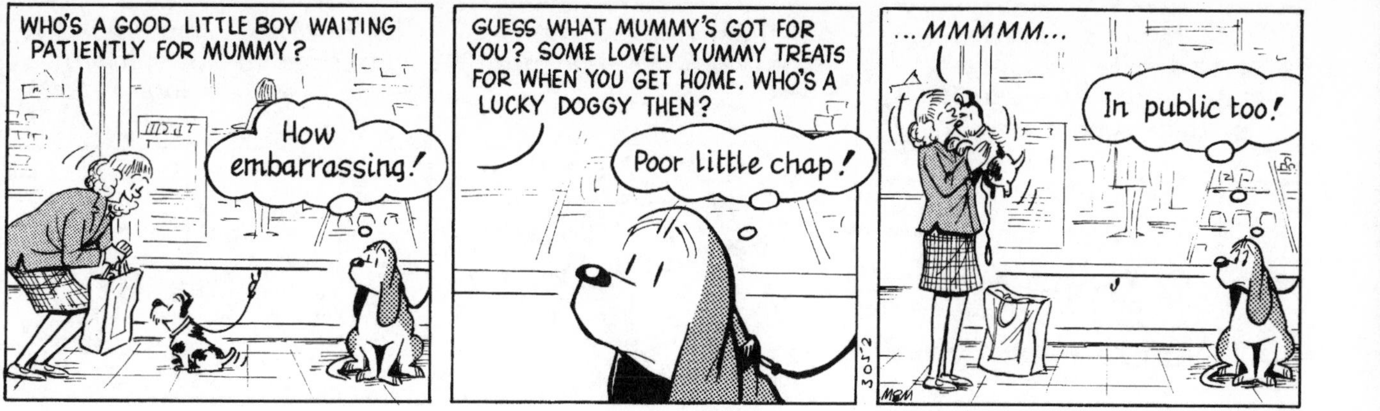
WHO'S A GOOD LITTLE BOY WAITING PATIENTLY FOR MUMMY?
How embarrassing!
GUESS WHAT MUMMY'S GOT FOR YOU? SOME LOVELY YUMMY TREATS FOR WHEN YOU GET HOME. WHO'S A LUCKY DOGGY THEN?
Poor little chap!
...MMMMM...
In public too!

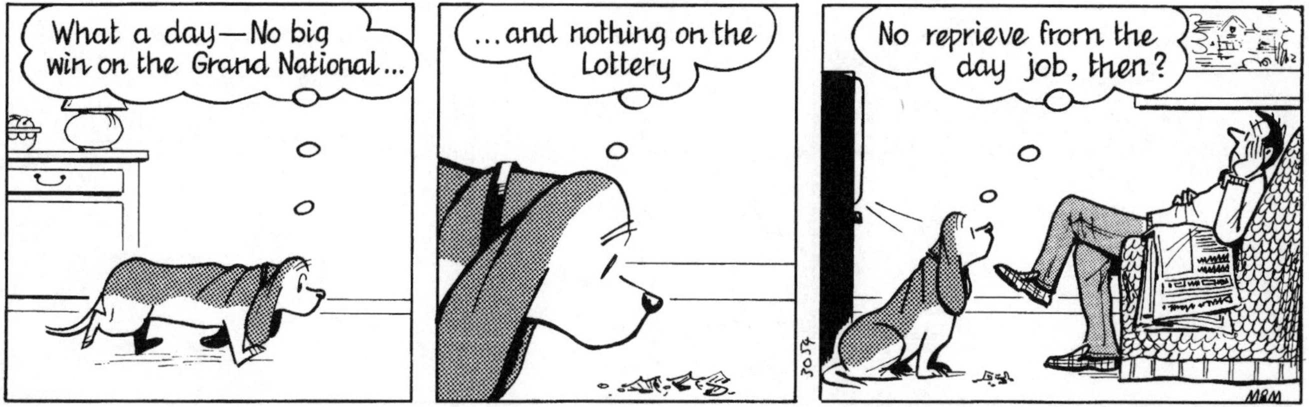
What a day—No big win on the Grand National...
...and nothing on the Lottery
No reprieve from the day job, then?

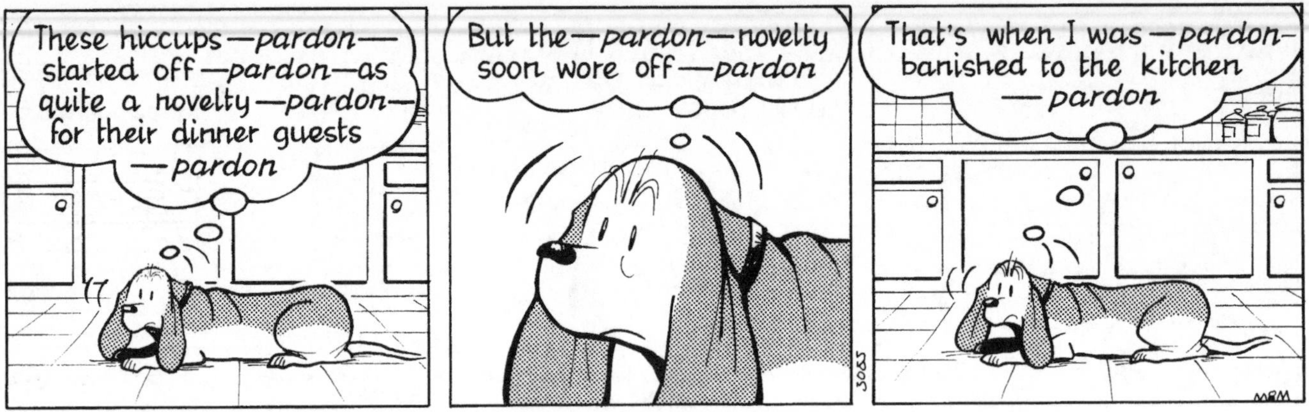
These hiccups—*pardon*—started off—*pardon*—as quite a novelty—*pardon*—for their dinner guests—*pardon*
But the—*pardon*—novelty soon wore off—*pardon*
That's when I was—*pardon*—banished to the kitchen—*pardon*

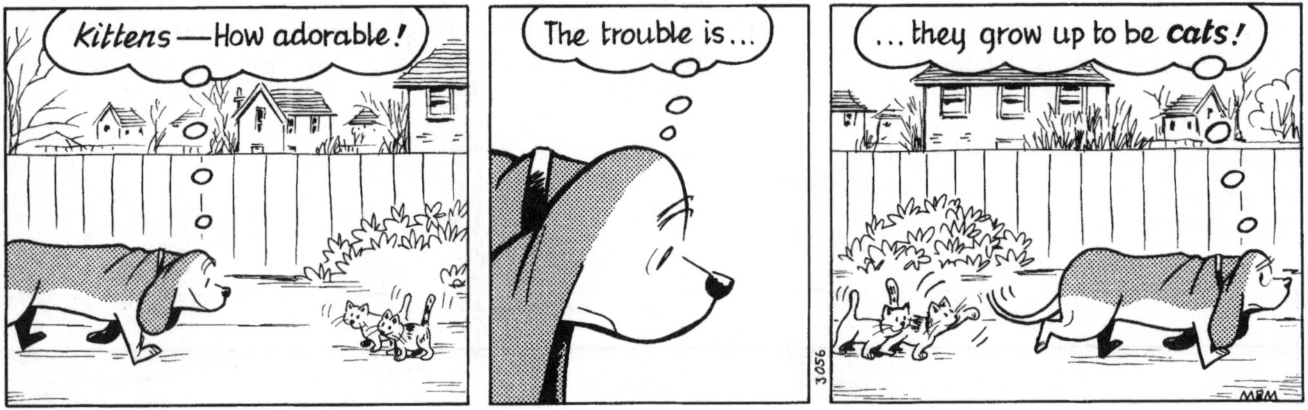
Kittens—How adorable!
The trouble is...
...they grow up to be **cats**!

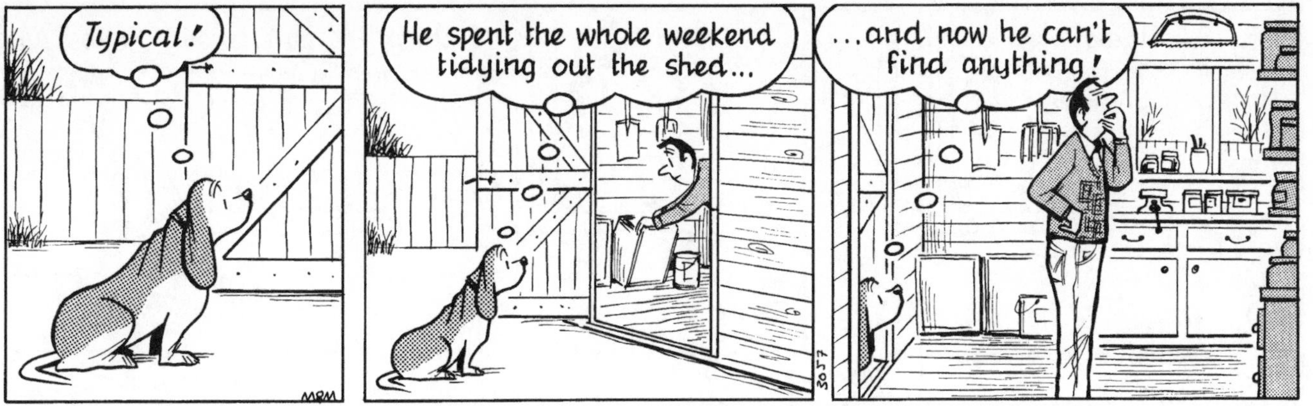
Typical!
He spent the whole weekend tidying out the shed...
...and now he can't find anything!

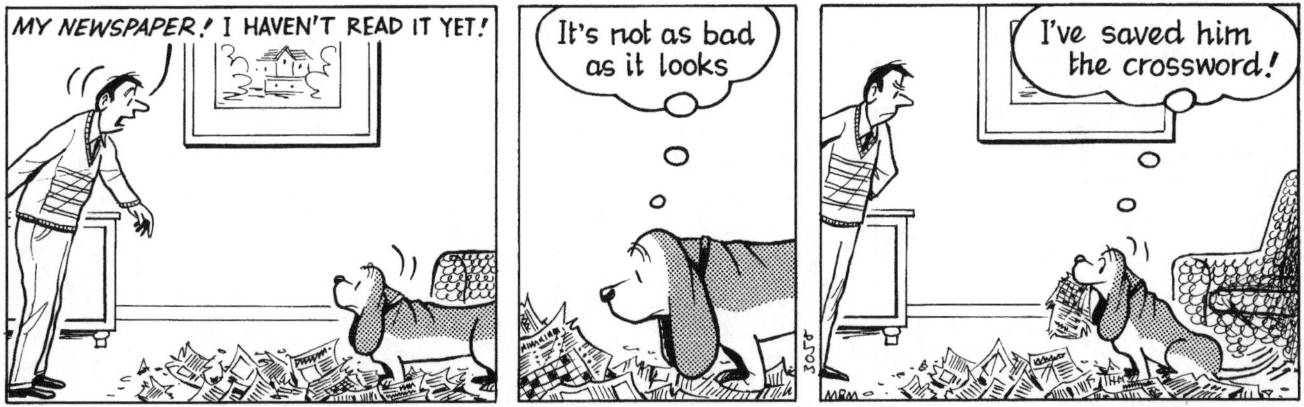
MY NEWSPAPER! I HAVEN'T READ IT YET!
It's not as bad as it looks
I've saved him the crossword!

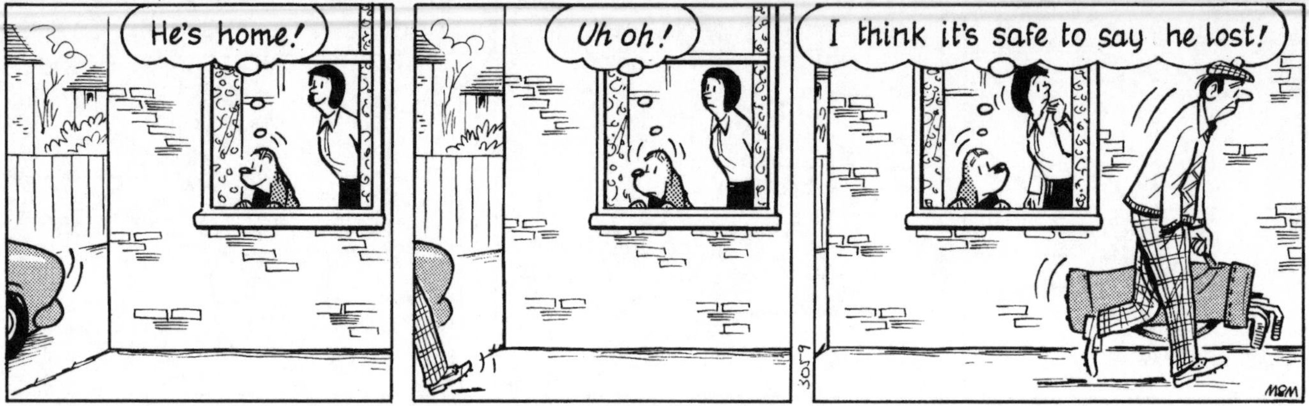
He's home!
Uh oh!
I think it's safe to say he lost!
3059

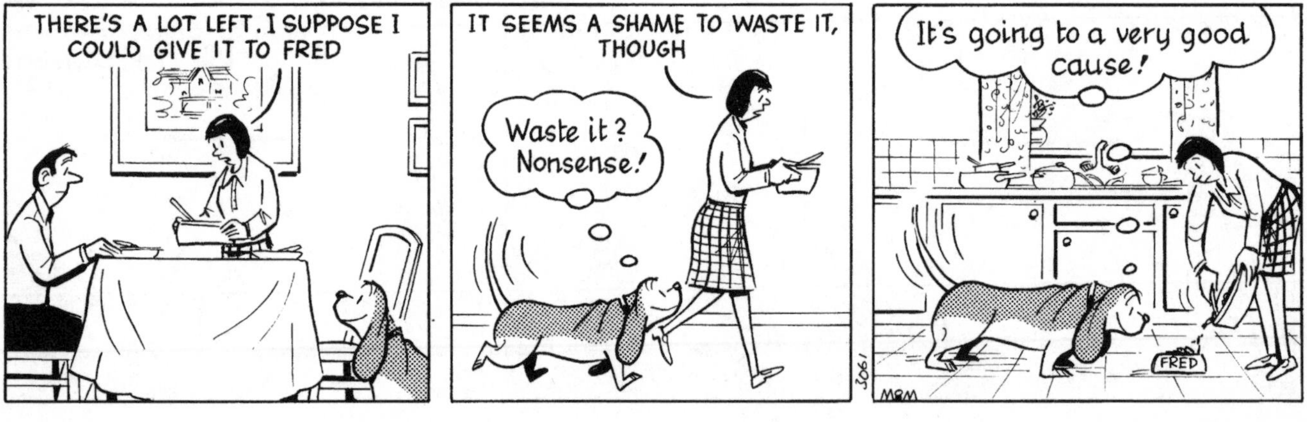
THERE'S A LOT LEFT. I SUPPOSE I COULD GIVE IT TO FRED
IT SEEMS A SHAME TO WASTE IT, THOUGH
Waste it? Nonsense!
It's going to a very good cause!
FRED
3061

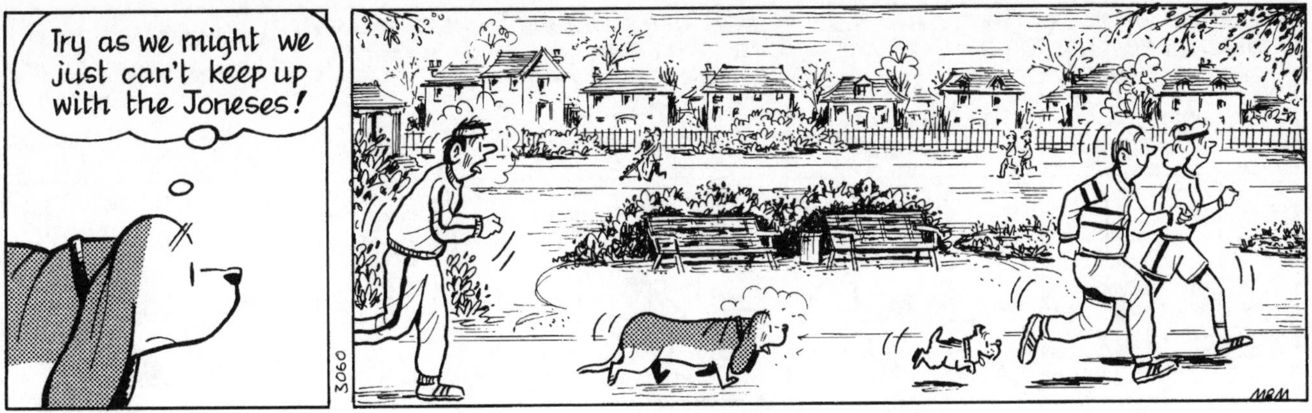
Try as we might we just can't keep up with the Joneses!
3060
M&M

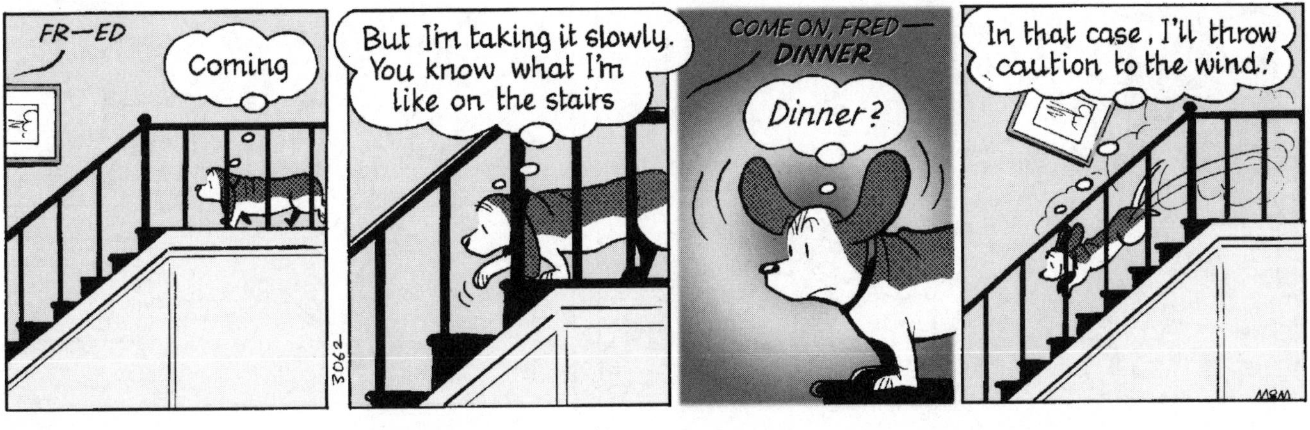
FR—ED
Coming
But I'm taking it slowly. You know what I'm like on the stairs
3062
COME ON, FRED— DINNER
Dinner?
In that case, I'll throw caution to the wind!
M&M

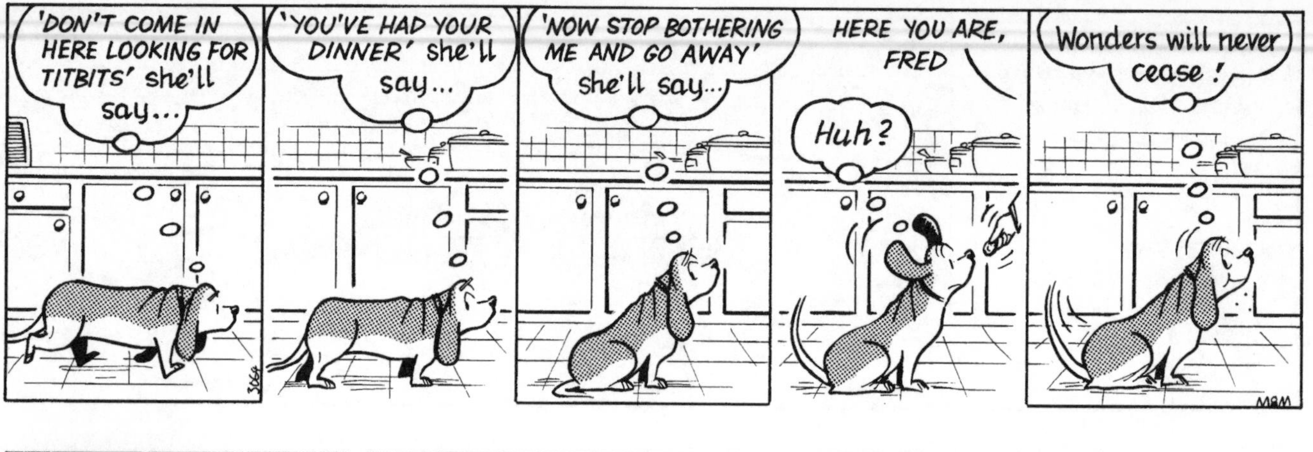
'DON'T COME IN HERE LOOKING FOR TITBITS' she'll say...
'YOU'VE HAD YOUR DINNER' she'll say...
'NOW STOP BOTHERING ME AND GO AWAY' she'll say...
HERE YOU ARE, FRED
Huh?
Wonders will never cease!

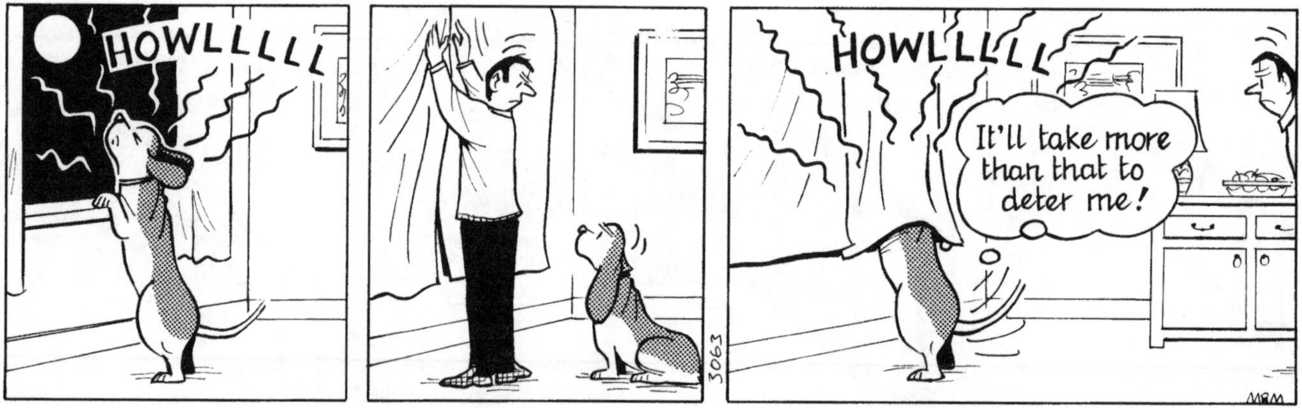
HOWLLLLLL
HOWLLLLL
It'll take more than that to deter me!

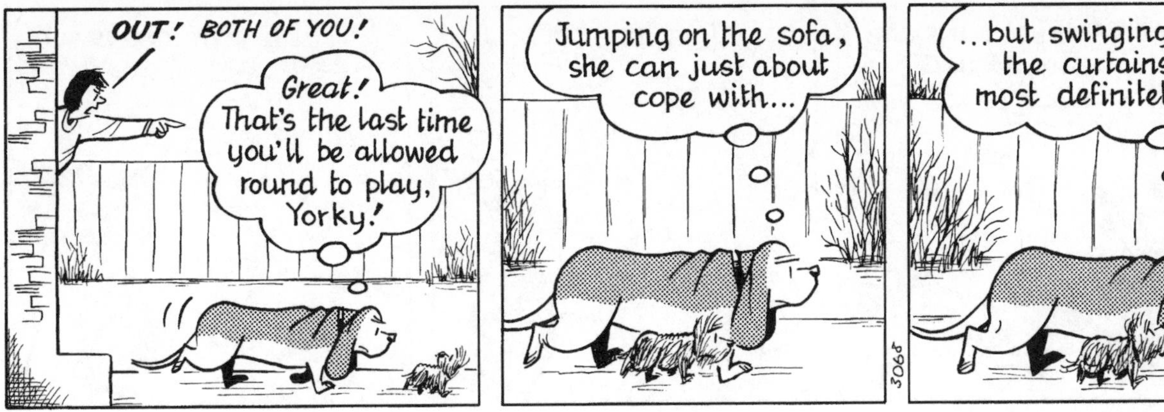
OUT! BOTH OF YOU!
Great! That's the last time you'll be allowed round to play, Yorky!
Jumping on the sofa, she can just about cope with...
...but swinging from the curtains, she most definitely can't!

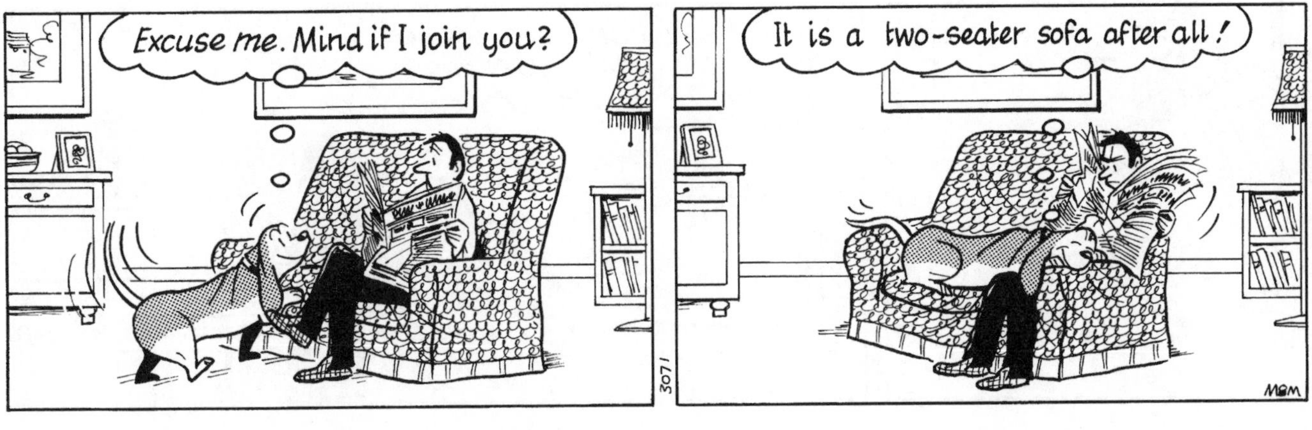
Excuse me. Mind if I join you?
It is a two-seater sofa after all!

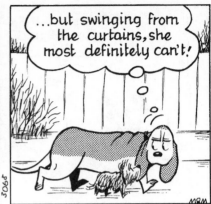

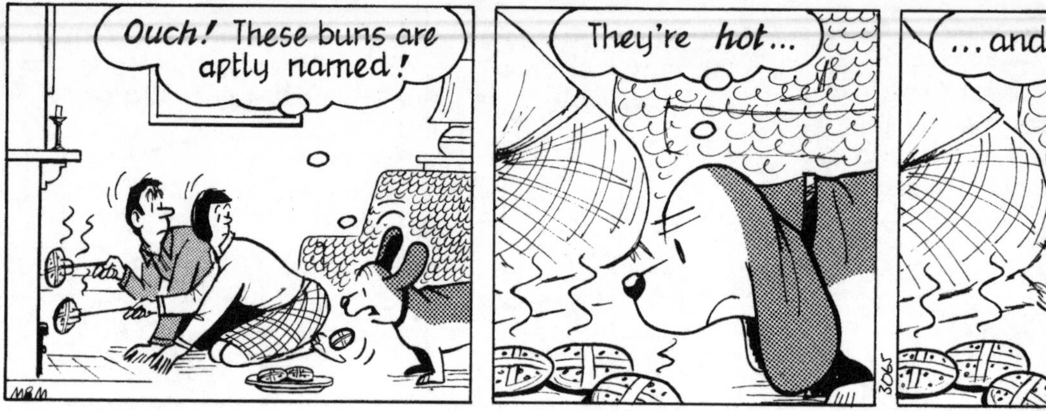
Ouch! These buns are aptly named!
They're hot...
...and I'm cross!
MBM
3065

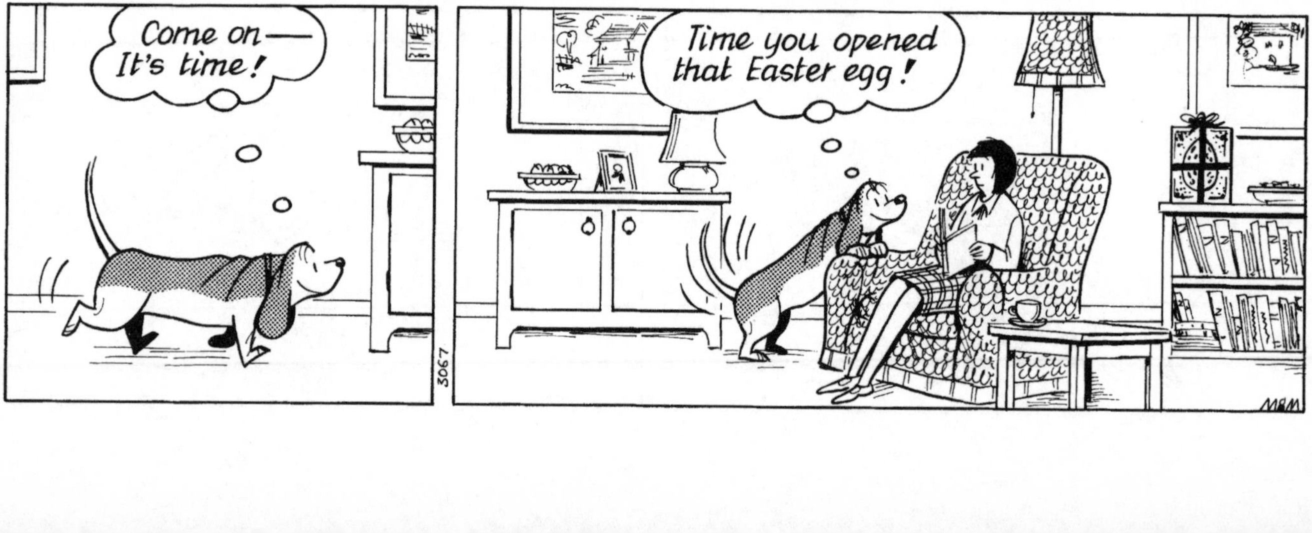
Come on— It's time!
Time you opened that Easter egg!
3067
MBM

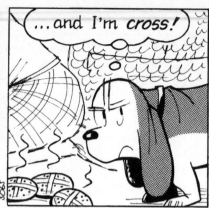

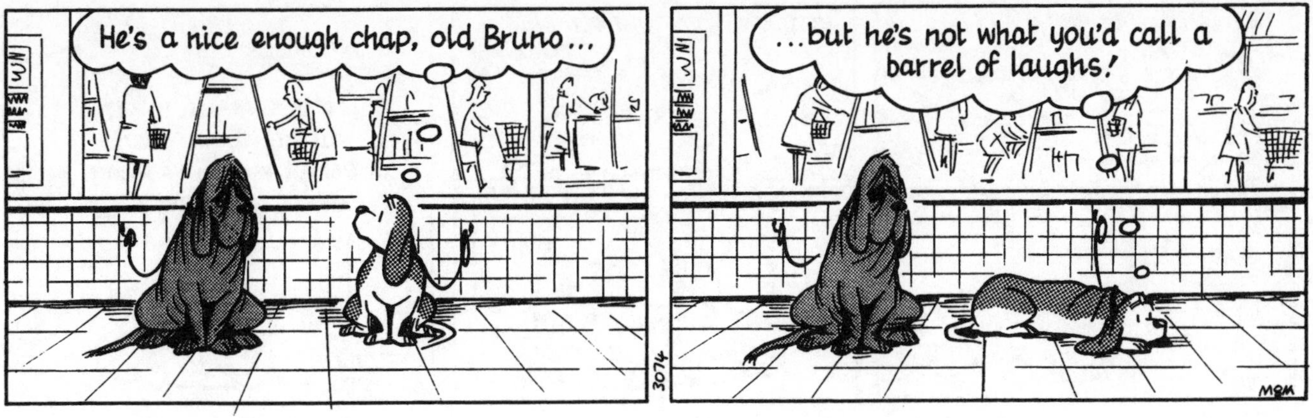
He's a nice enough chap, old Bruno...
3074
...but he's not what you'd call a barrel of laughs!
MGM

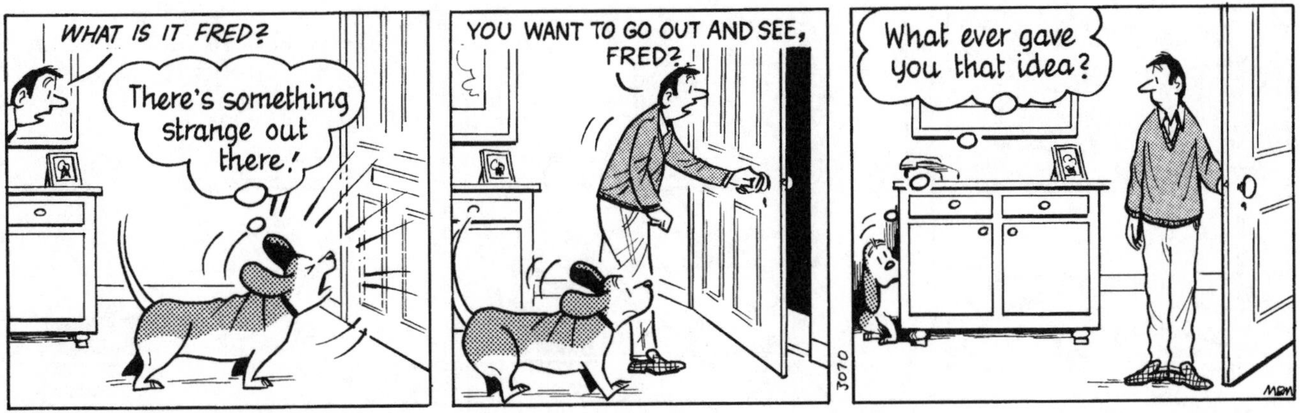
WHAT IS IT FRED?
There's something strange out there!
YOU WANT TO GO OUT AND SEE, FRED?
3070
What ever gave you that idea?
MGM

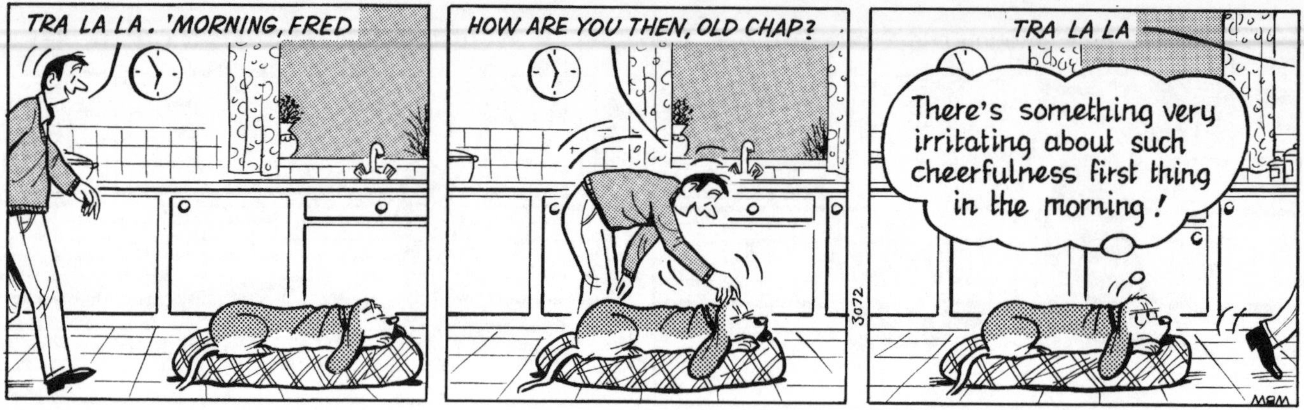
TRA LA LA. 'MORNING, FRED
HOW ARE YOU THEN, OLD CHAP?
3072
TRA LA LA
There's something very irritating about such cheerfulness first thing in the morning!

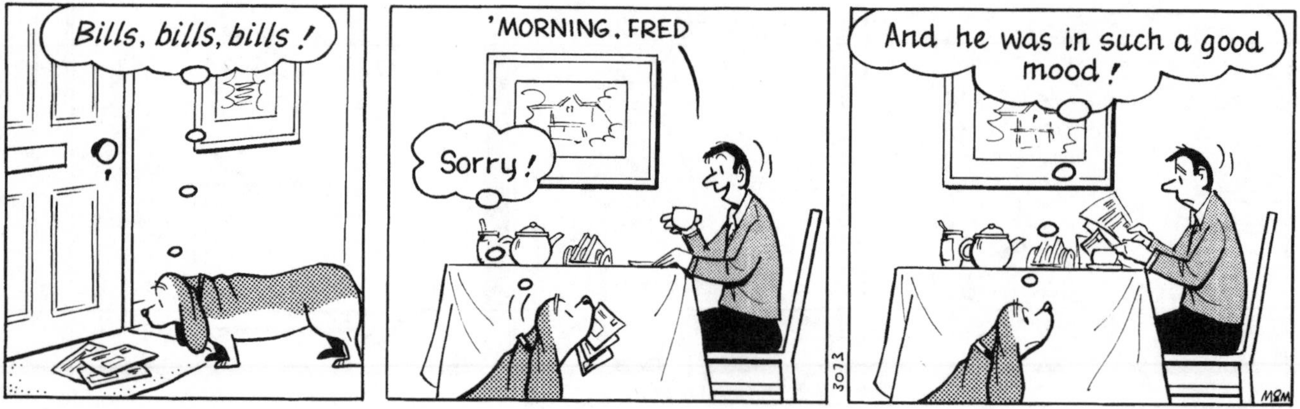
Bills, bills, bills!
'MORNING. FRED
Sorry!
3073
And he was in such a good mood!

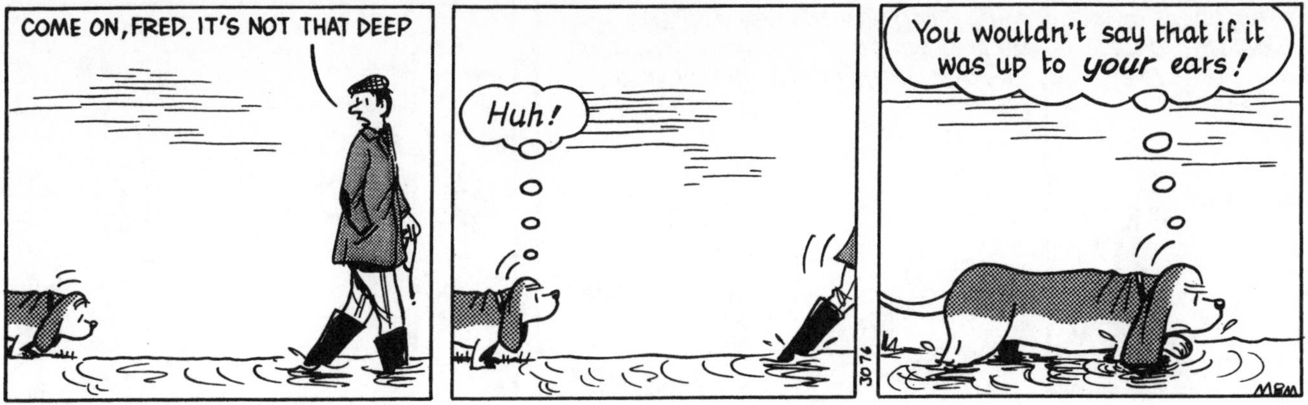
COME ON, FRED. IT'S NOT THAT DEEP
Huh!
You wouldn't say that if it was up to *your* ears!
3076
MBM

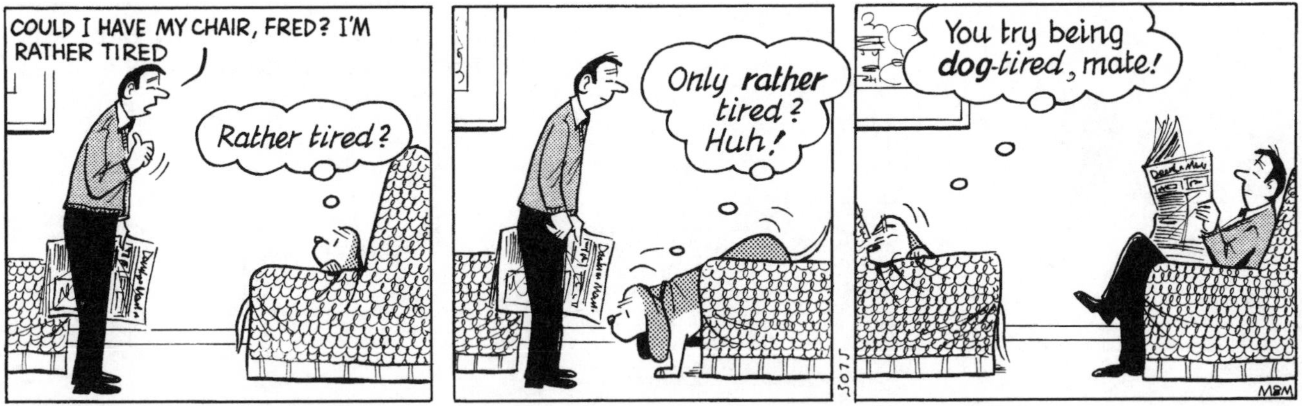
COULD I HAVE MY CHAIR, FRED? I'M RATHER TIRED
Rather tired?
Only **rather** tired? Huh!
You try being **dog**-tired, mate!
3075
MBM

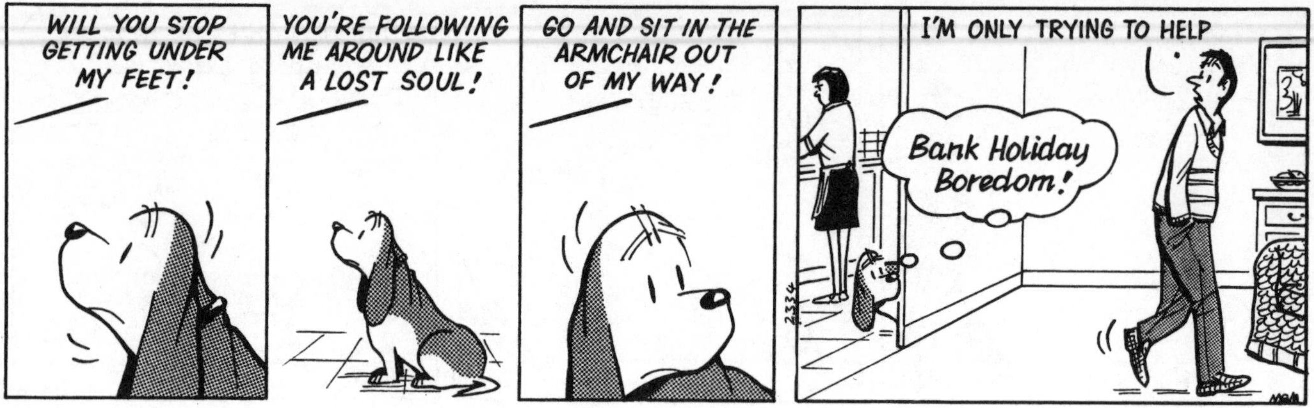
WILL YOU STOP GETTING UNDER MY FEET!
YOU'RE FOLLOWING ME AROUND LIKE A LOST SOUL!
GO AND SIT IN THE ARMCHAIR OUT OF MY WAY!
Bank Holiday Boredom!
I'M ONLY TRYING TO HELP

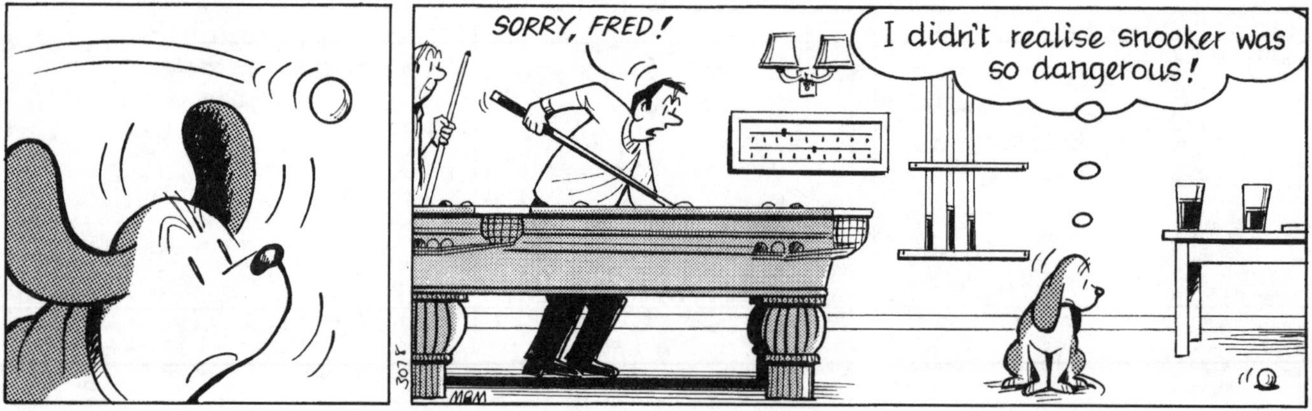
SORRY, FRED!
I didn't realise snooker was so dangerous!

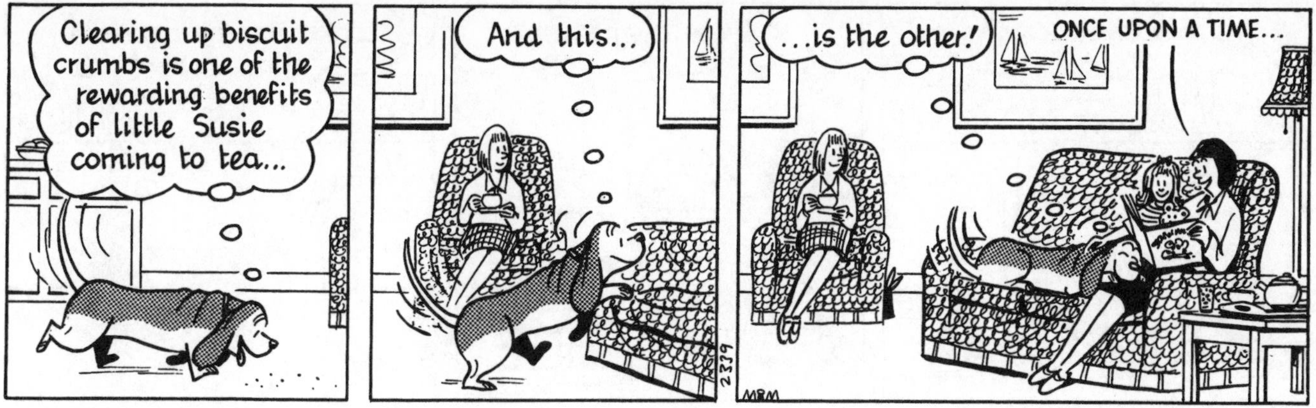
Clearing up biscuit crumbs is one of the rewarding benefits of little Susie coming to tea...
And this...
...is the other!
ONCE UPON A TIME...
2339

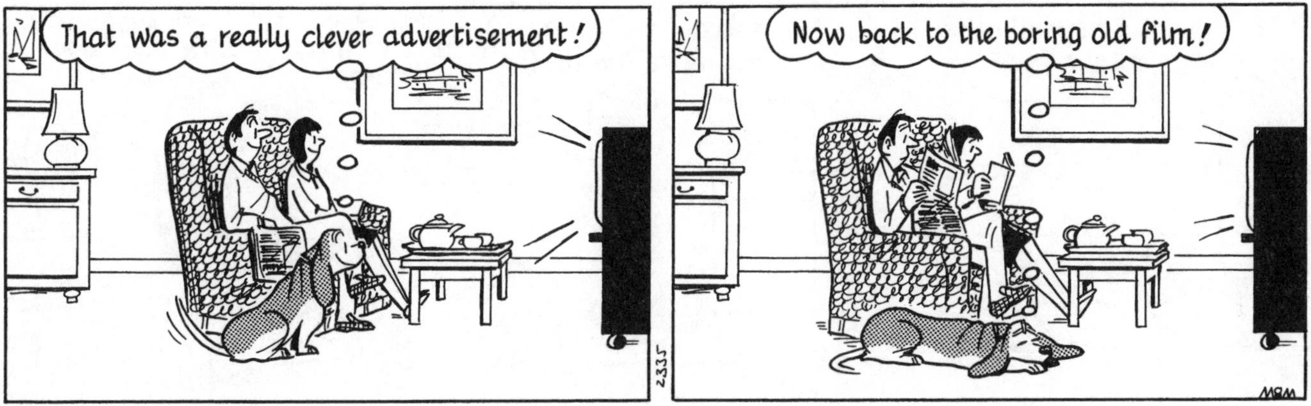
That was a really clever advertisement!
2335
Now back to the boring old film!

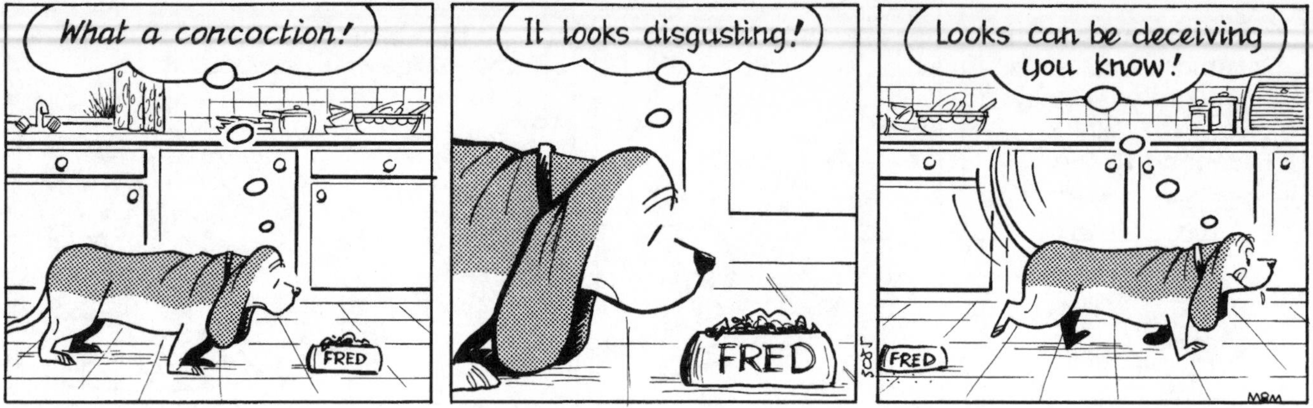
What a concoction!
It looks disgusting!
Looks can be deceiving you know!
FRED
FRED
FRED
MRM

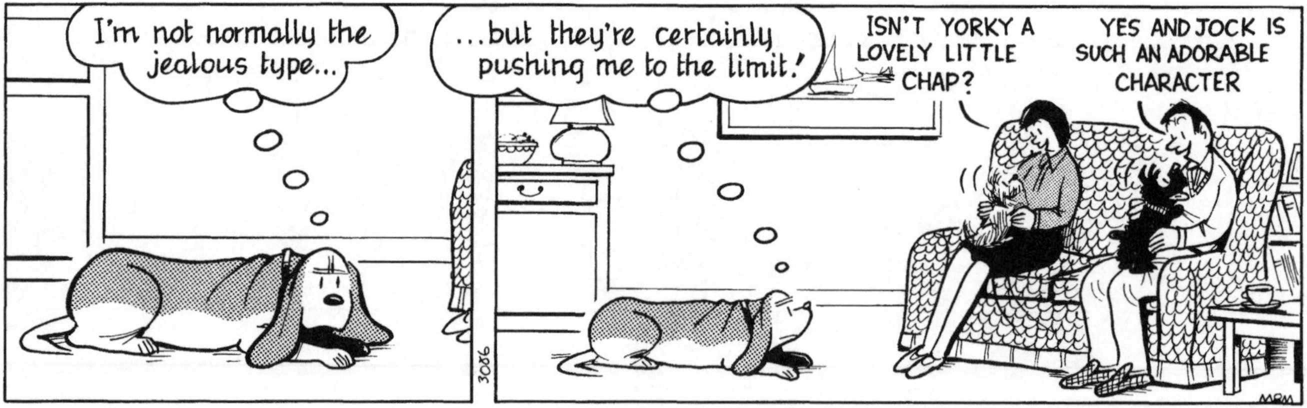
I'm not normally the jealous type...
...but they're certainly pushing me to the limit!
ISN'T YORKY A LOVELY LITTLE CHAP?
YES AND JOCK IS SUCH AN ADORABLE CHARACTER
MRM

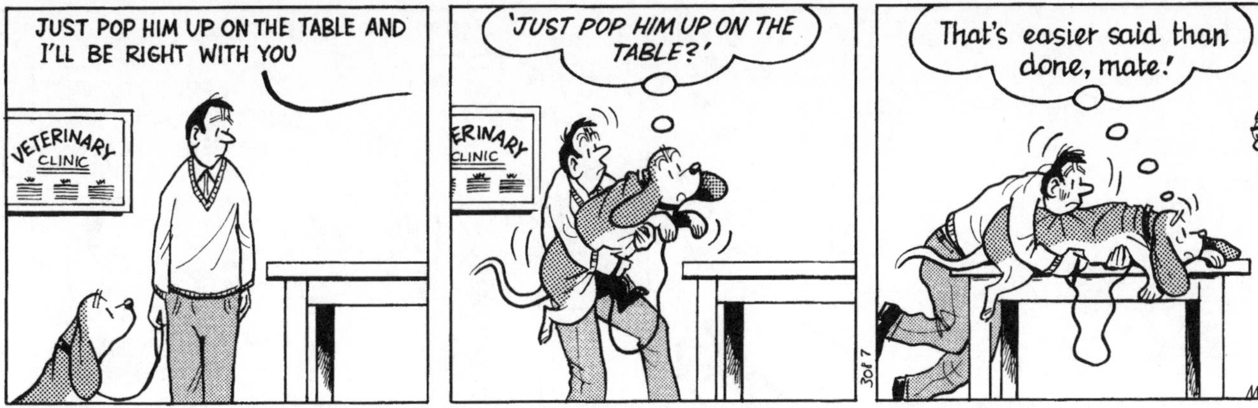
JUST POP HIM UP ON THE TABLE AND I'LL BE RIGHT WITH YOU
VETERINARY CLINIC
'JUST POP HIM UP ON THE TABLE?'
That's easier said than done, mate!

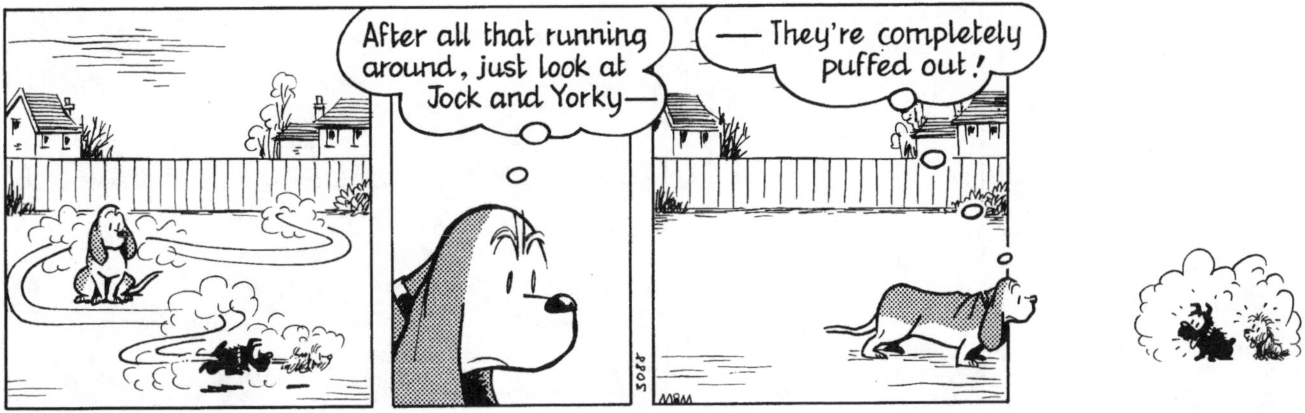
After all that running around, just look at Jock and Yorky—
— They're completely puffed out!

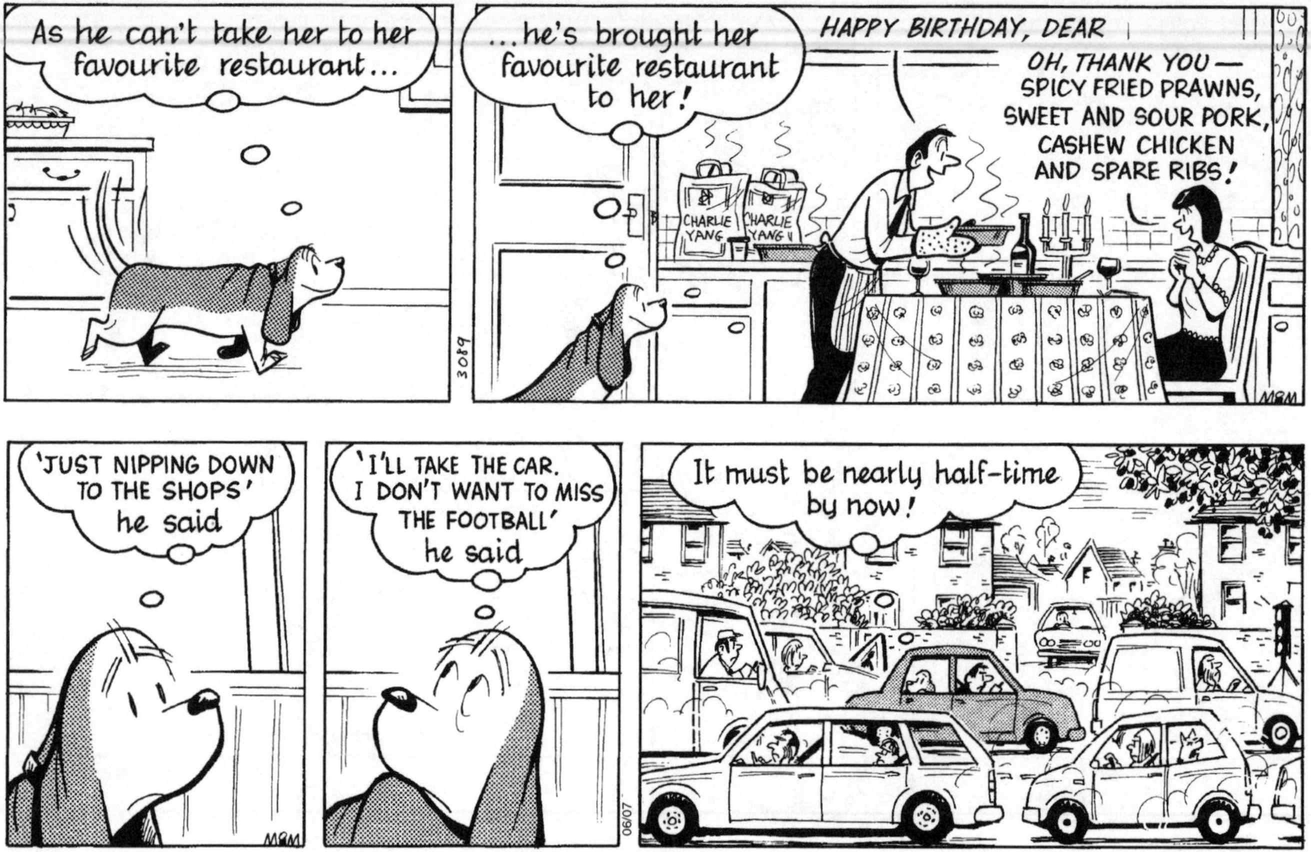
As he can't take her to her favourite restaurant...
...he's brought her favourite restaurant to her!
HAPPY BIRTHDAY, DEAR
OH, THANK YOU — SPICY FRIED PRAWNS, SWEET AND SOUR PORK, CASHEW CHICKEN AND SPARE RIBS!
CHARLIE YANG
CHARLIE YANG
'JUST NIPPING DOWN TO THE SHOPS' he said
'I'LL TAKE THE CAR. I DON'T WANT TO MISS THE FOOTBALL' he said
It must be nearly half-time by now!

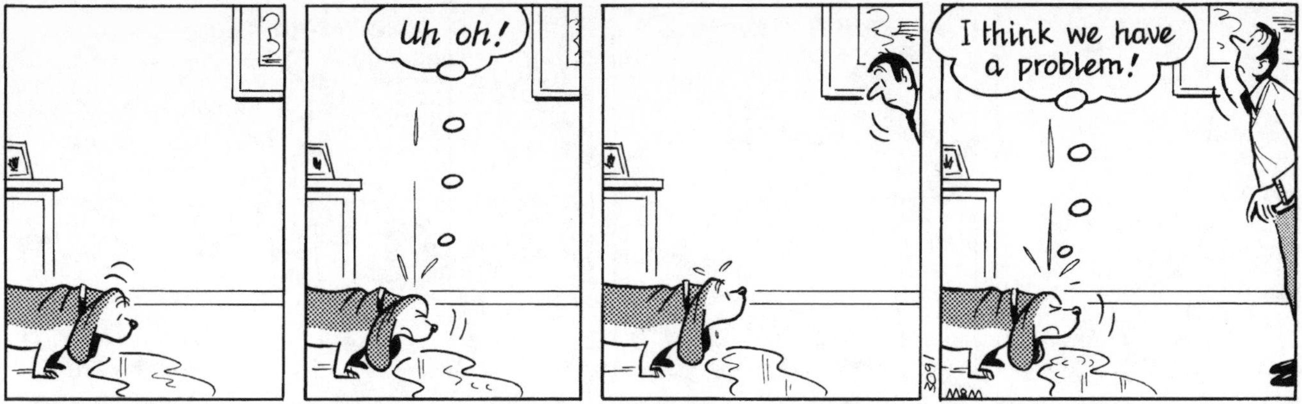
Uh oh!
I think we have a problem!
3091

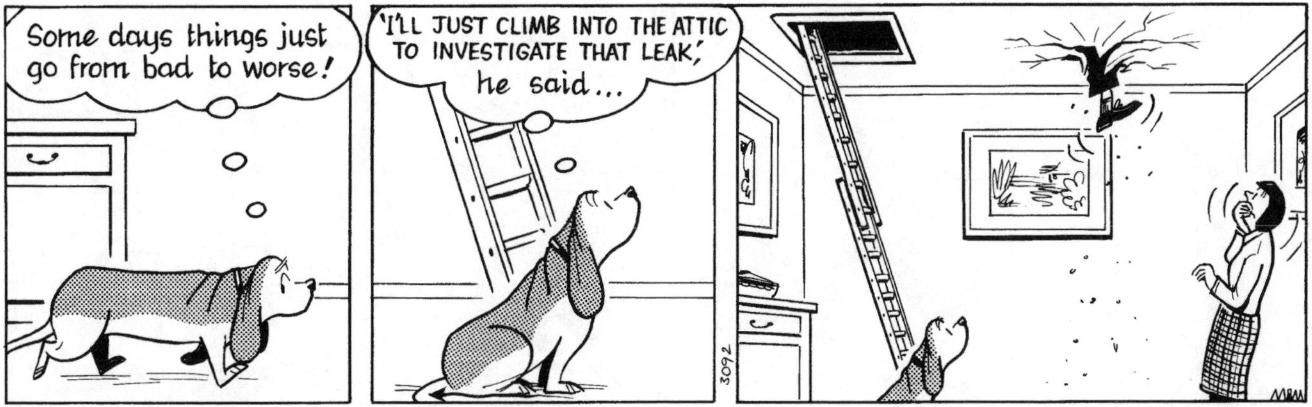
Some days things just go from bad to worse!
'I'LL JUST CLIMB INTO THE ATTIC TO INVESTIGATE THAT LEAK,' he said...
3092

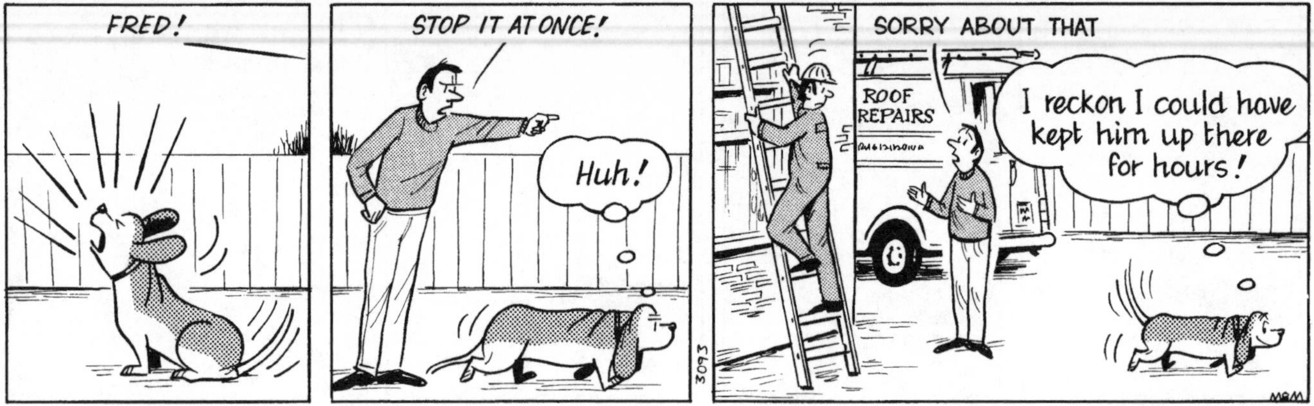
FRED!
STOP IT AT ONCE!
Huh!
SORRY ABOUT THAT
ROOF REPAIRS
I reckon I could have kept him up there for hours!
3093
MBM

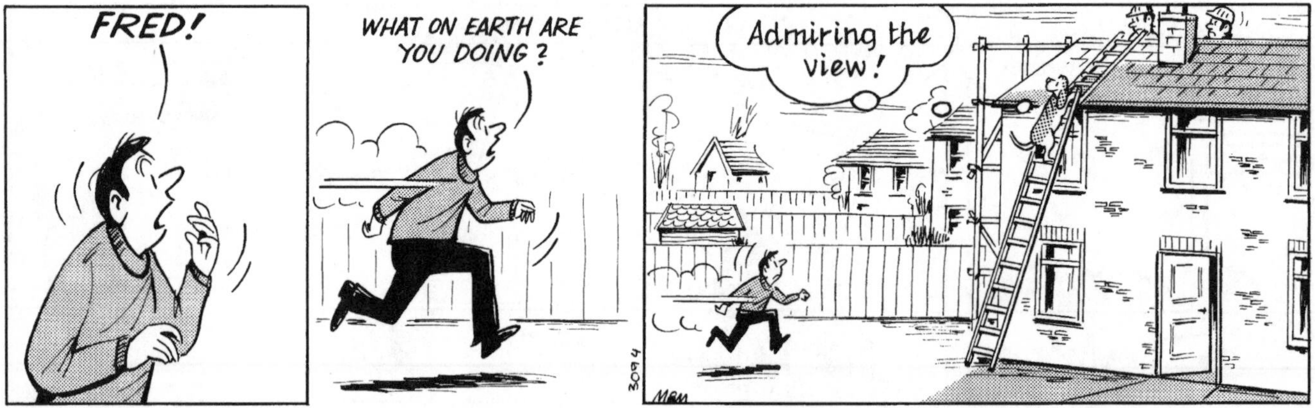
FRED!
WHAT ON EARTH ARE YOU DOING?
Admiring the view!
3094
MBM

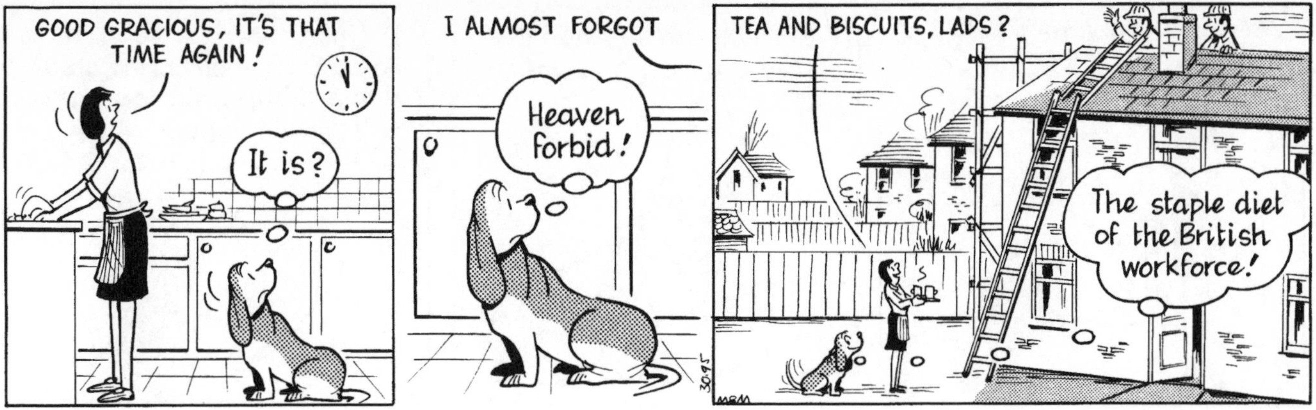
GOOD GRACIOUS, IT'S THAT TIME AGAIN!
It is?
I ALMOST FORGOT
Heaven forbid!
TEA AND BISCUITS, LADS?
The staple diet of the British workforce!

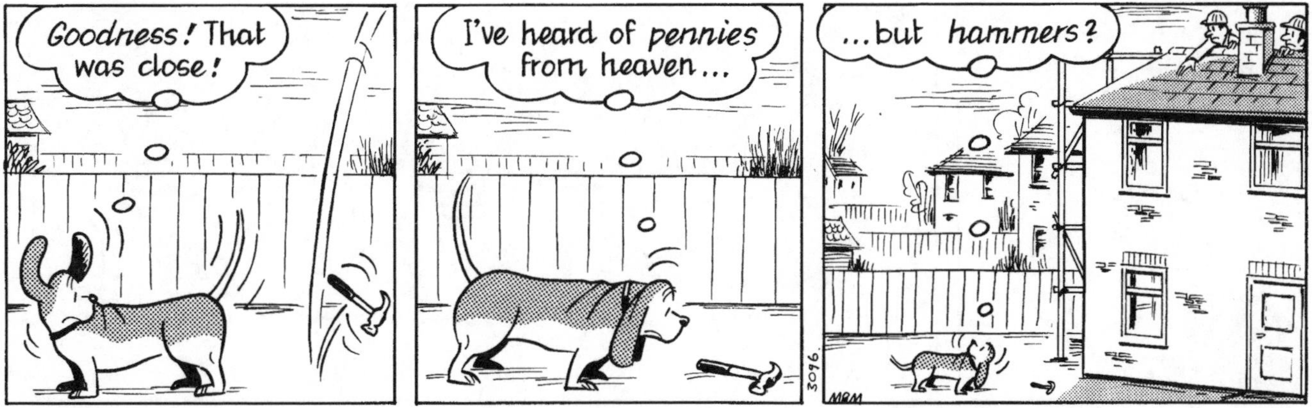
Goodness! That was close!
I've heard of pennies from heaven...
...but hammers?

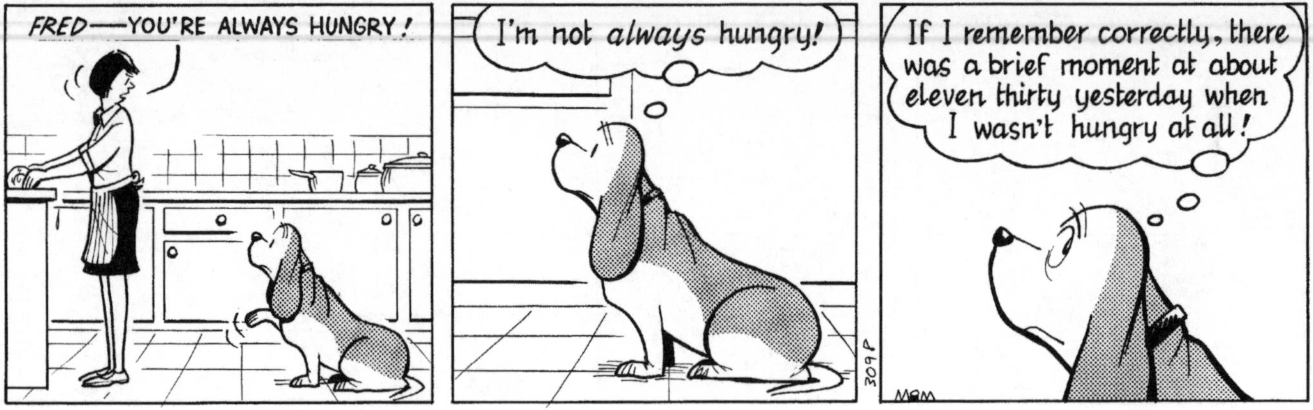
FRED—YOU'RE ALWAYS HUNGRY!
I'm not *always* hungry!
If I remember correctly, there was a brief moment at about eleven thirty yesterday when I wasn't hungry at all!

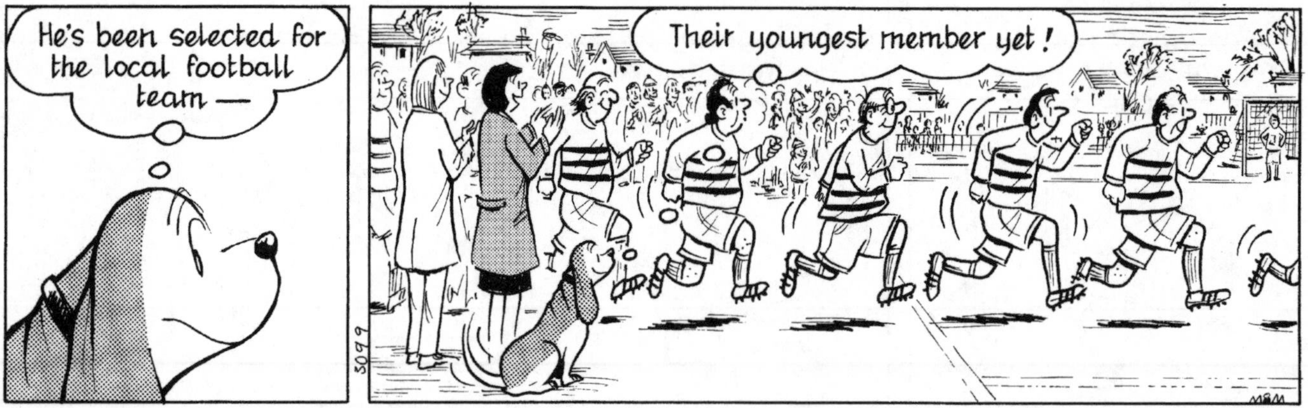
He's been selected for the local football team—
Their youngest member yet!

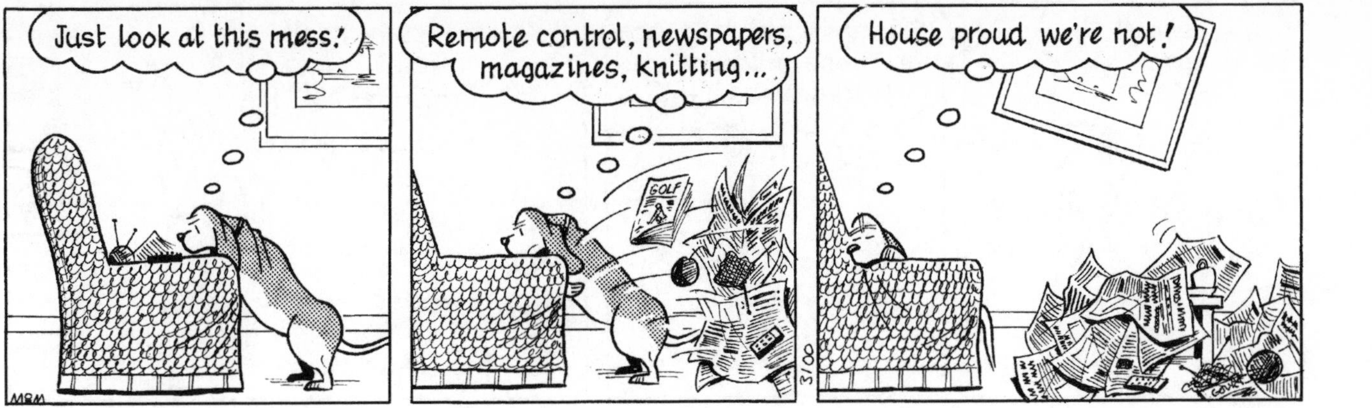
Just look at this mess!
Remote control, newspapers, magazines, knitting...
House proud we're not!

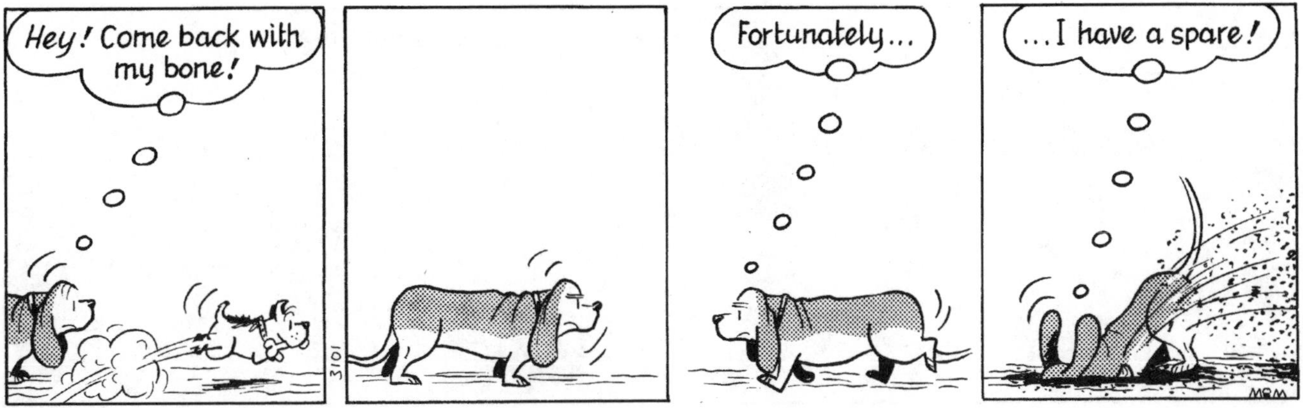
Hey! Come back with my bone!
Fortunately...
...I have a spare!

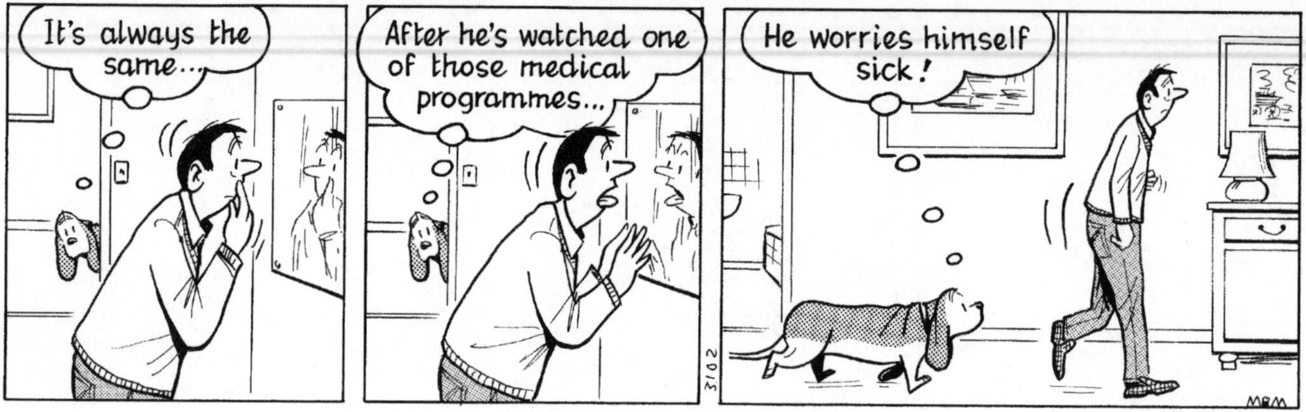
It's always the same...
After he's watched one of those medical programmes...
He worries himself sick!

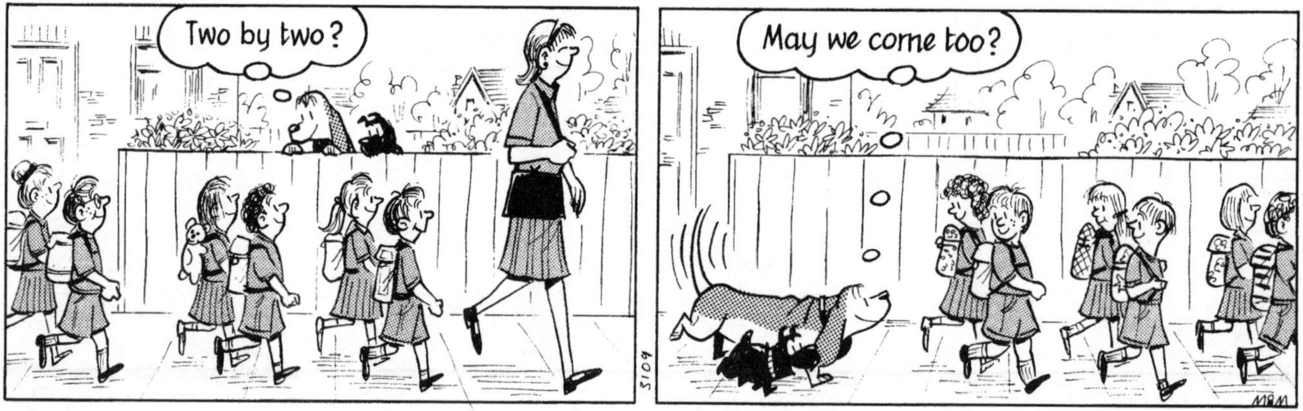
Two by two?
May we come too?

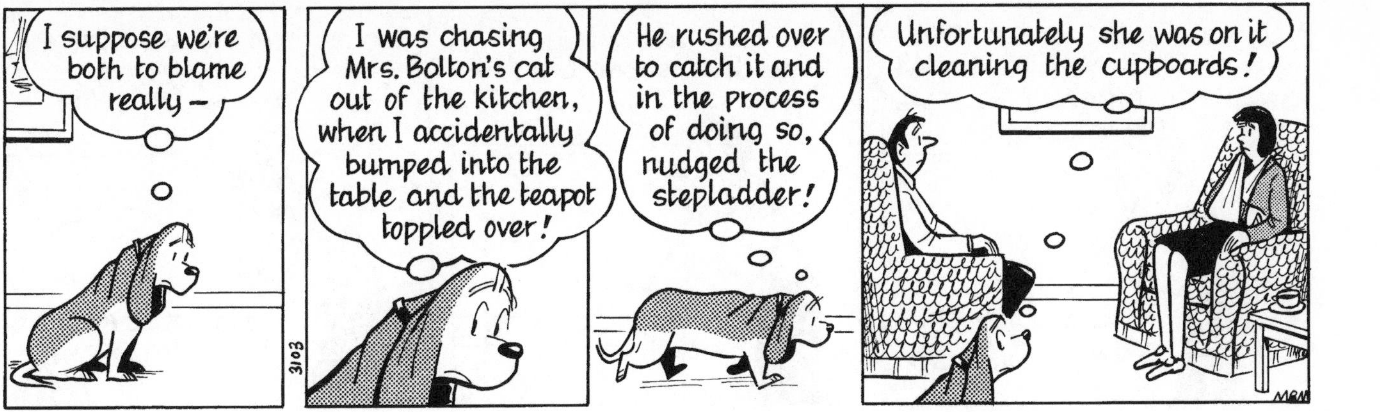
I suppose we're both to blame really –
I was chasing Mrs. Bolton's cat out of the kitchen, when I accidentally bumped into the table and the teapot toppled over!
3103
He rushed over to catch it and in the process of doing so, nudged the stepladder!
Unfortunately she was on it cleaning the cupboards!
MBM

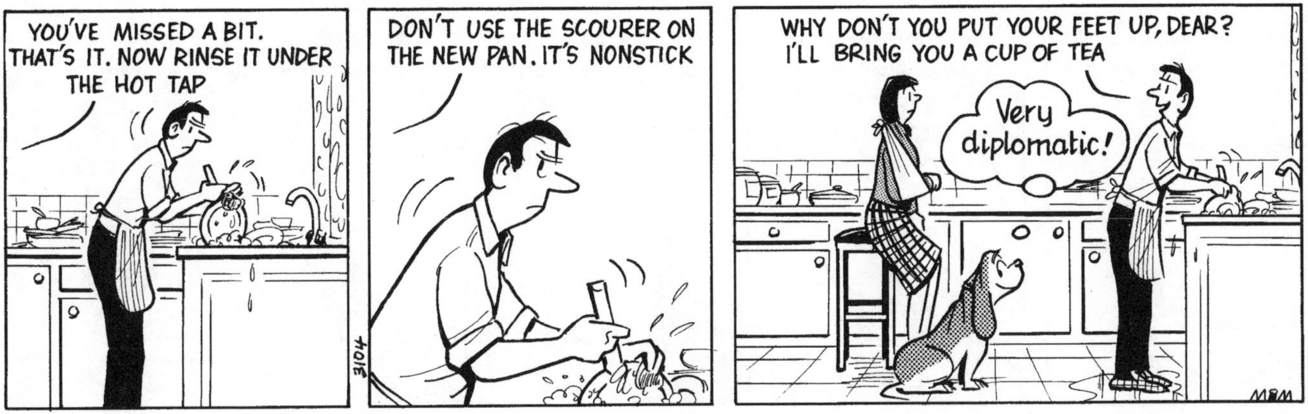
YOU'VE MISSED A BIT. THAT'S IT. NOW RINSE IT UNDER THE HOT TAP
DON'T USE THE SCOURER ON THE NEW PAN. IT'S NONSTICK
3104
WHY DON'T YOU PUT YOUR FEET UP, DEAR? I'LL BRING YOU A CUP OF TEA
Very diplomatic!
MBM

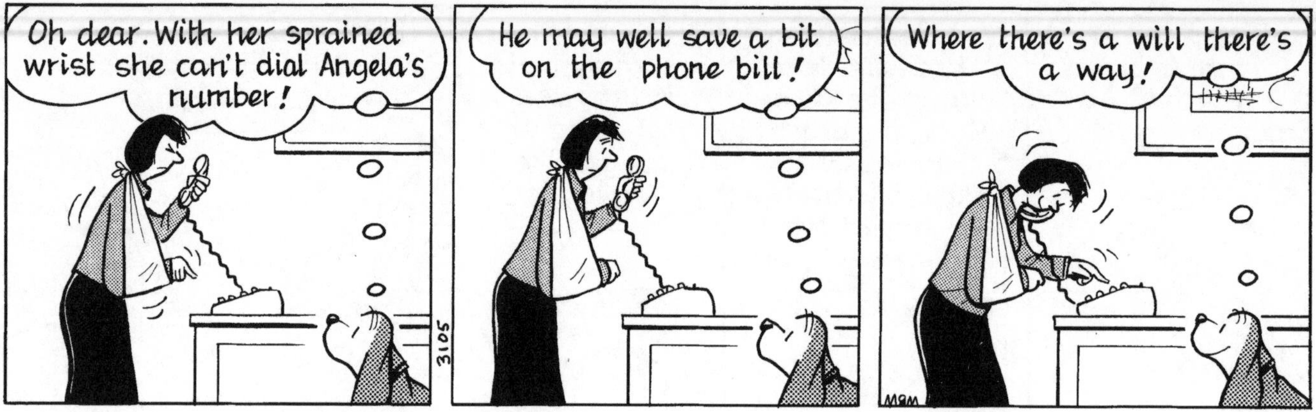
Oh dear. With her sprained wrist she can't dial Angela's number!
3105
He may well save a bit on the phone bill!
Where there's a will there's a way!
M&M

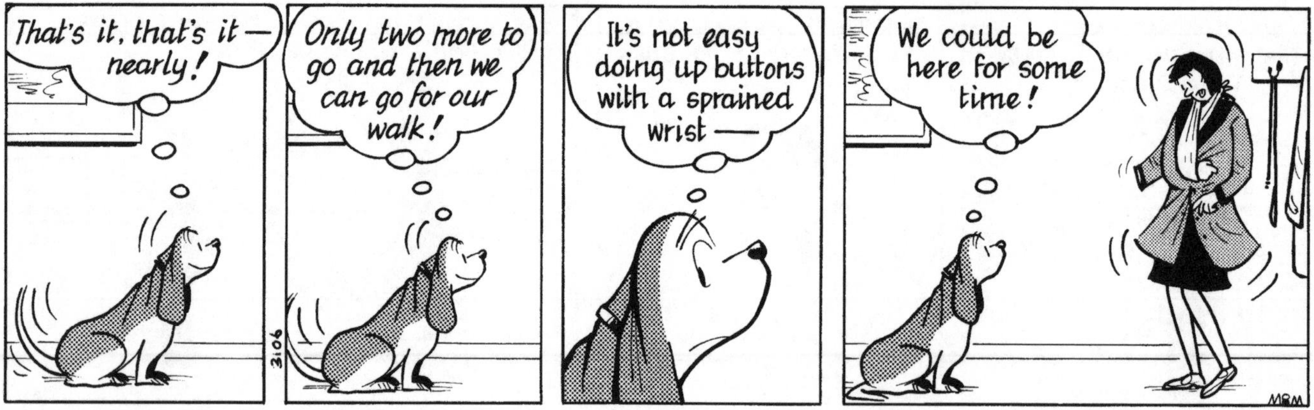
That's it, that's it — nearly!
Only two more to go and then we can go for our walk!
3106
It's not easy doing up buttons with a sprained wrist —
We could be here for some time!
M&M

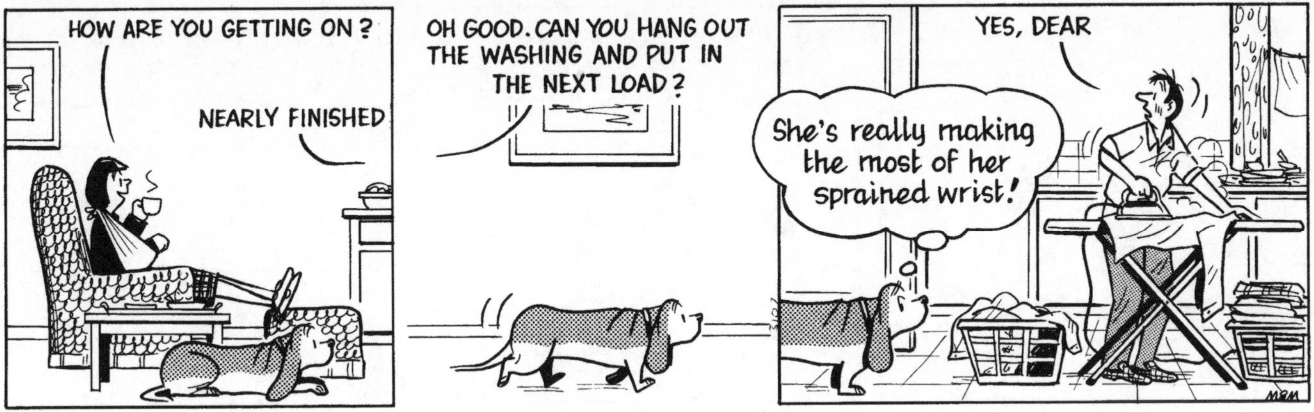
HOW ARE YOU GETTING ON ?
NEARLY FINISHED
OH GOOD. CAN YOU HANG OUT THE WASHING AND PUT IN THE NEXT LOAD ?
YES, DEAR
She's really making the most of her sprained wrist!

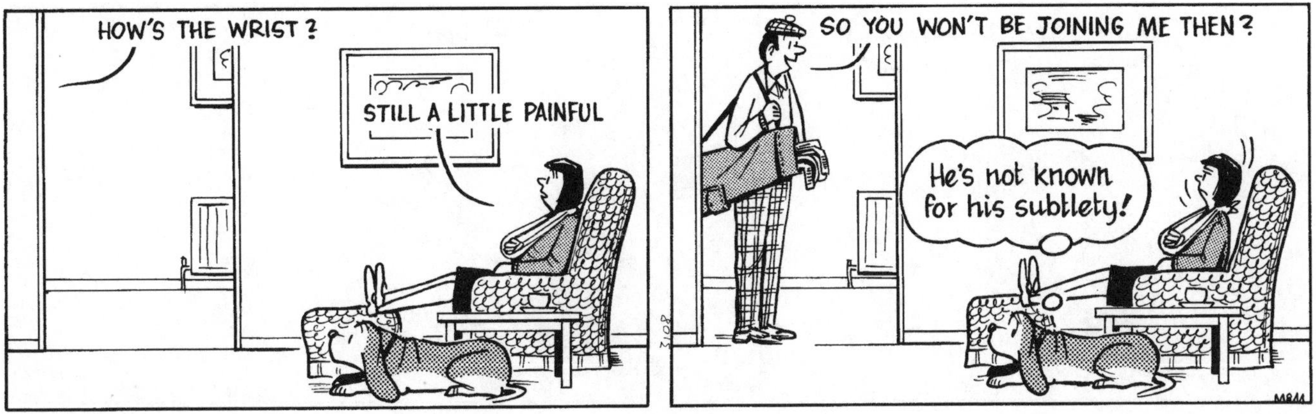
HOW'S THE WRIST ?
STILL A LITTLE PAINFUL
SO YOU WON'T BE JOINING ME THEN ?
He's not known for his subtlety!

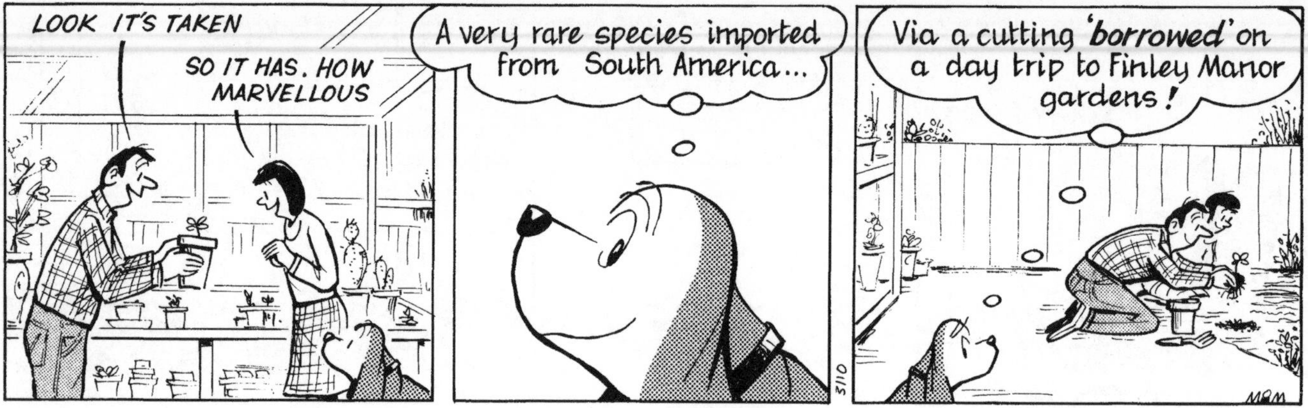
LOOK IT'S TAKEN
SO IT HAS. HOW MARVELLOUS
A very rare species imported from South America...
Via a cutting 'borrowed' on a day trip to Finley Manor gardens!
3/10

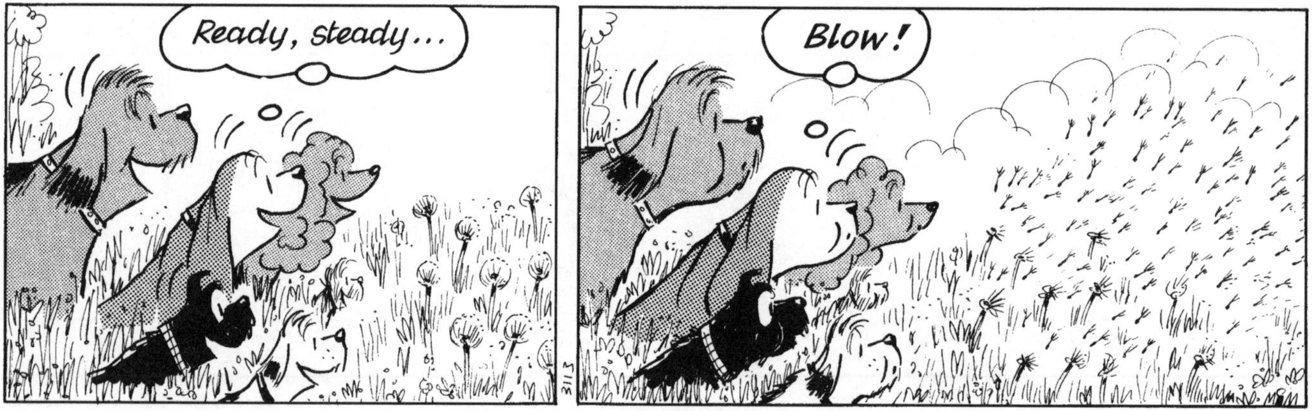
Ready, steady...
Blow!
3/13

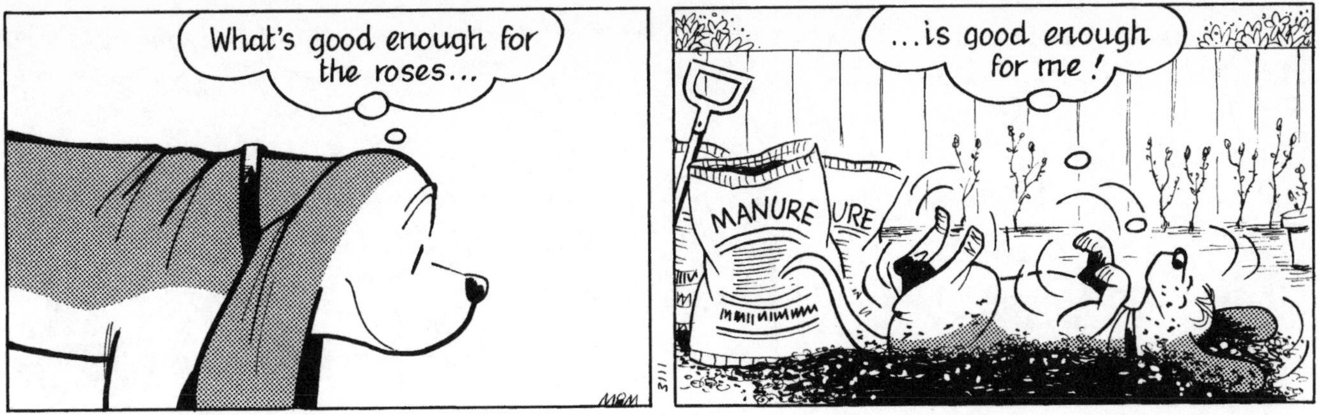
What's good enough for the roses...
MANURE
URE
...is good enough for me!

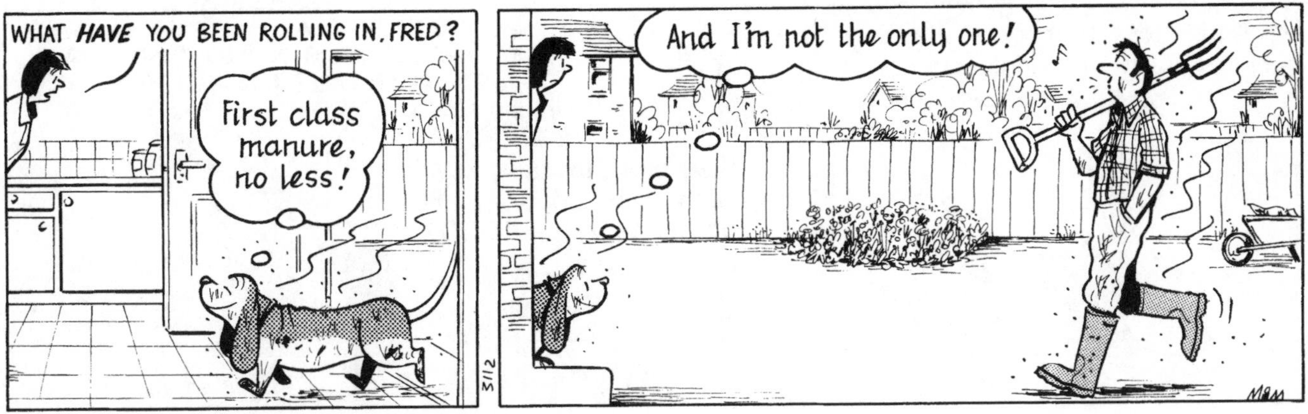
WHAT HAVE YOU BEEN ROLLING IN, FRED?
First class manure, no less!
And I'm not the only one!

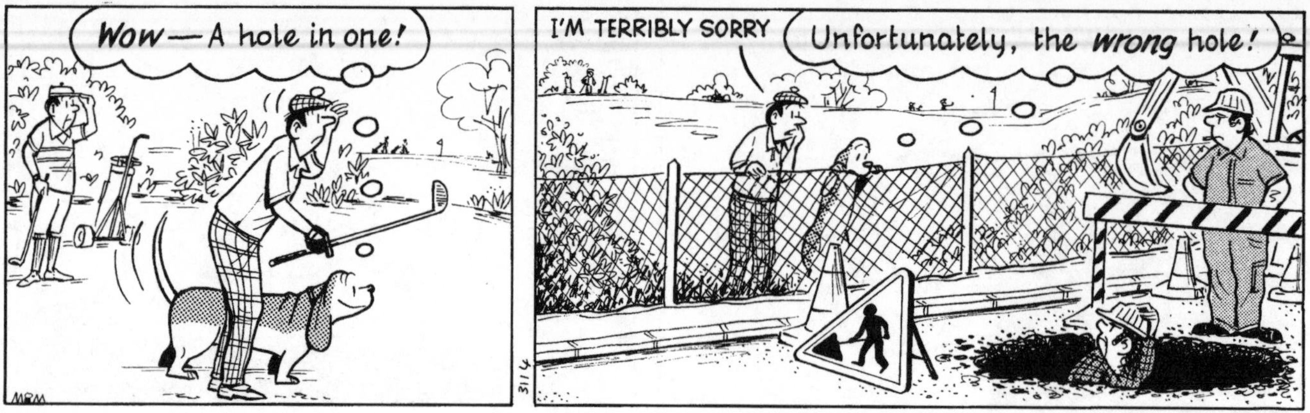
Wow — A hole in one!
I'M TERRIBLY SORRY
Unfortunately, the wrong hole!
3114

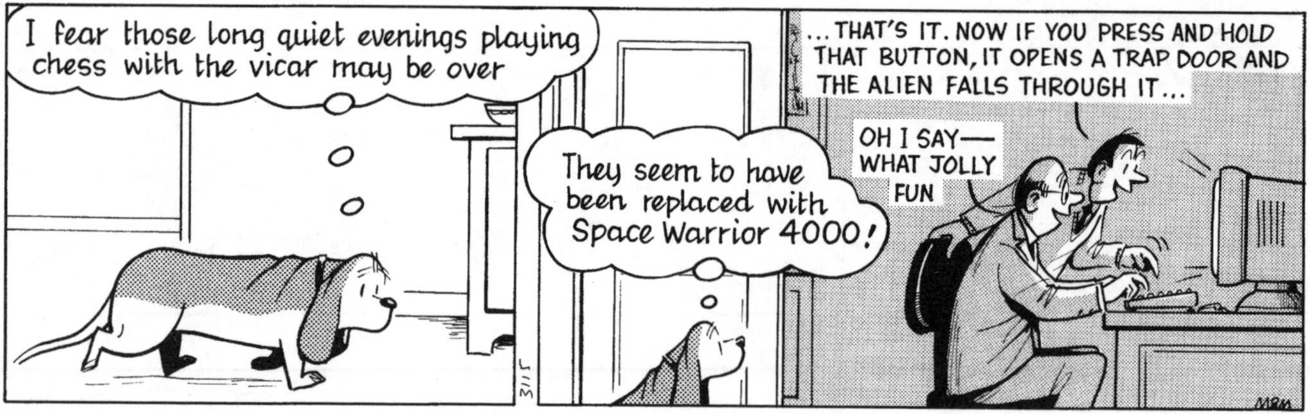
I fear those long quiet evenings playing chess with the vicar may be over
...THAT'S IT. NOW IF YOU PRESS AND HOLD THAT BUTTON, IT OPENS A TRAP DOOR AND THE ALIEN FALLS THROUGH IT...
OH I SAY— WHAT JOLLY FUN
They seem to have been replaced with Space Warrior 4000!
3115

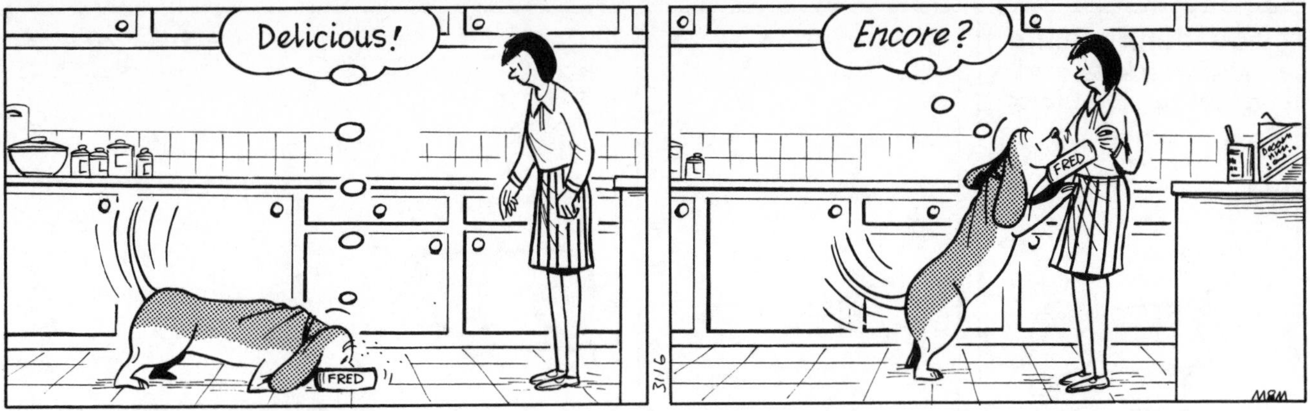
Delicious!
FRED
Encore?
FRED
3116
M&M

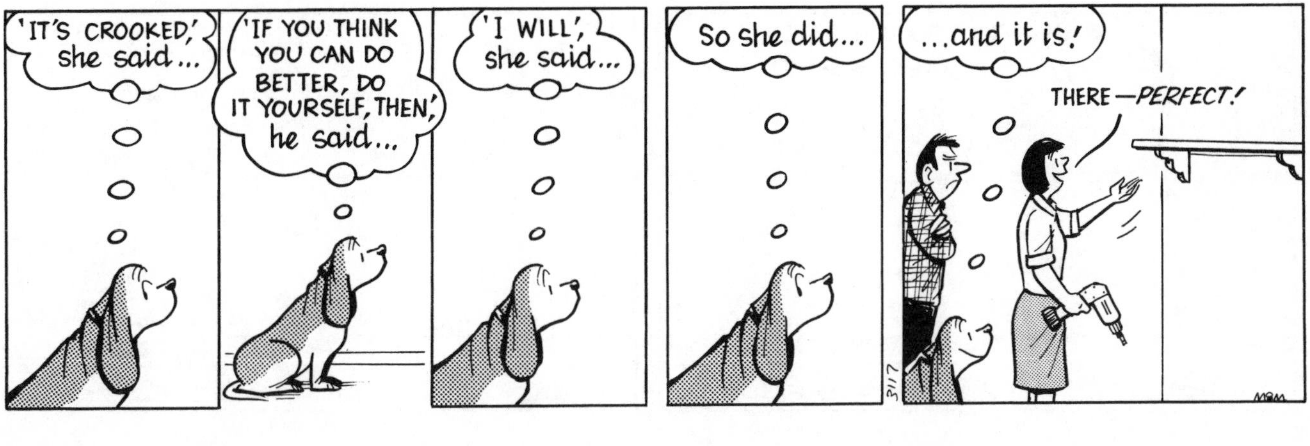
'IT'S CROOKED,' she said...
'IF YOU THINK YOU CAN DO BETTER, DO IT YOURSELF, THEN,' he said...
'I WILL', she said...
So she did...
...and it is!
THERE—PERFECT!
3117
M&M

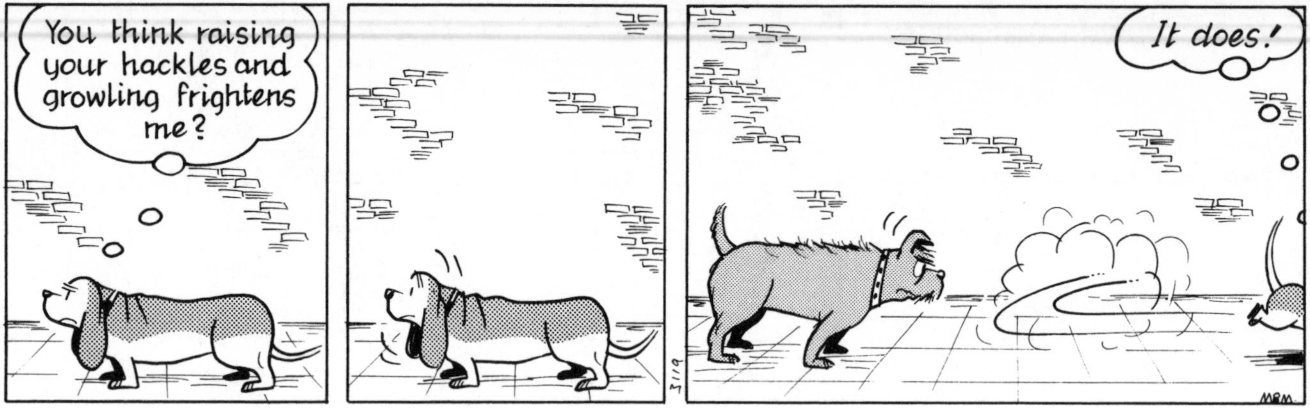
You think raising your hackles and growling frightens me?
It does!
3119
MBM

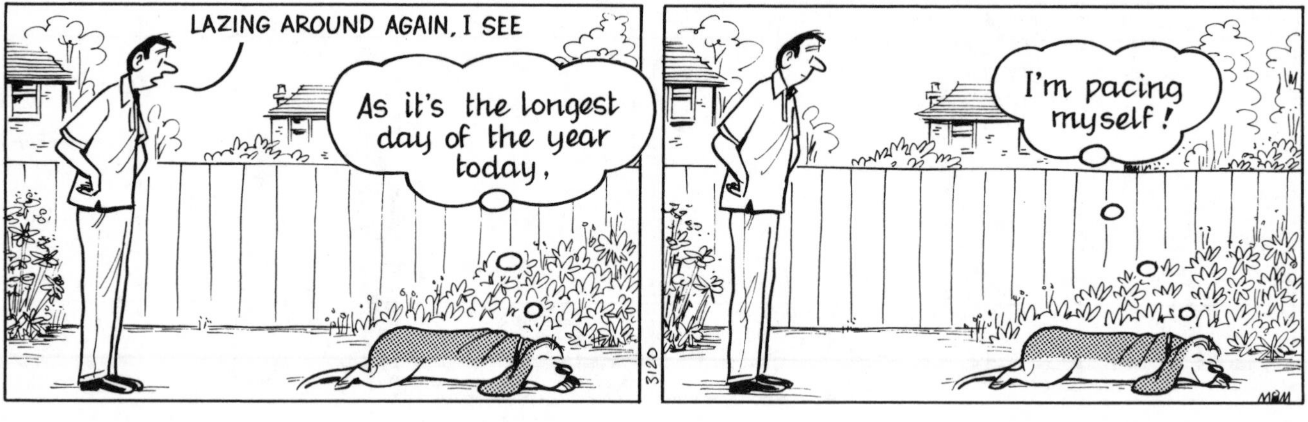
LAZING AROUND AGAIN, I SEE
As it's the longest day of the year today,
I'm pacing myself!
3120
MBM

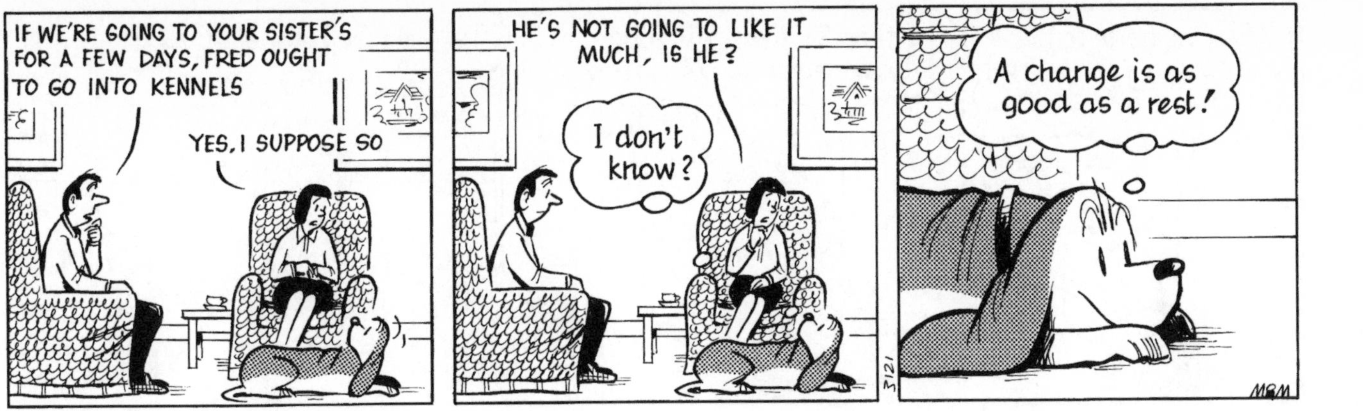
IF WE'RE GOING TO YOUR SISTER'S FOR A FEW DAYS, FRED OUGHT TO GO INTO KENNELS
YES, I SUPPOSE SO
HE'S NOT GOING TO LIKE IT MUCH, IS HE?
I don't know?
A change is as good as a rest!
3121
M&M

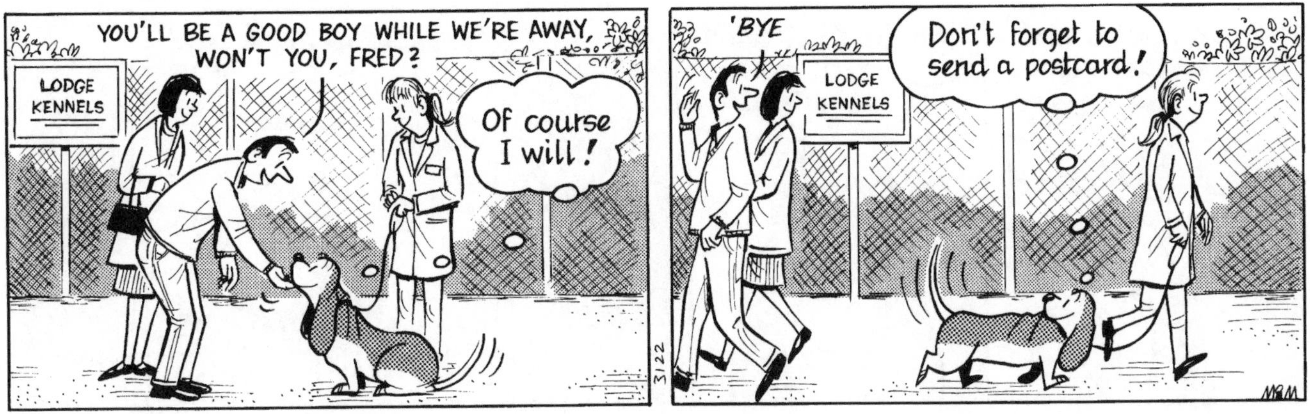
YOU'LL BE A GOOD BOY WHILE WE'RE AWAY, WON'T YOU, FRED?
LODGE KENNELS
Of course I will!
3122
'BYE
LODGE KENNELS
Don't forget to send a postcard!
M&M

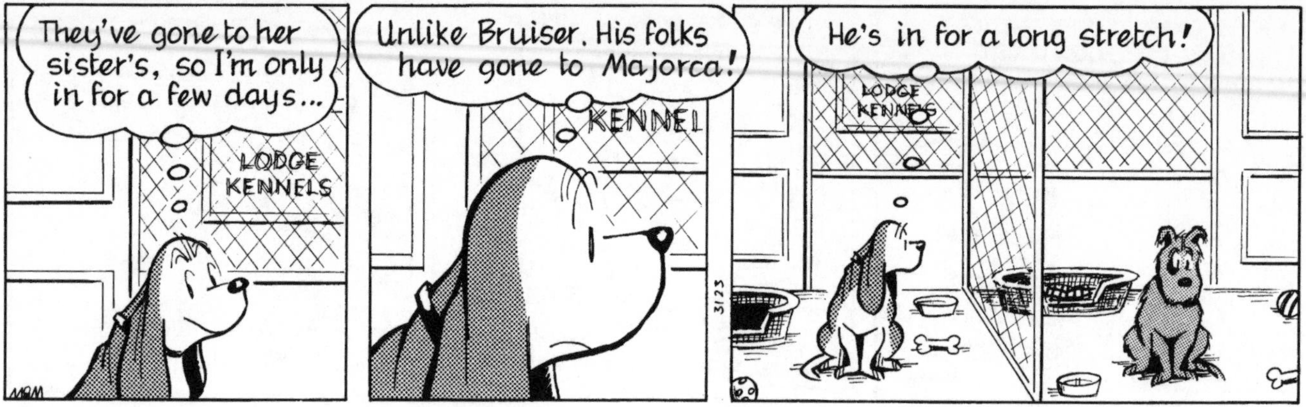
They've gone to her sister's, so I'm only in for a few days...
LODGE KENNELS
Unlike Bruiser. His folks have gone to Majorca!
KENNEL
3/23
He's in for a long stretch!

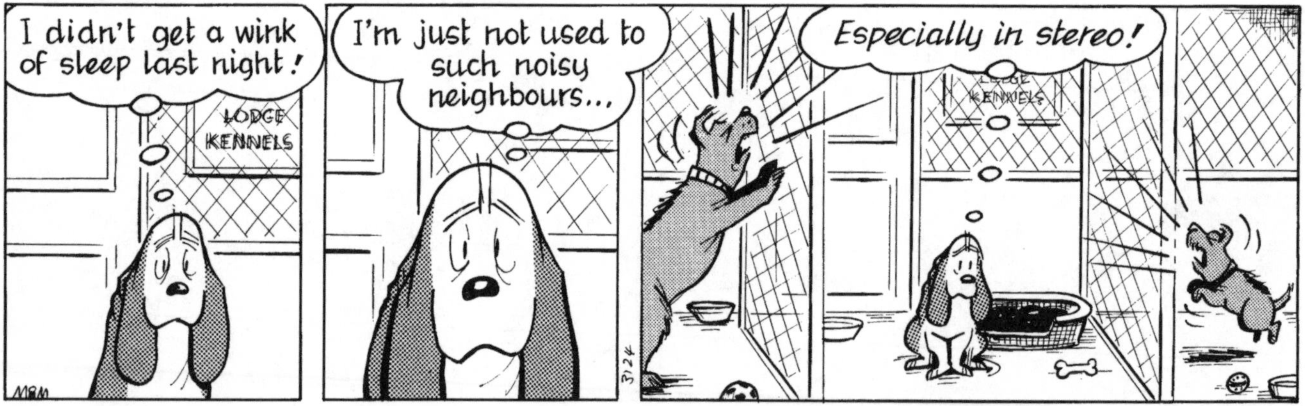
I didn't get a wink of sleep last night!
LODGE KENNELS
I'm just not used to such noisy neighbours...
3/24
Especially in stereo!

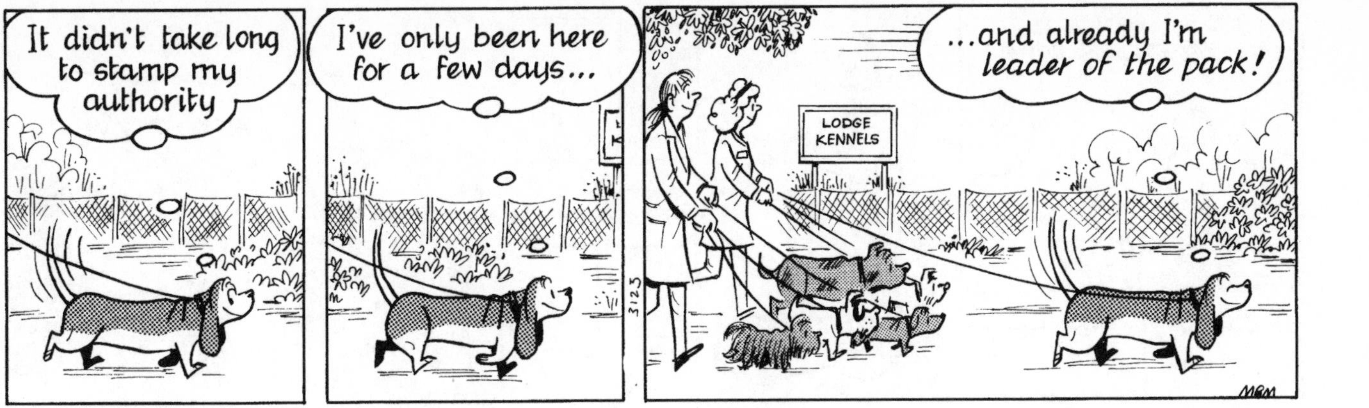
It didn't take long to stamp my authority
I've only been here for a few days...
3125
LODGE KENNELS
...and already I'm *leader of the pack!*
MBM

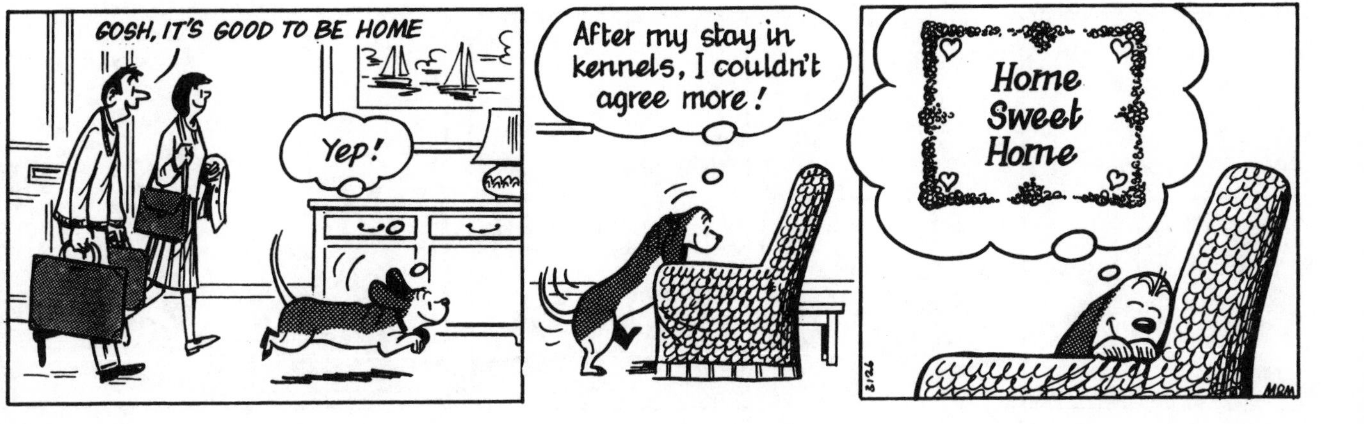
GOSH, IT'S GOOD TO BE HOME
Yep!
After my stay in kennels, I couldn't agree more!
Home Sweet Home
3126
MBM

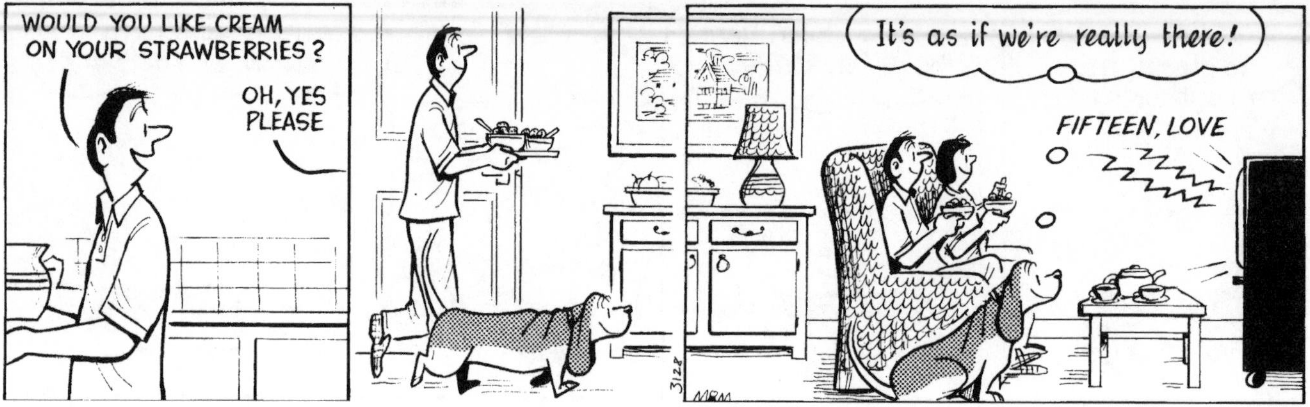
WOULD YOU LIKE CREAM ON YOUR STRAWBERRIES ?
OH, YES PLEASE
It's as if we're really there!
FIFTEEN, LOVE
3128

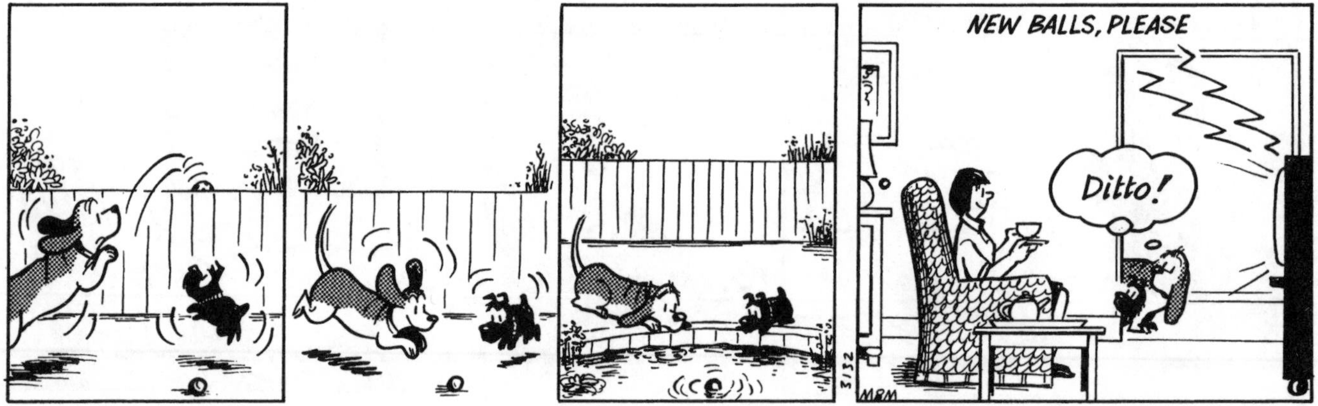
NEW BALLS, PLEASE
Ditto!
3132

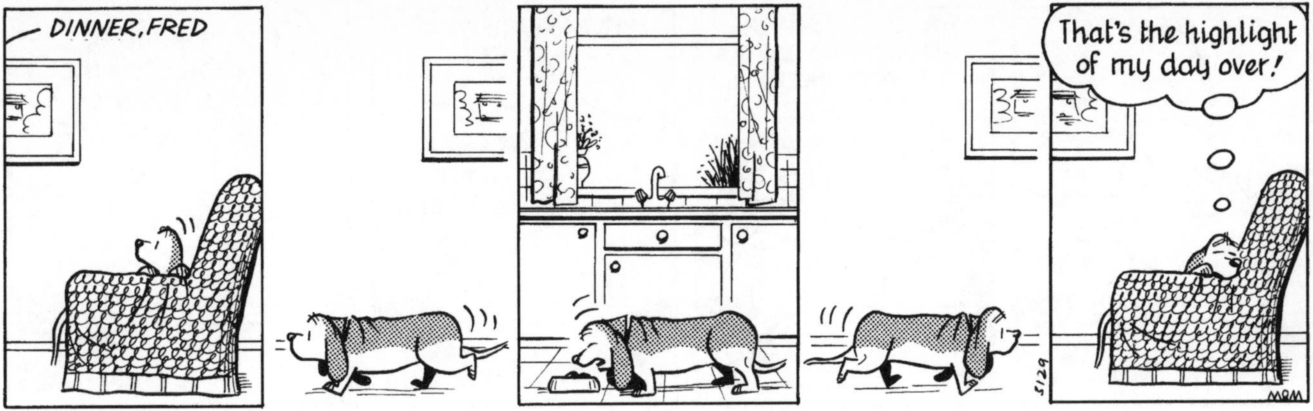
DINNER, FRED
That's the highlight of my day over!

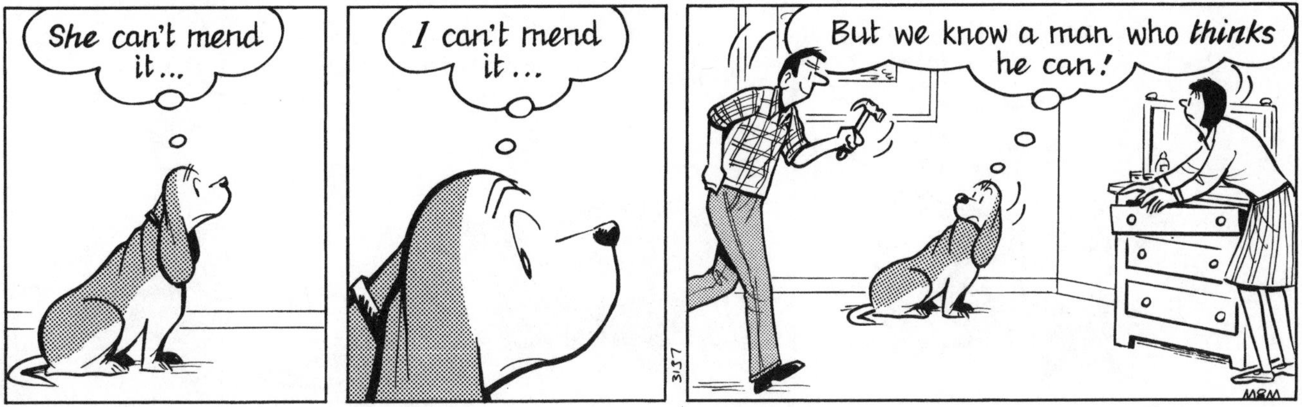
She can't mend it...
I can't mend it...
But we know a man who *thinks* he can!

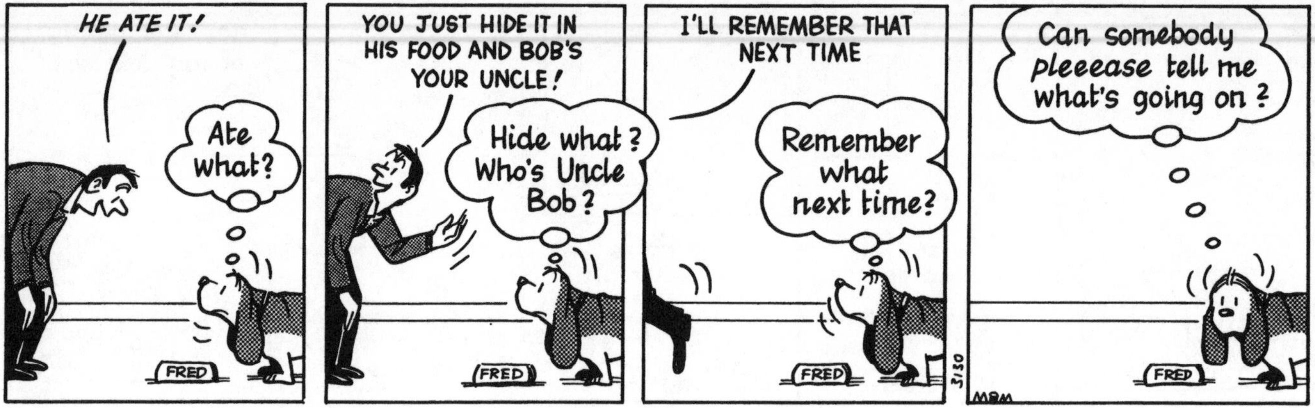
HE ATE IT!
Ate what?
FRED
YOU JUST HIDE IT IN HIS FOOD AND BOB'S YOUR UNCLE!
Hide what? Who's Uncle Bob?
FRED
I'LL REMEMBER THAT NEXT TIME
Remember what next time?
FRED
3/30
Can somebody pleeease tell me what's going on?
FRED
MBM

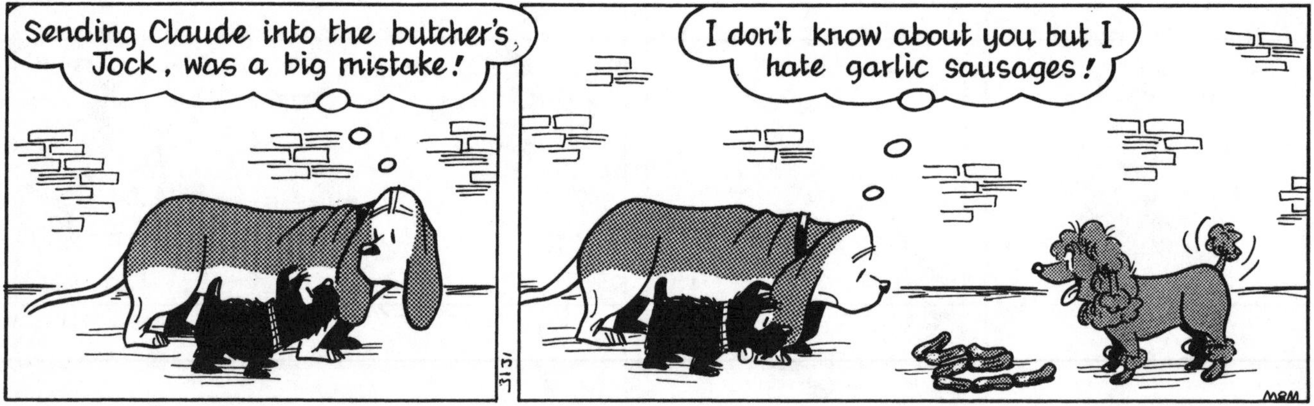
Sending Claude into the butcher's, Jock, was a big mistake!
3/31
I don't know about you but I hate garlic sausages!
MBM

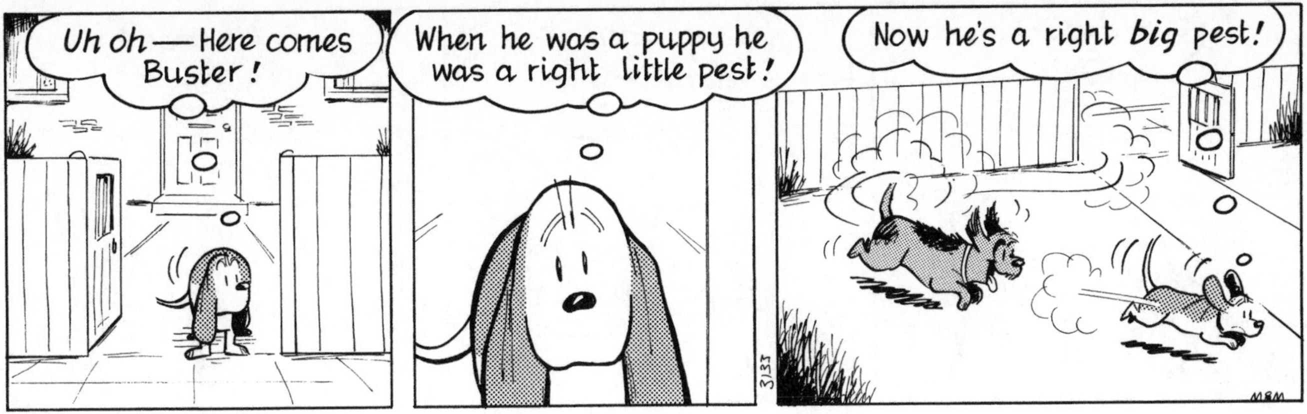
Uh oh — Here comes Buster!
When he was a puppy he was a right little pest!
Now he's a right *big* pest!

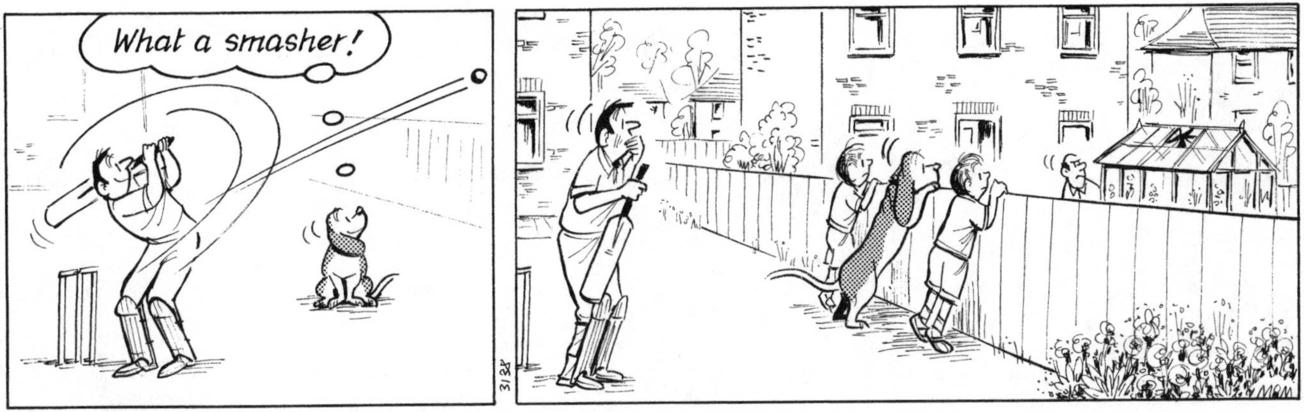
What a smasher!

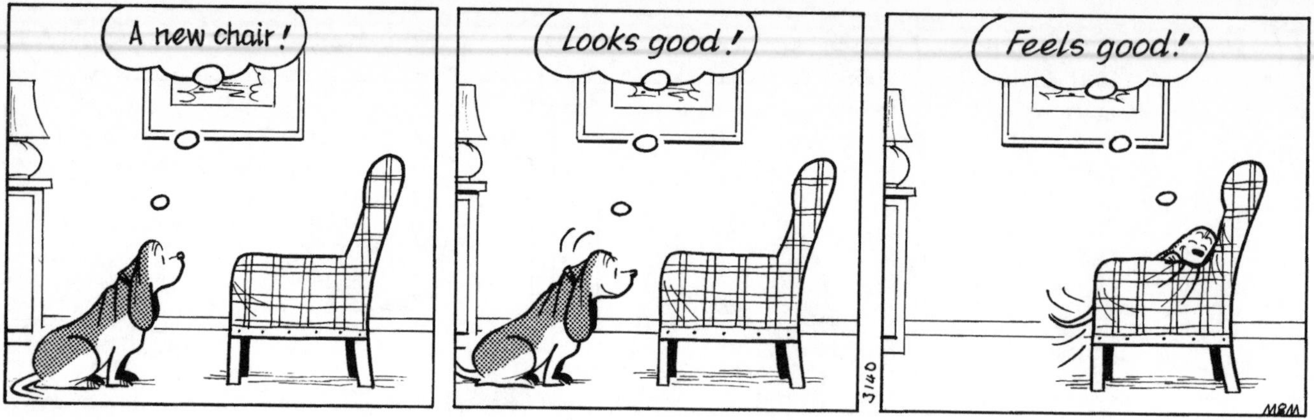
A new chair!
Looks good!
Feels good!

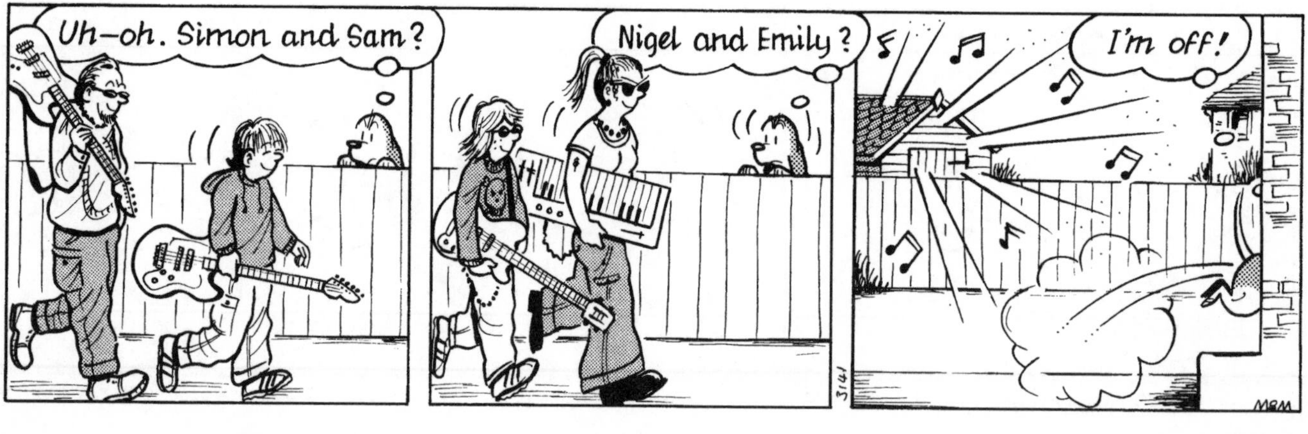
Uh-oh. Simon and Sam?
Nigel and Emily?
I'm off!

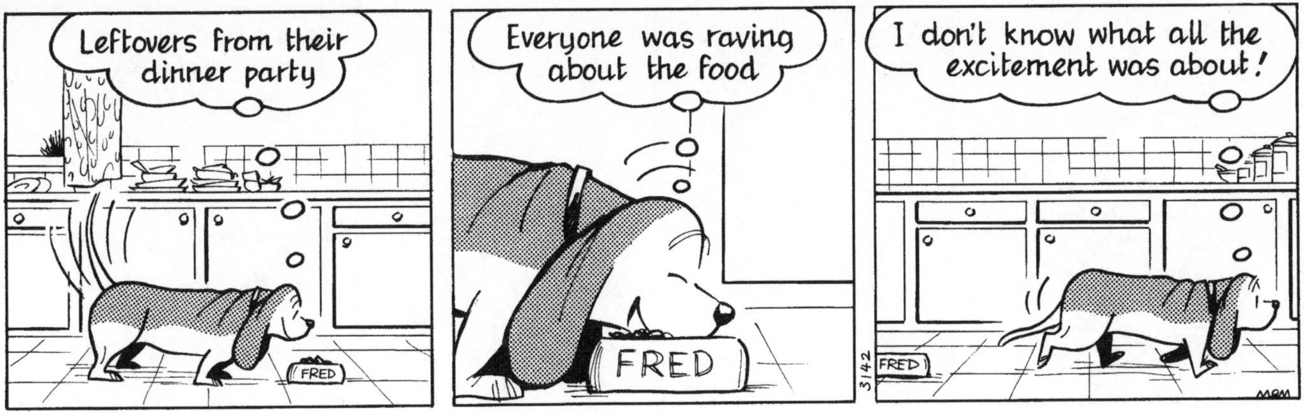
Leftovers from their dinner party
FRED
Everyone was raving about the food
FRED
3142
I don't know what all the excitement was about!
FRED

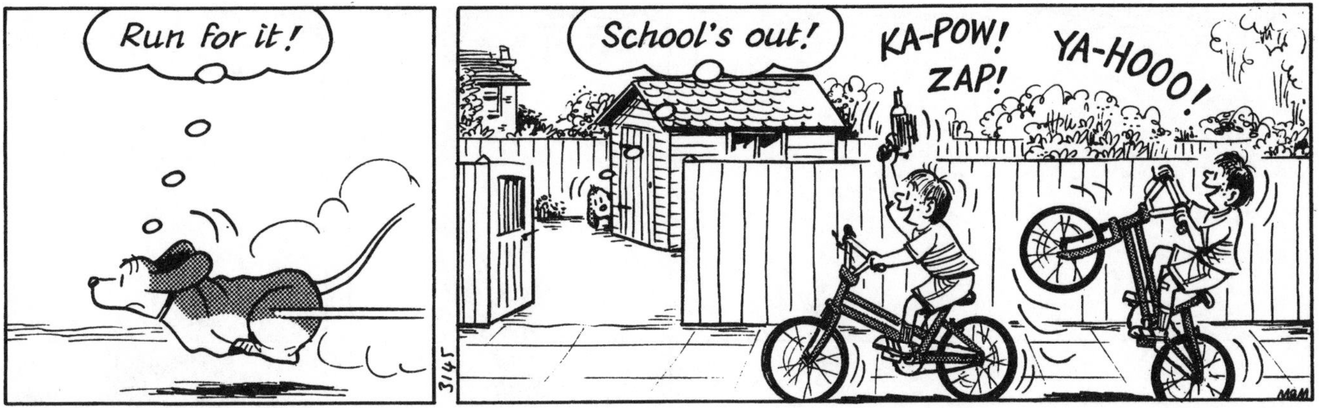
Run for it!
3145
School's out!
KA-POW! ZAP!
YA-HOOO!

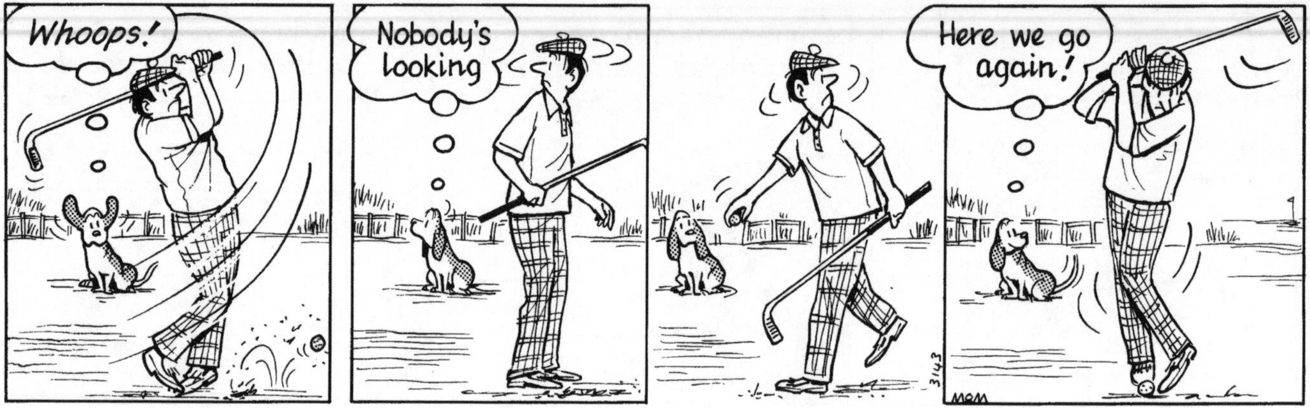
Whoops!
Nobody's looking
Here we go again!

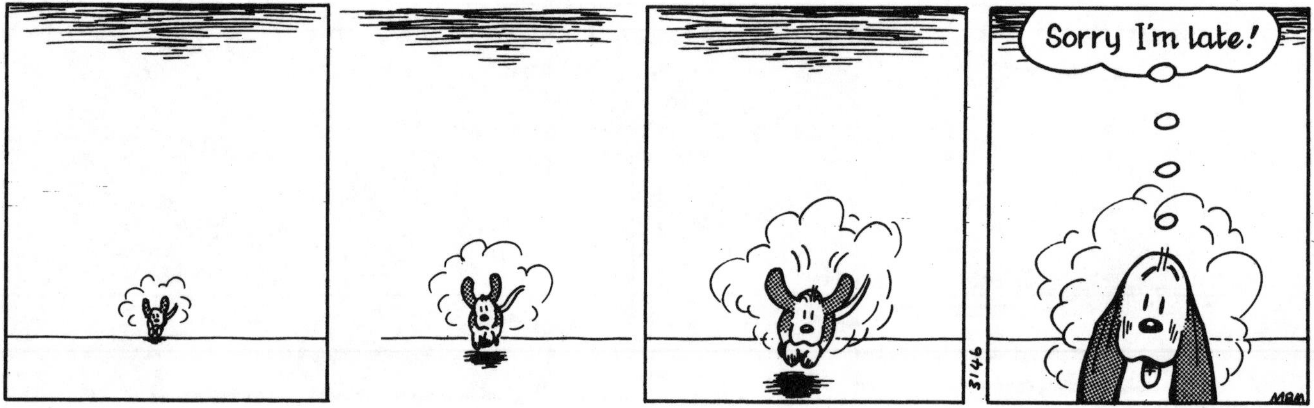
Sorry I'm late!

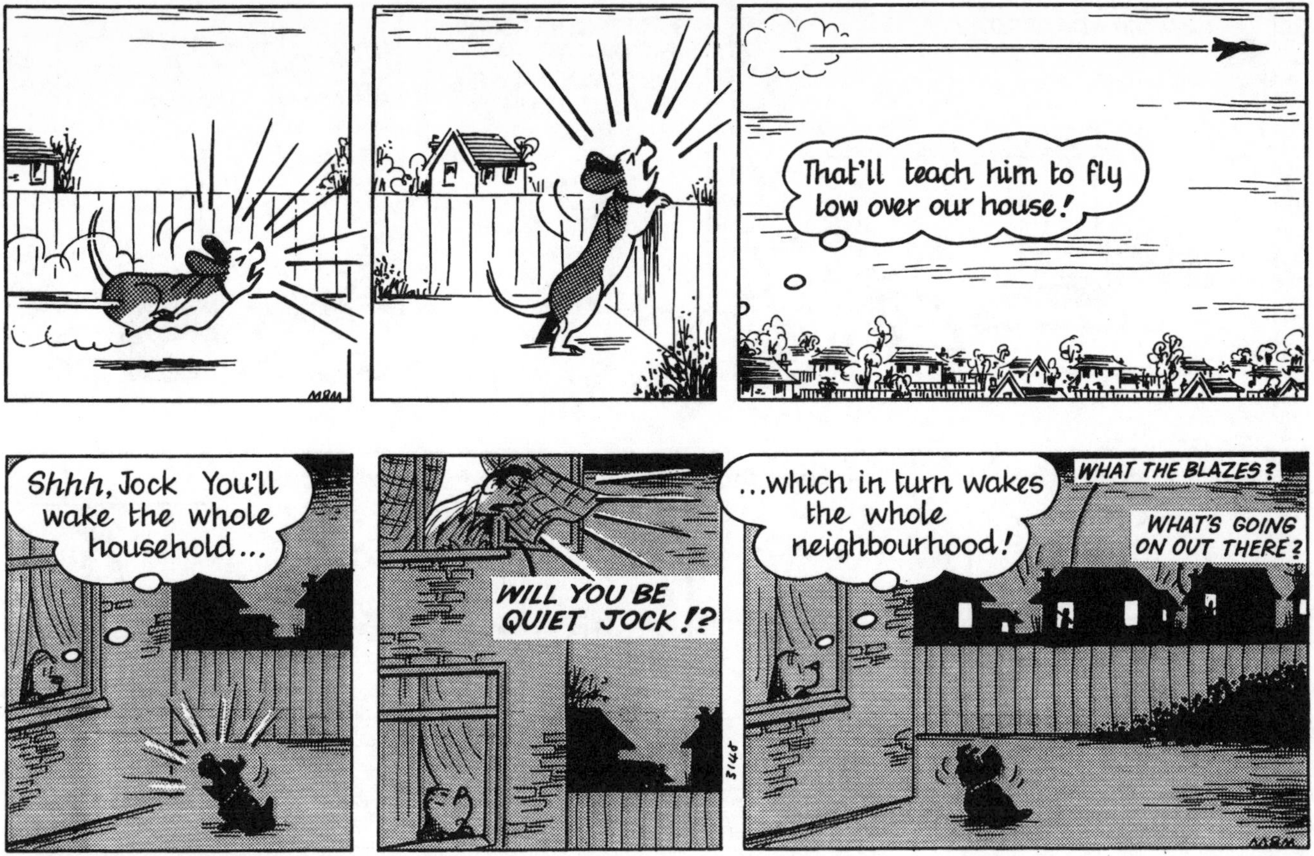
That'll teach him to fly low over our house!
Shhh, Jock You'll wake the whole household...
WILL YOU BE QUIET JOCK!?
...which in turn wakes the whole neighbourhood!
WHAT THE BLAZES?
WHAT'S GOING ON OUT THERE?

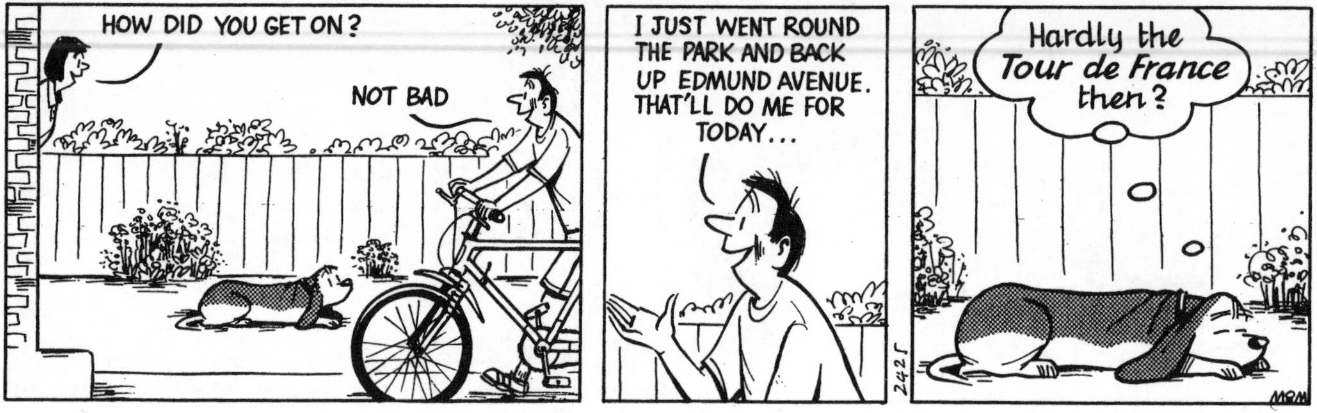
HOW DID YOU GET ON?
NOT BAD
I JUST WENT ROUND THE PARK AND BACK UP EDMUND AVENUE. THAT'LL DO ME FOR TODAY...
Hardly the *Tour de France* then?

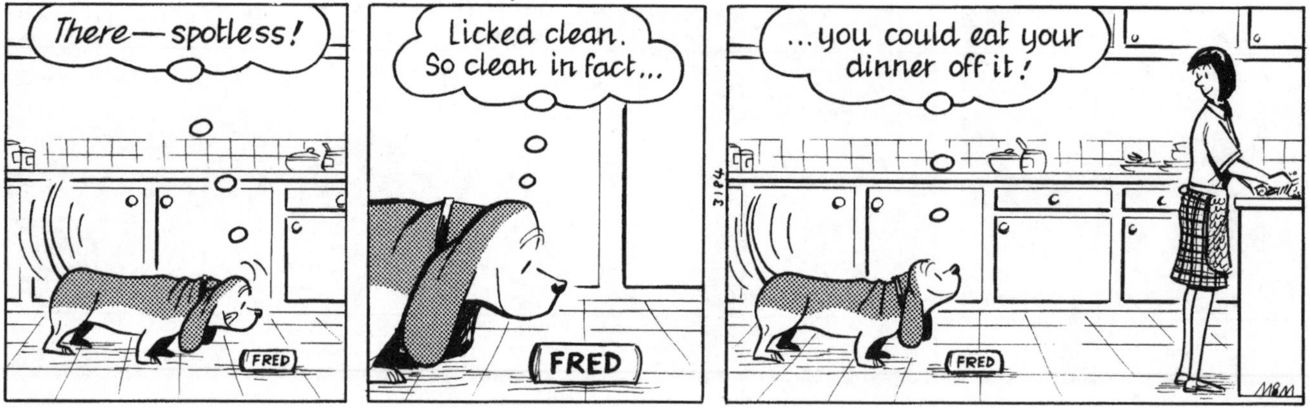
There—spotless!
FRED
Licked clean. So clean in fact...
FRED
...you could eat your dinner off it!
FRED

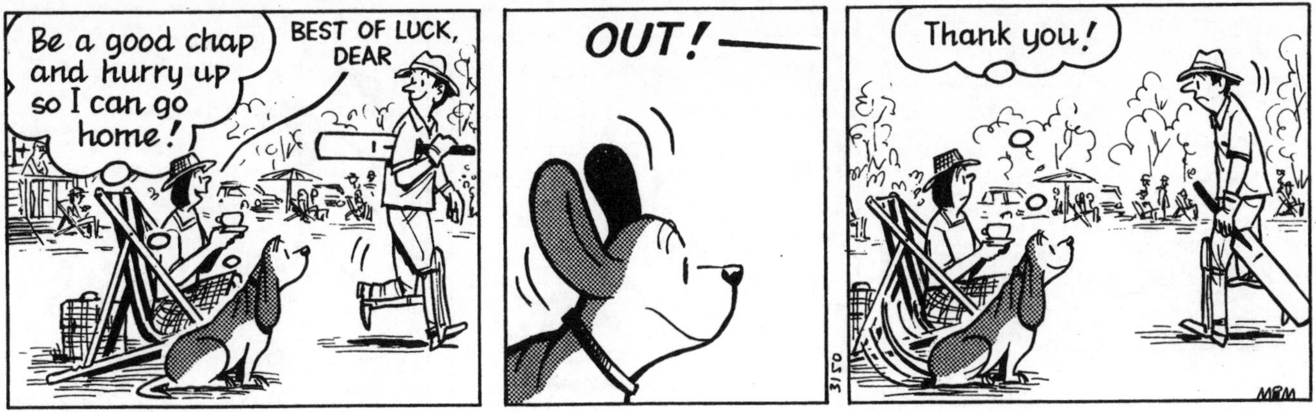
Be a good chap and hurry up so I can go home!
BEST OF LUCK, DEAR
OUT!
Thank you!

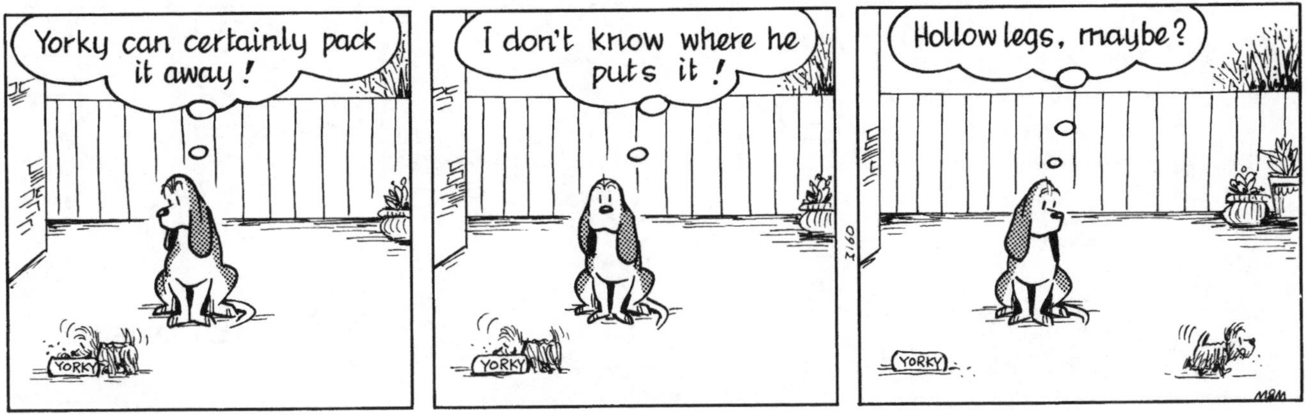
Yorky can certainly pack it away!
YORKY
I don't know where he puts it!
YORKY
Hollow legs, maybe?
YORKY

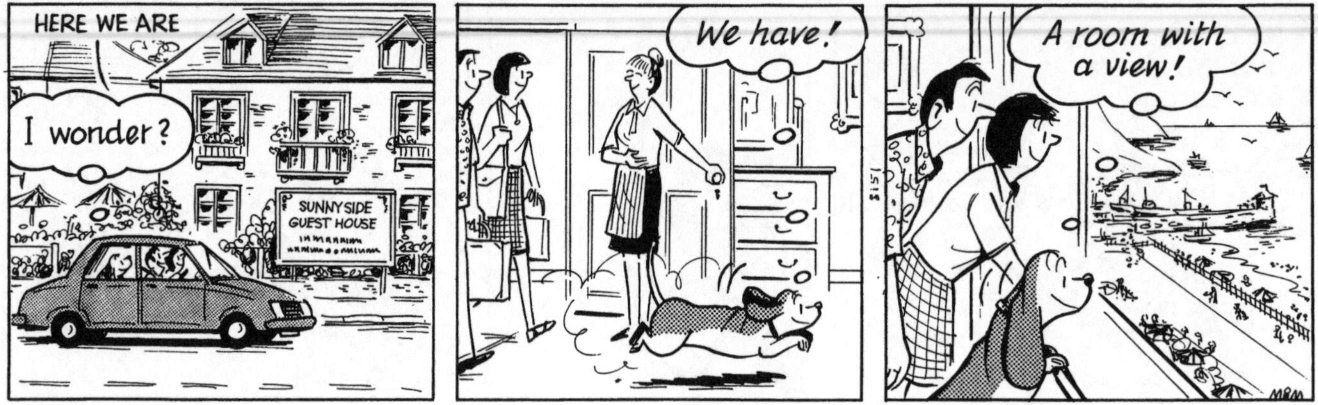
HERE WE ARE
I wonder?
SUNNYSIDE GUEST HOUSE
We have!
A room with a view!

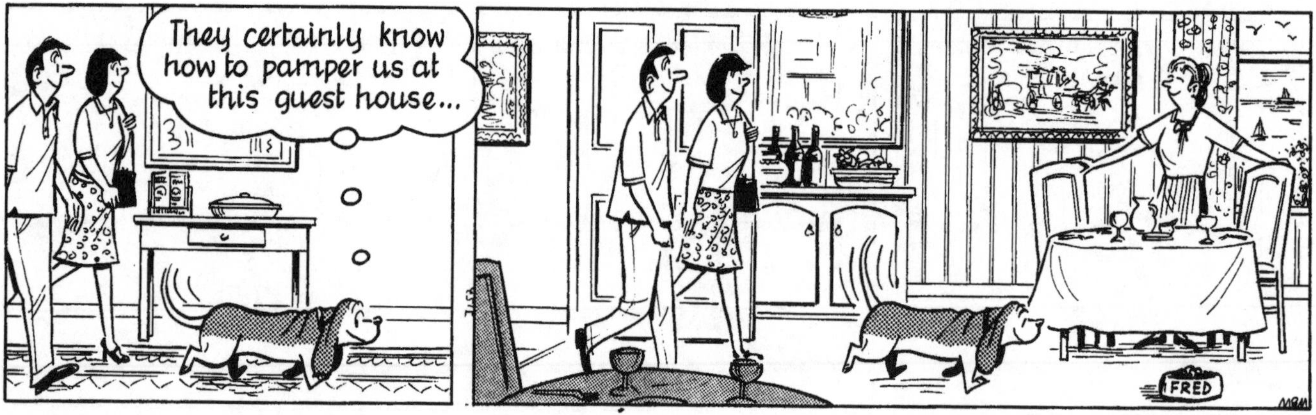
They certainly know how to pamper us at this guest house...
FRED

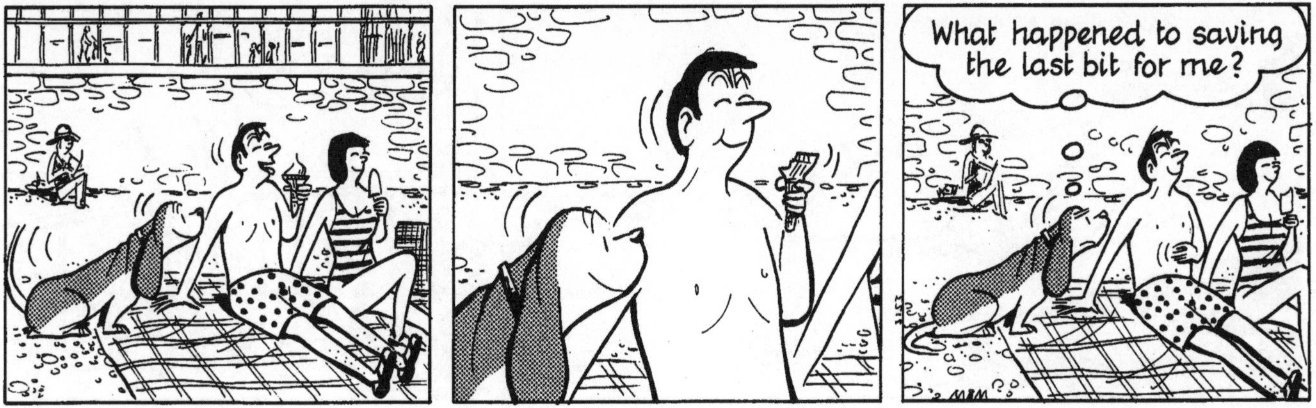
What happened to saving the last bit for me?

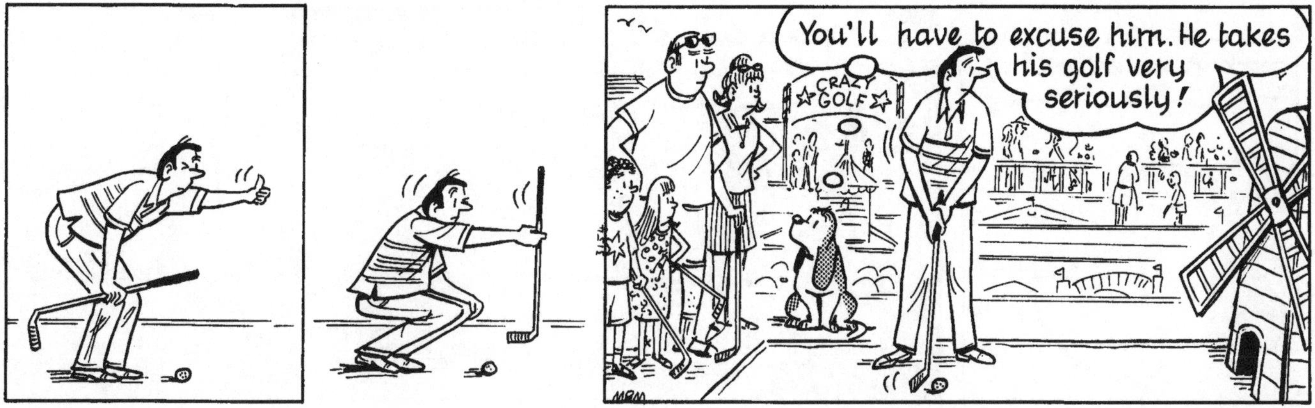
CRAZY GOLF
You'll have to excuse him. He takes his golf very seriously!

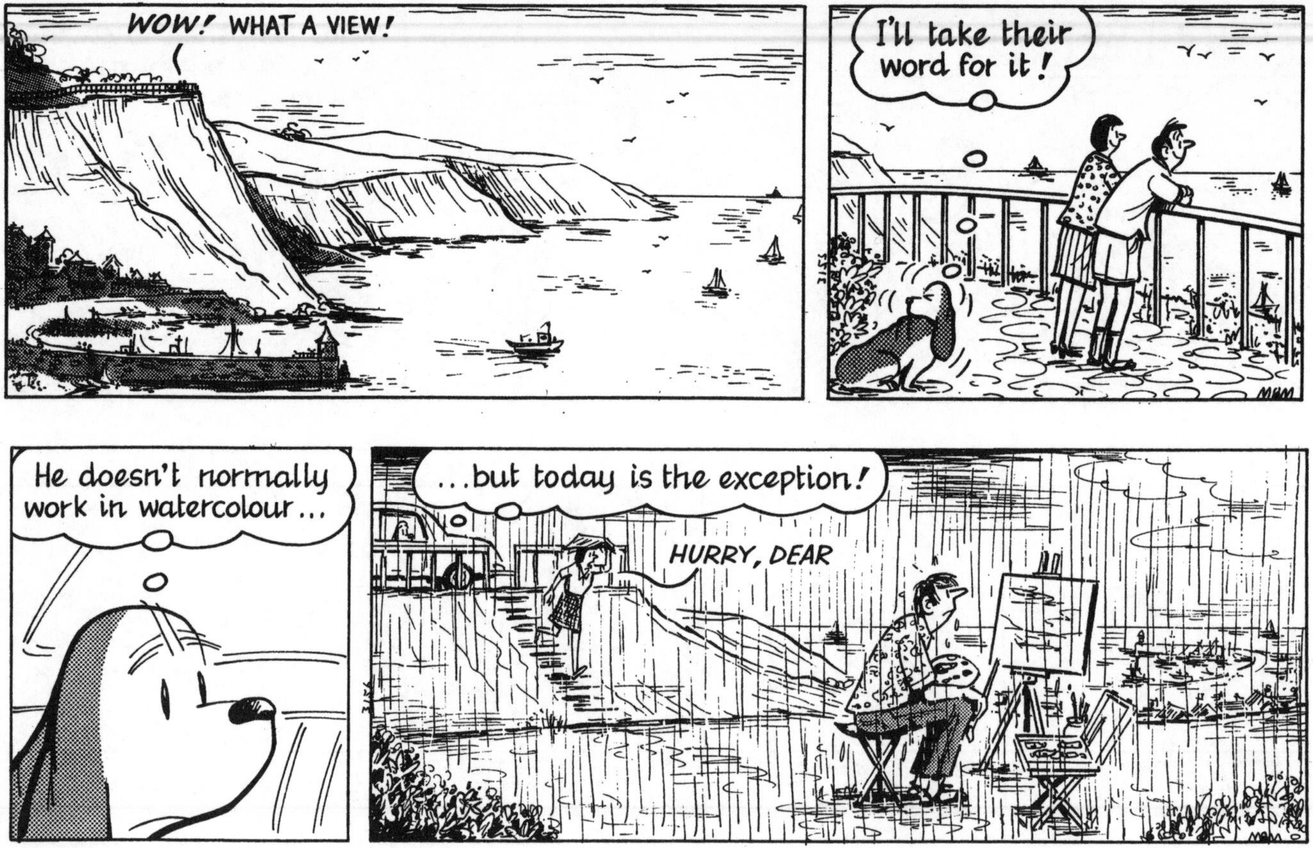
WOW! WHAT A VIEW!
I'll take their word for it!
He doesn't normally work in watercolour...
...but today is the exception!
HURRY, DEAR

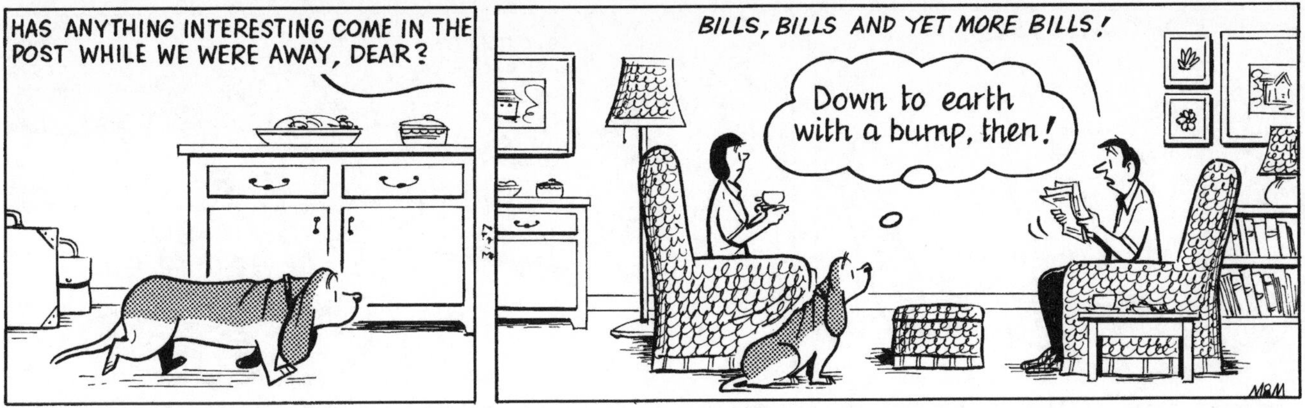
HAS ANYTHING INTERESTING COME IN THE POST WHILE WE WERE AWAY, DEAR?
BILLS, BILLS AND YET MORE BILLS!
Down to earth with a bump, then!

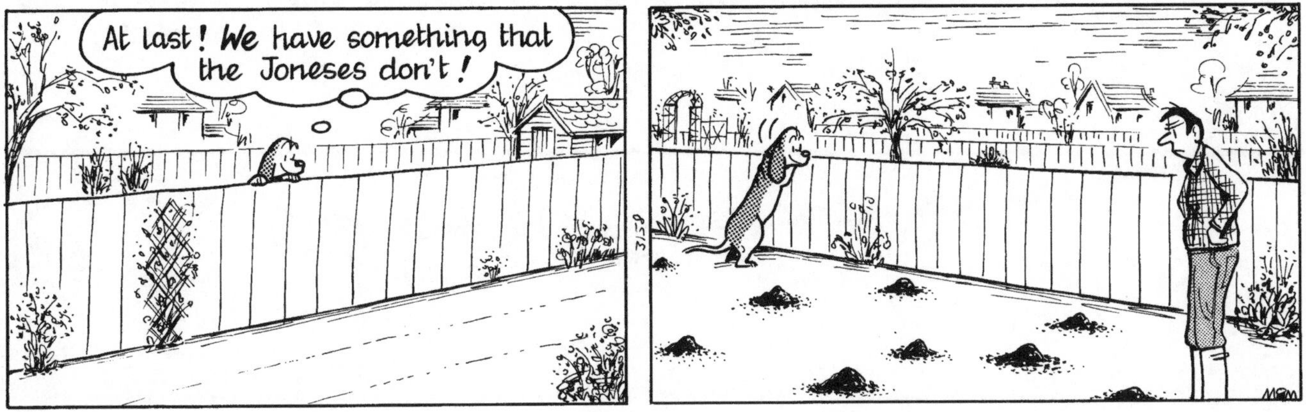
At last! We have something that the Joneses don't!

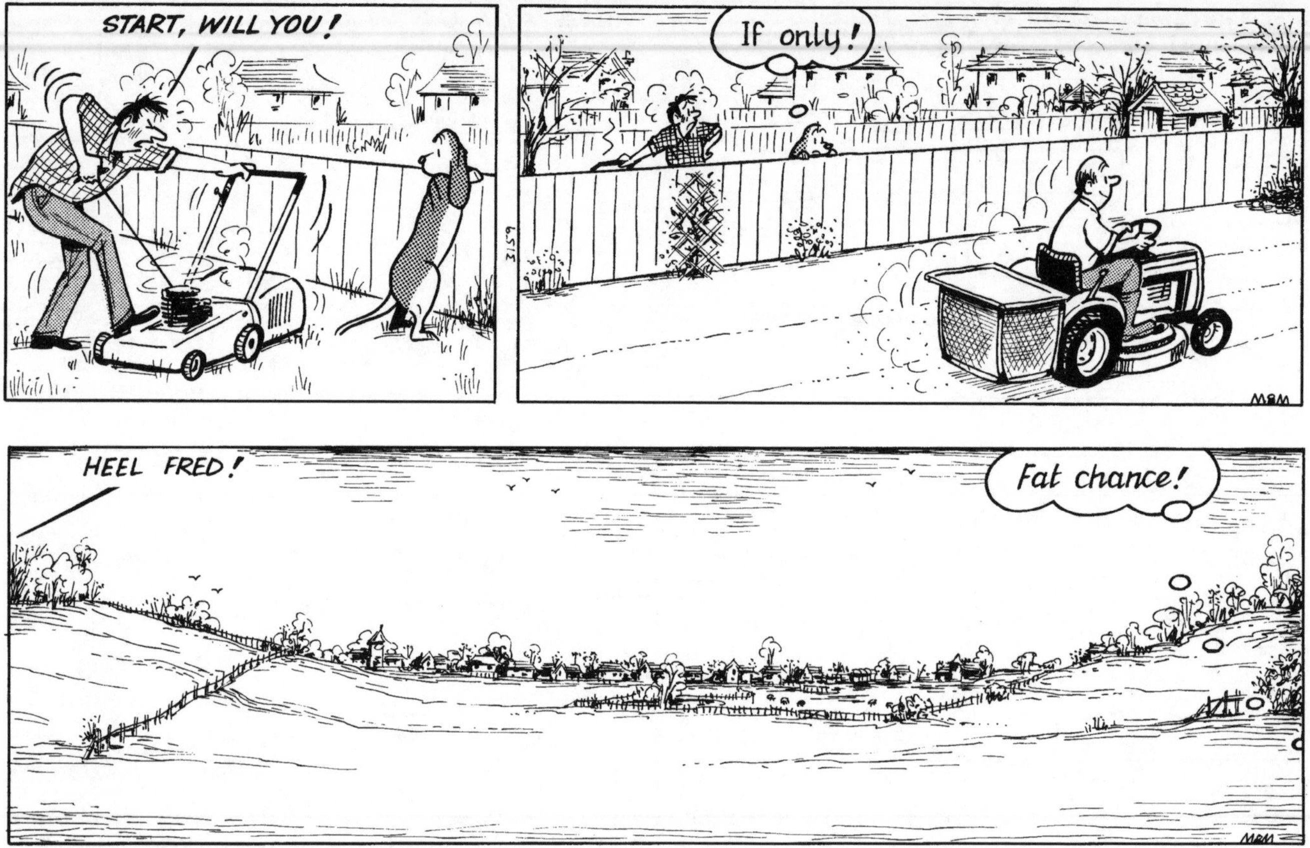
START, WILL YOU!
If only!
HEEL FRED!
Fat chance!

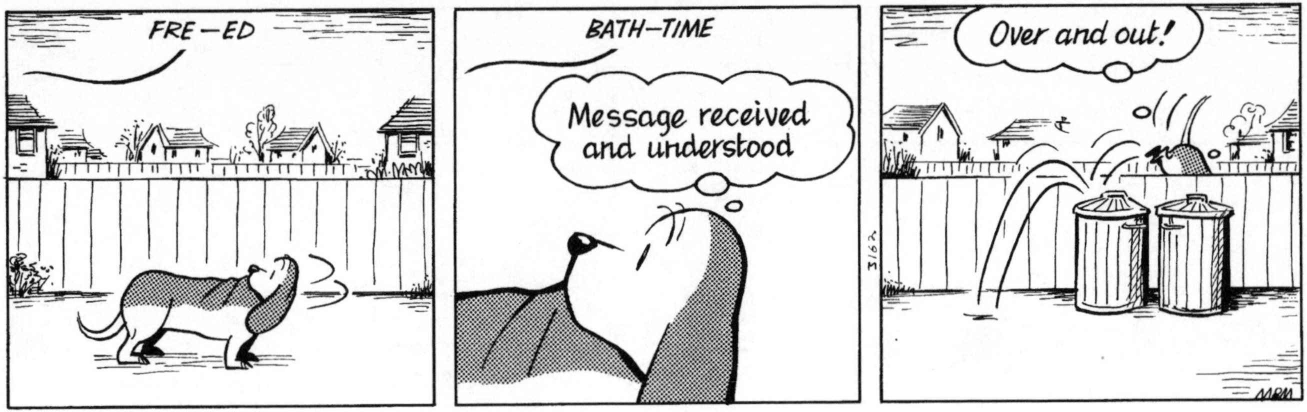
FRE—ED
BATH—TIME
Message received and understood
Over and out!
3162

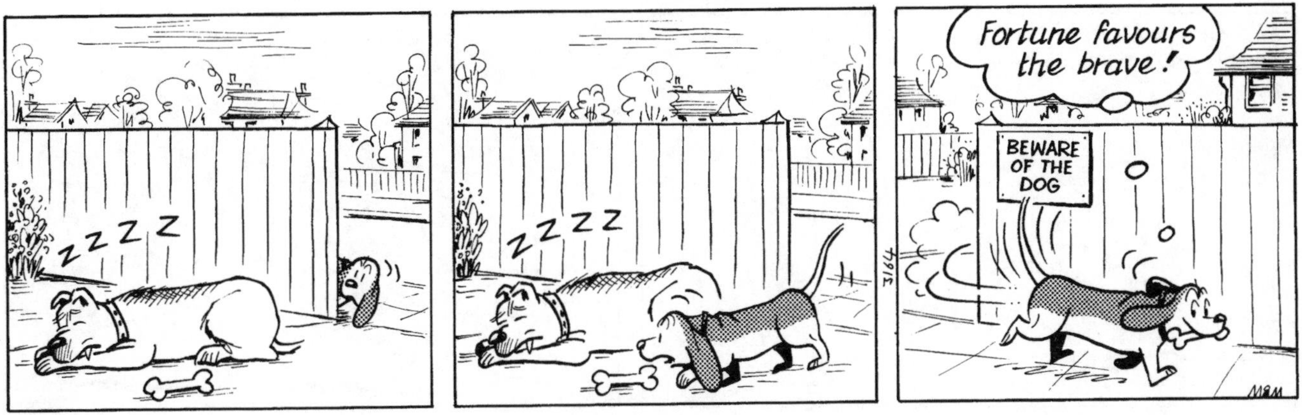
ZZZZZ
ZZZZZ
3164
BEWARE OF THE DOG
Fortune favours the brave!

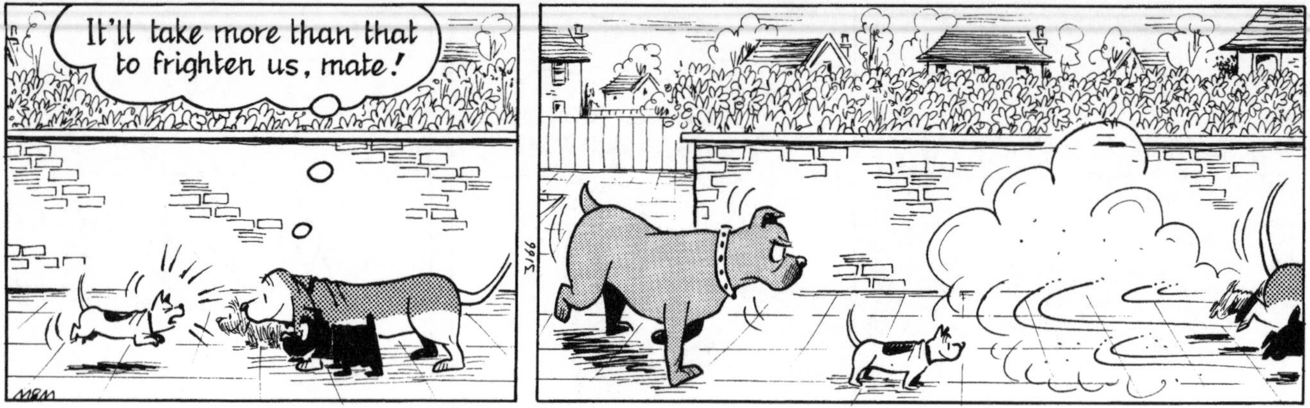
It'll take more than that to frighten us, mate!

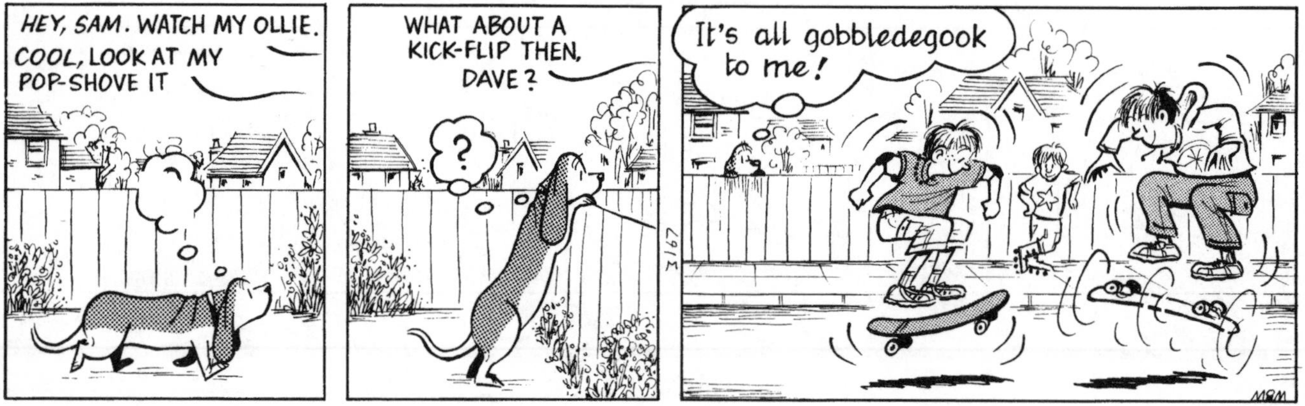
HEY, SAM. WATCH MY OLLIE.
COOL, LOOK AT MY POP-SHOVE IT
WHAT ABOUT A KICK-FLIP THEN, DAVE?
?
It's all gobbledegook to me!

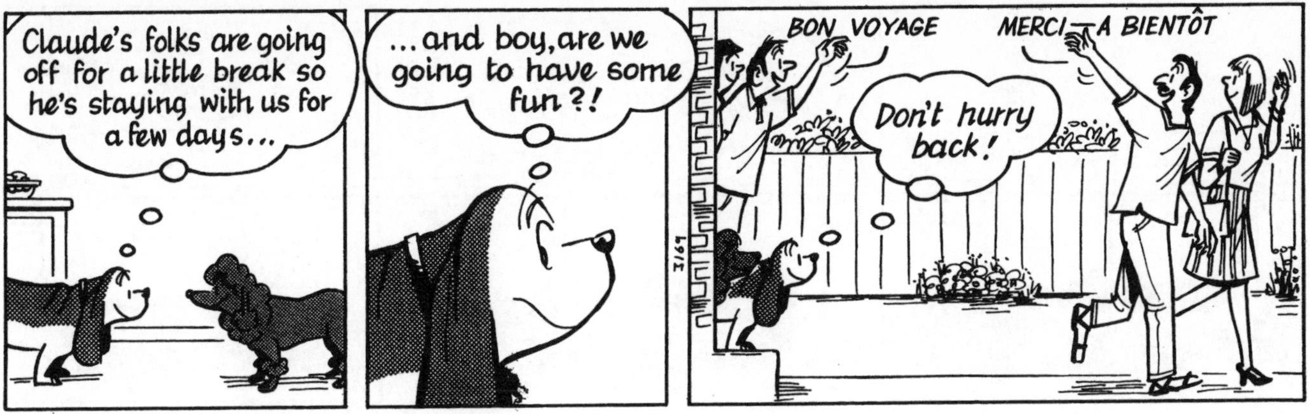

Claude's folks are going off for a little break so he's staying with us for a few days...
...and boy, are we going to have some fun?!
BON VOYAGE
MERCI — A BIENTÔT
Don't hurry back!

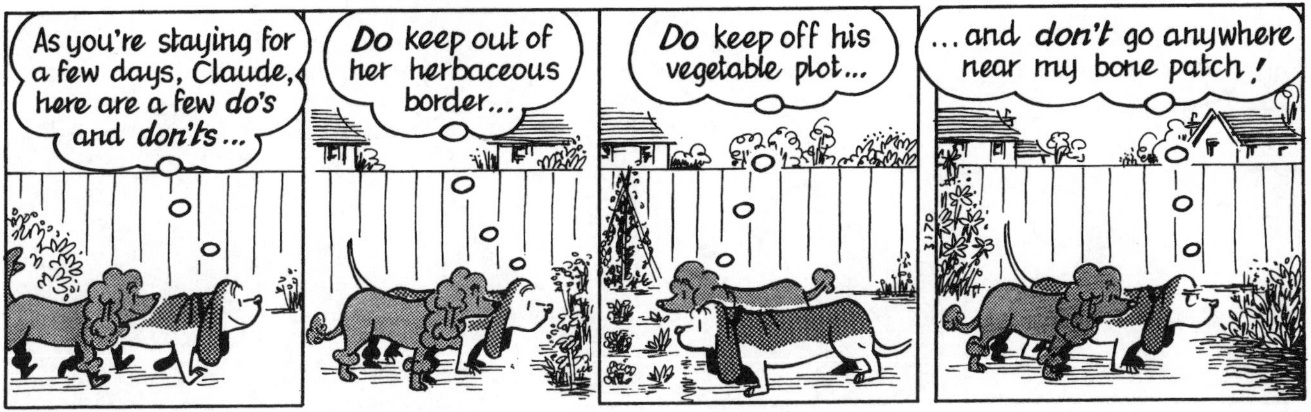

As you're staying for a few days, Claude, here are a few *do's* and *don'ts*...
Do keep out of her herbaceous border...
Do keep off his vegetable plot...
...and **don't** go anywhere near my bone patch!

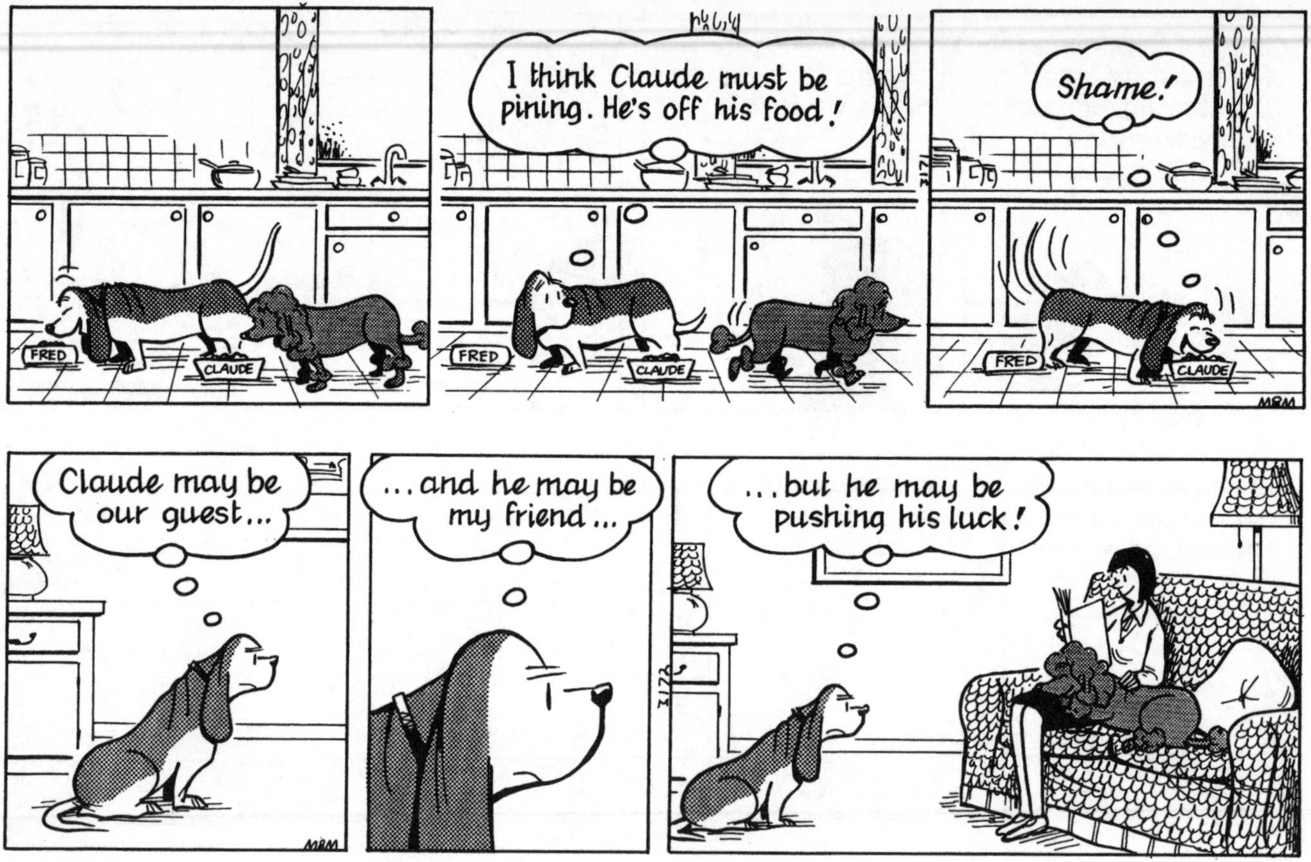
FRED
CLAUDE
I think Claude must be pining. He's off his food!
FRED
CLAUDE
Shame!
FRED
CLAUDE
MBM
Claude may be our guest...
MBM
...and he may be my friend...
...but he may be pushing his luck!

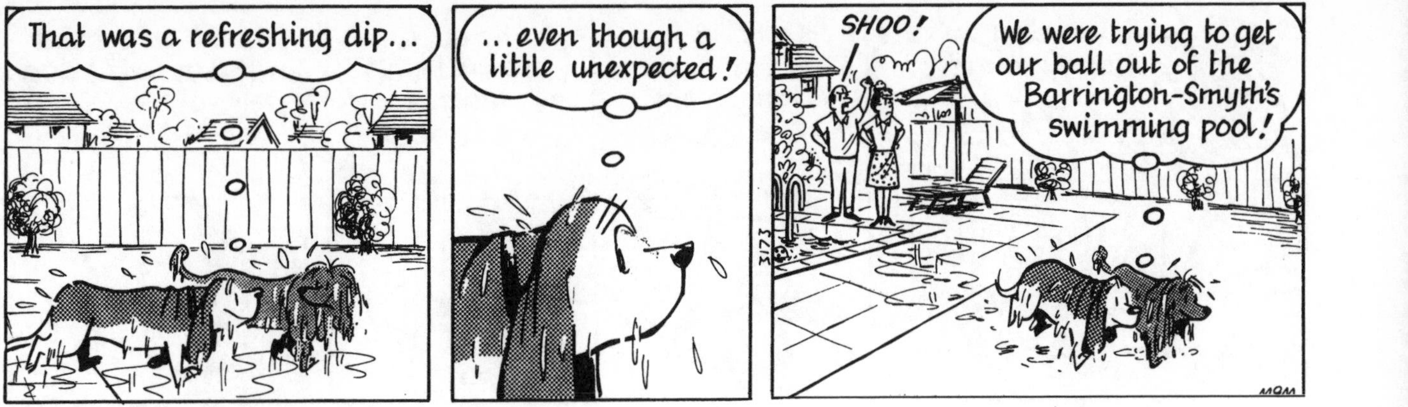
That was a refreshing dip...
...even though a little unexpected!
SHOO!
We were trying to get our ball out of the Barrington-Smyth's swimming pool!
3173

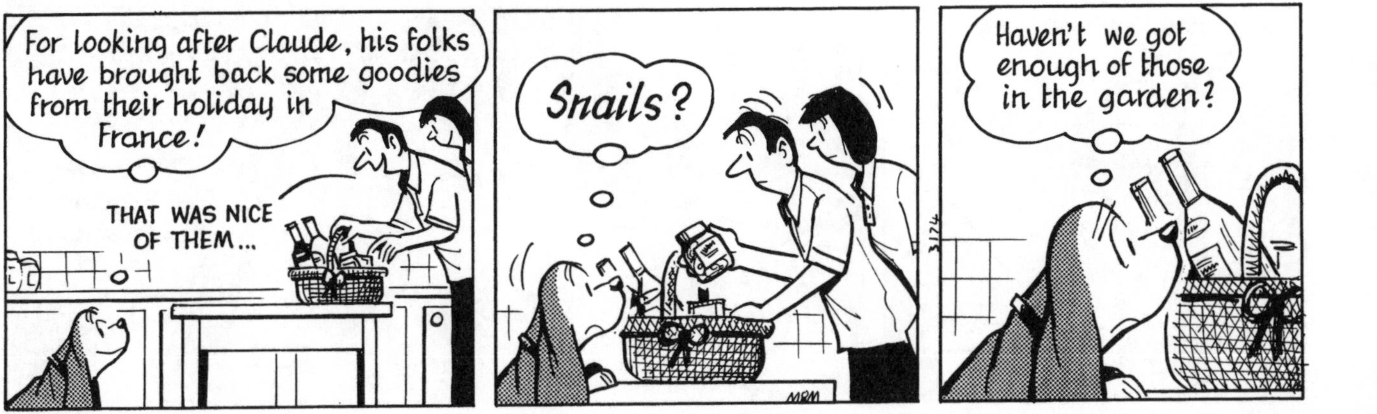
For looking after Claude, his folks have brought back some goodies from their holiday in France!
THAT WAS NICE OF THEM...
Snails?
Haven't we got enough of those in the garden?
3174

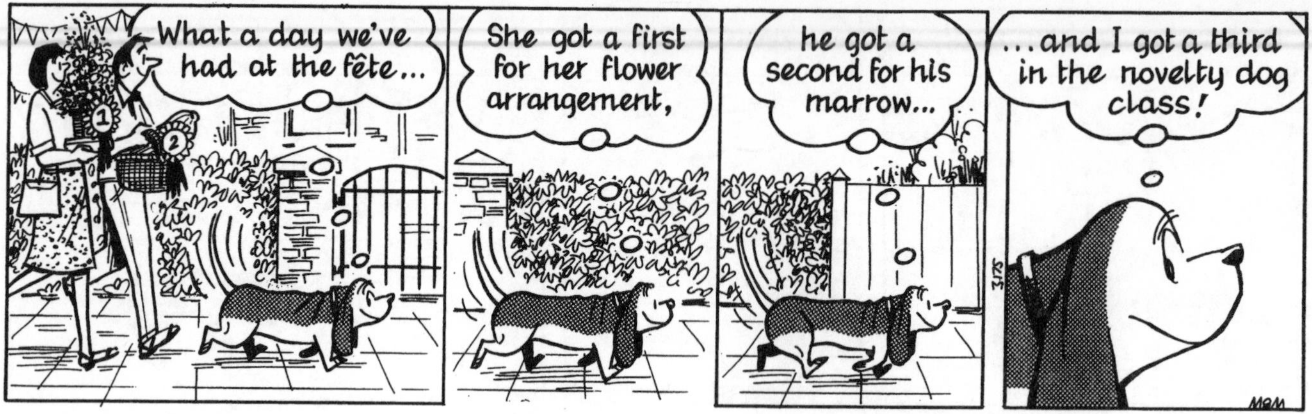
What a day we've had at the fête...
She got a first for her flower arrangement,
he got a second for his marrow...
...and I got a third in the novelty dog class!

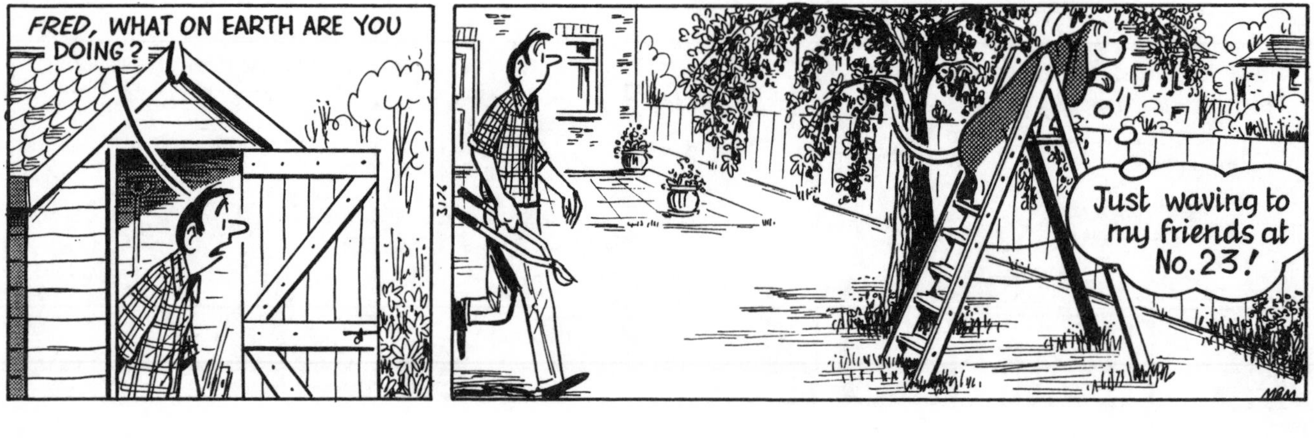
FRED, WHAT ON EARTH ARE YOU DOING?
Just waving to my friends at No.23!

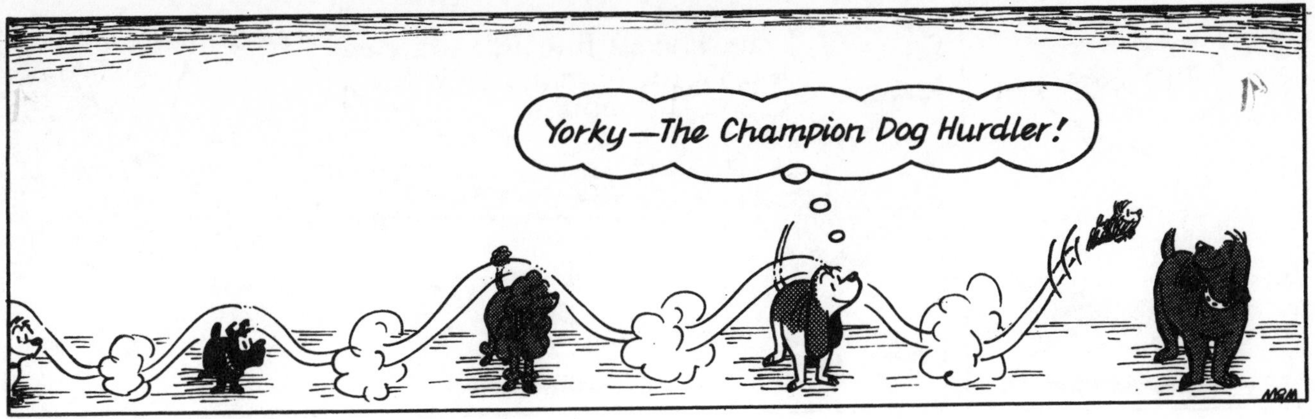
Yorky—The Champion Dog Hurdler!
MGM

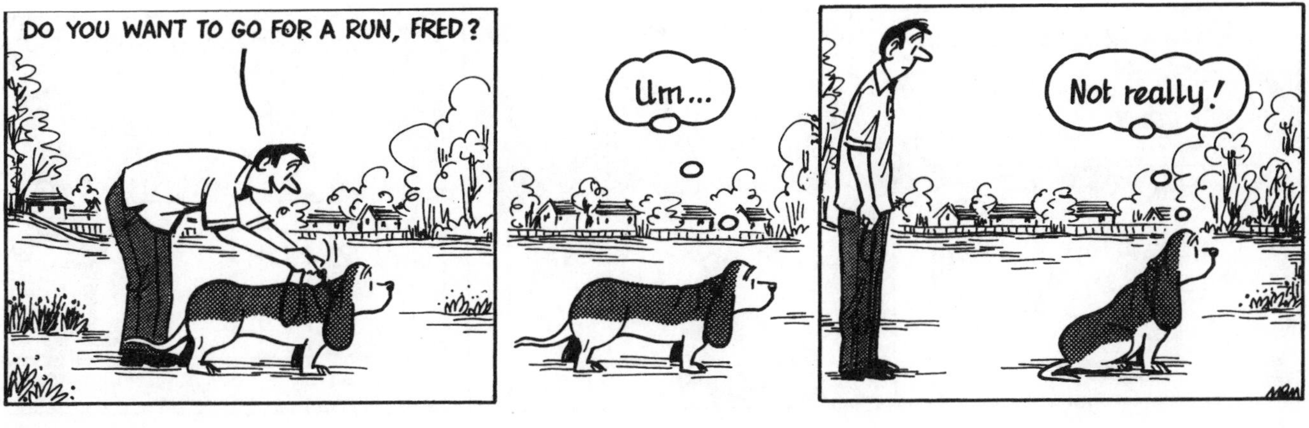
DO YOU WANT TO GO FOR A RUN, FRED?
Um...
Not really!
MGM

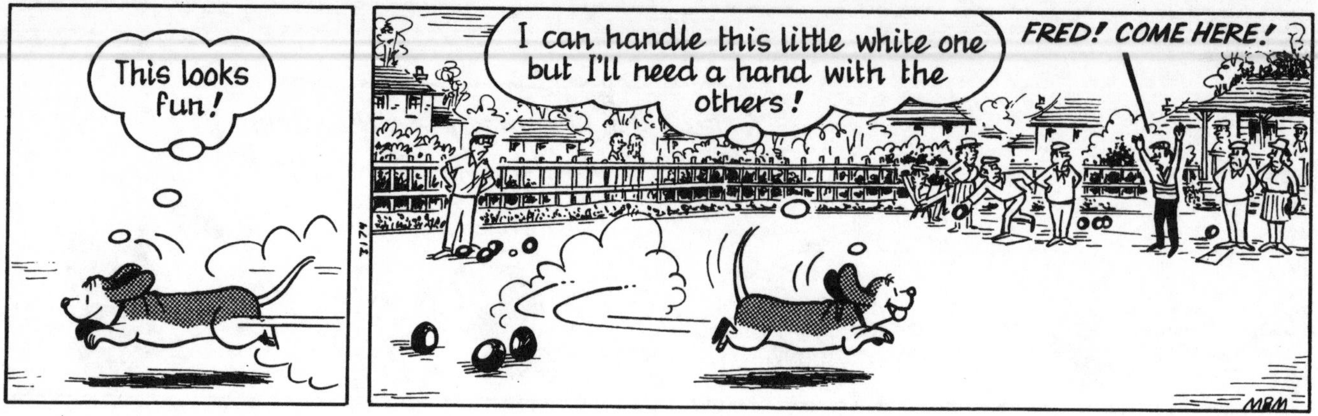
This looks fun!
3174
I can handle this little white one but I'll need a hand with the others!
FRED! COME HERE!
MBM

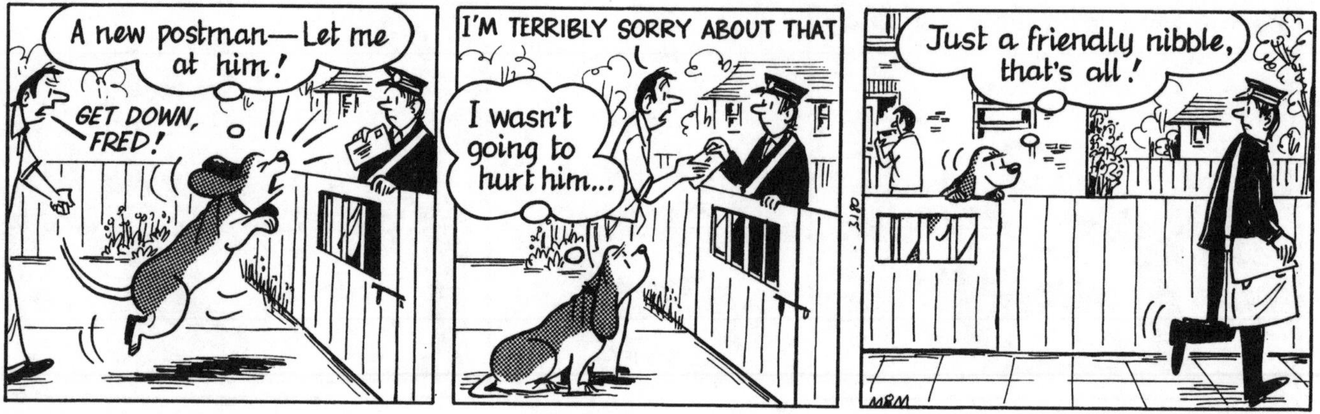
A new postman—Let me at him!
GET DOWN, FRED!
I'M TERRIBLY SORRY ABOUT THAT
I wasn't going to hurt him...
3180
Just a friendly nibble, that's all!
MBM

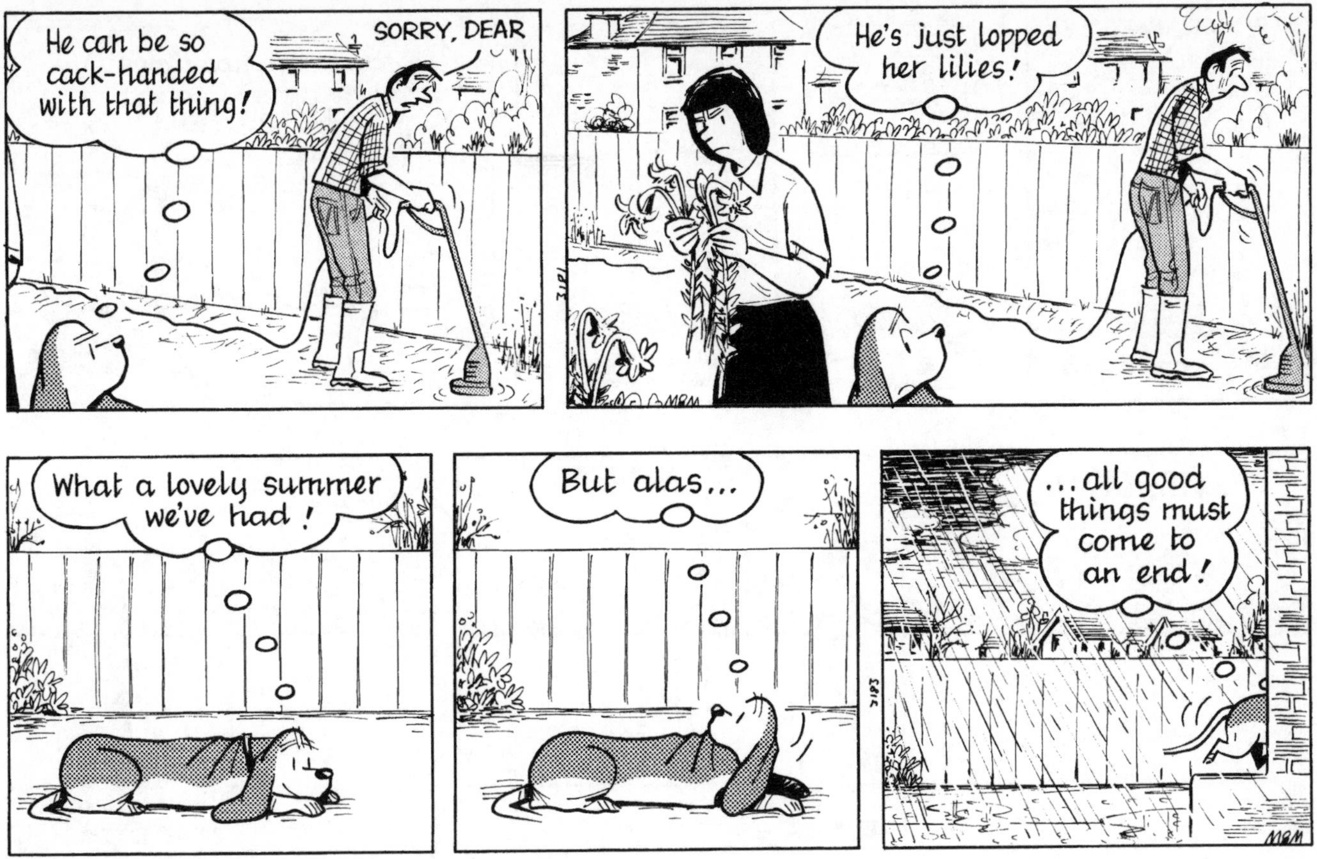
He can be so cack-handed with that thing!
SORRY, DEAR
He's just lopped her lilies!
What a lovely summer we've had!
But alas...
...all good things must come to an end!

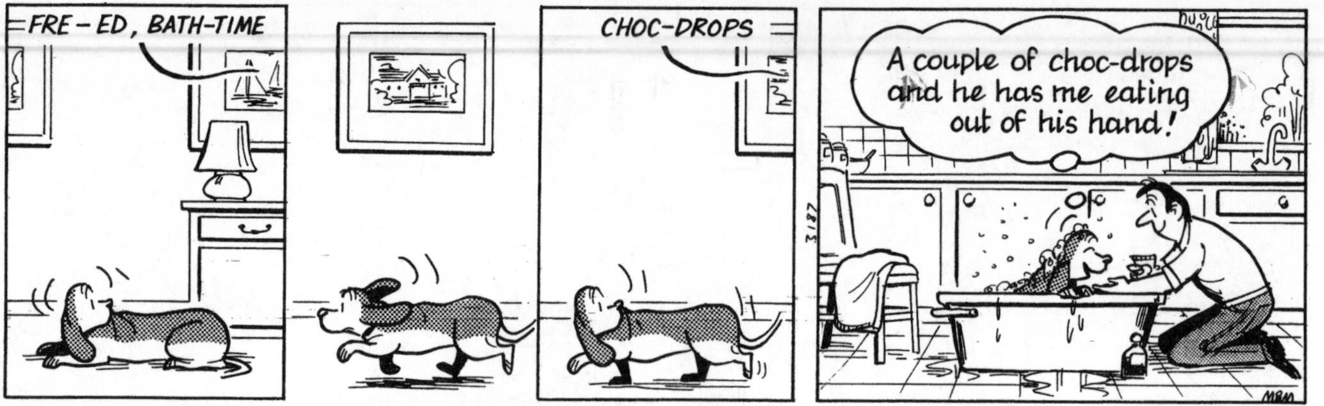
FRE-ED, BATH-TIME
CHOC-DROPS
A couple of choc-drops and he has me eating out of his hand!

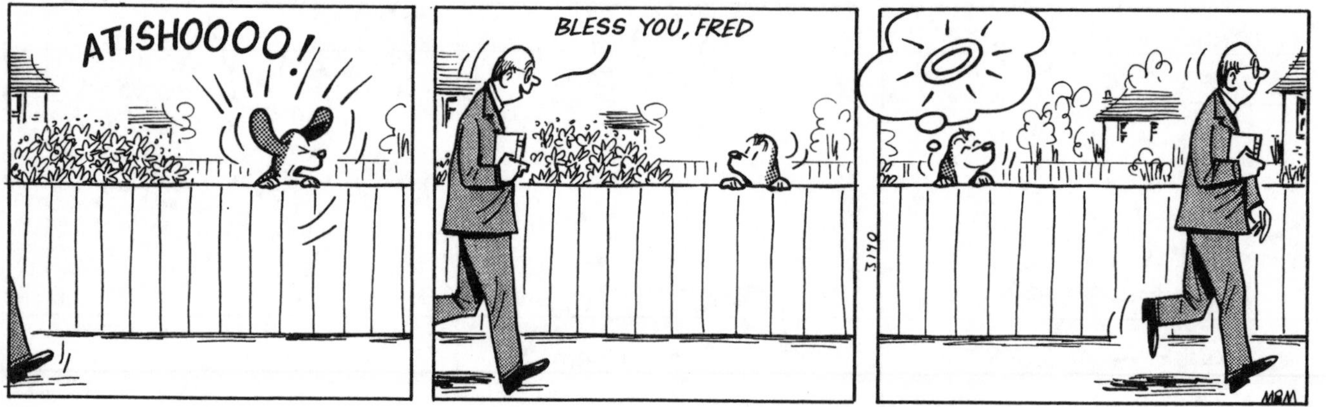
ATISHOOOO!
BLESS YOU, FRED

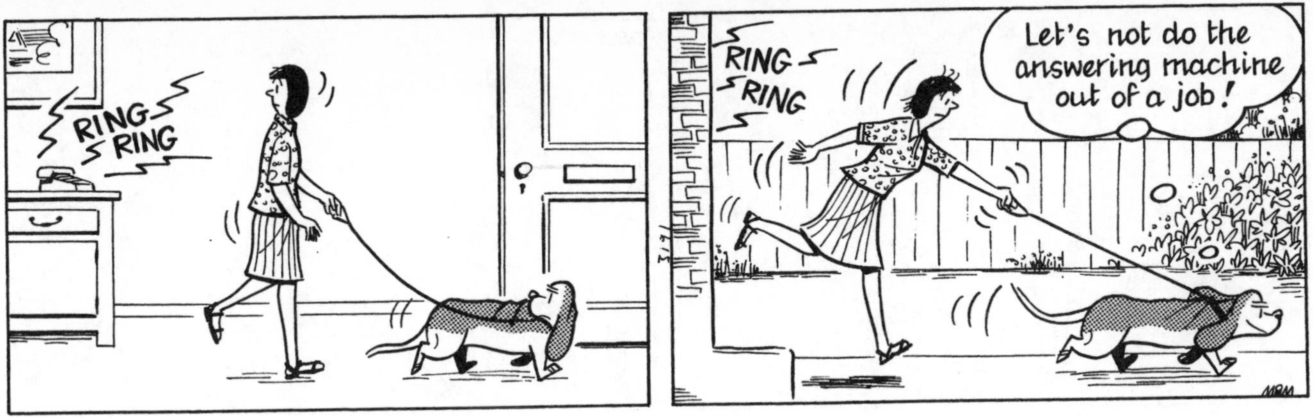
RING RING
RING RING
Let's not do the answering machine out of a job!
MBM

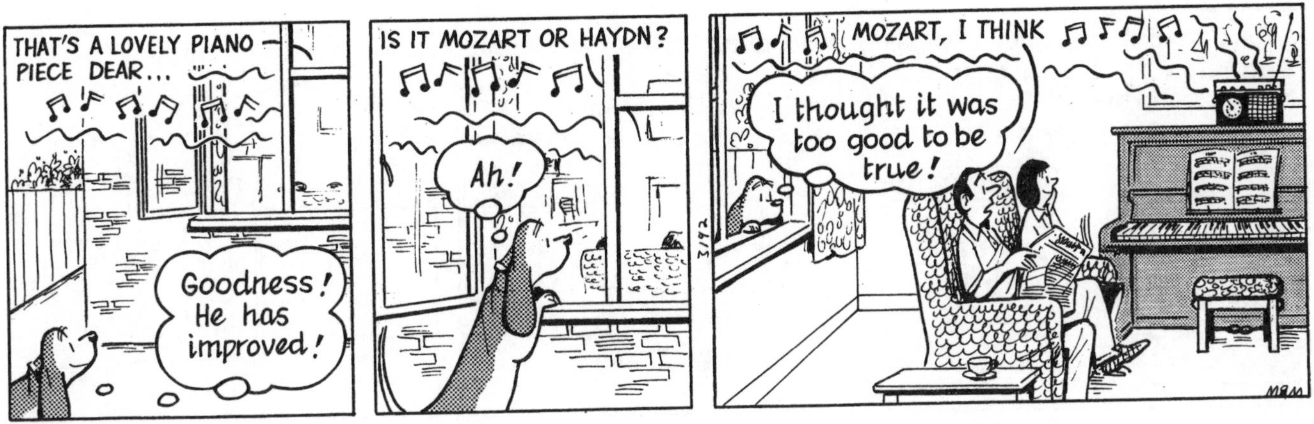
THAT'S A LOVELY PIANO PIECE DEAR...
Goodness! He has improved!
IS IT MOZART OR HAYDN?
Ah!
MOZART, I THINK
I thought it was too good to be true!
MBM

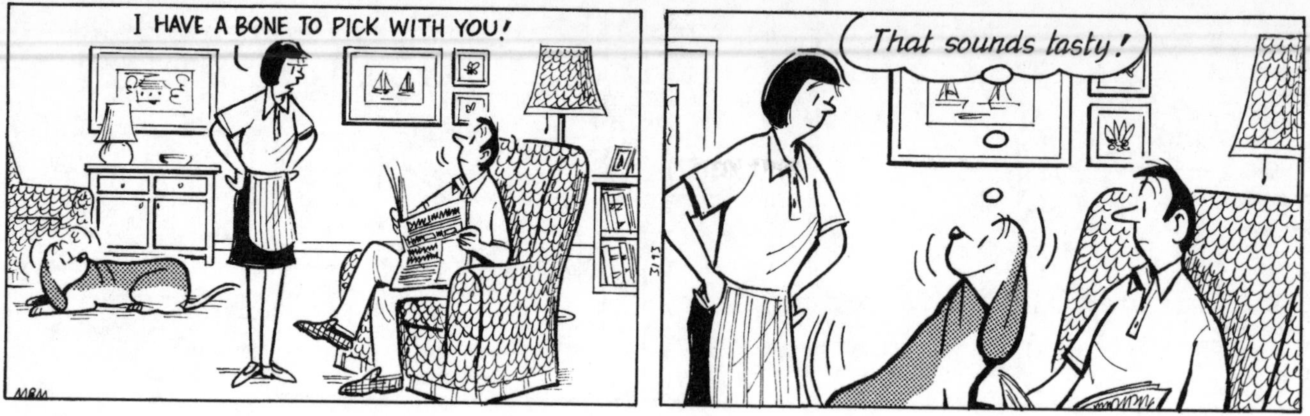
I HAVE A BONE TO PICK WITH YOU!
That sounds tasty!

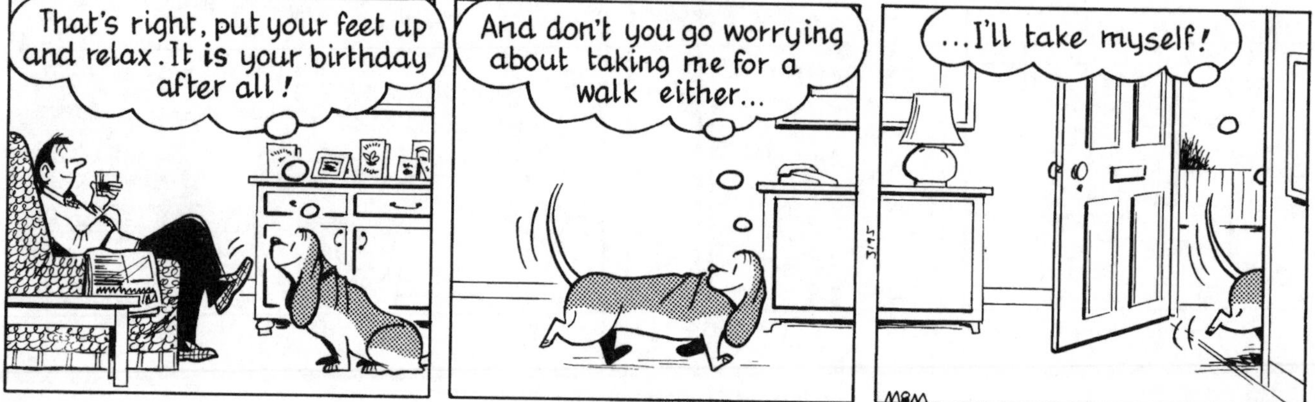
That's right, put your feet up and relax. It is your birthday after all!
And don't you go worrying about taking me for a walk either...
...I'll take myself!

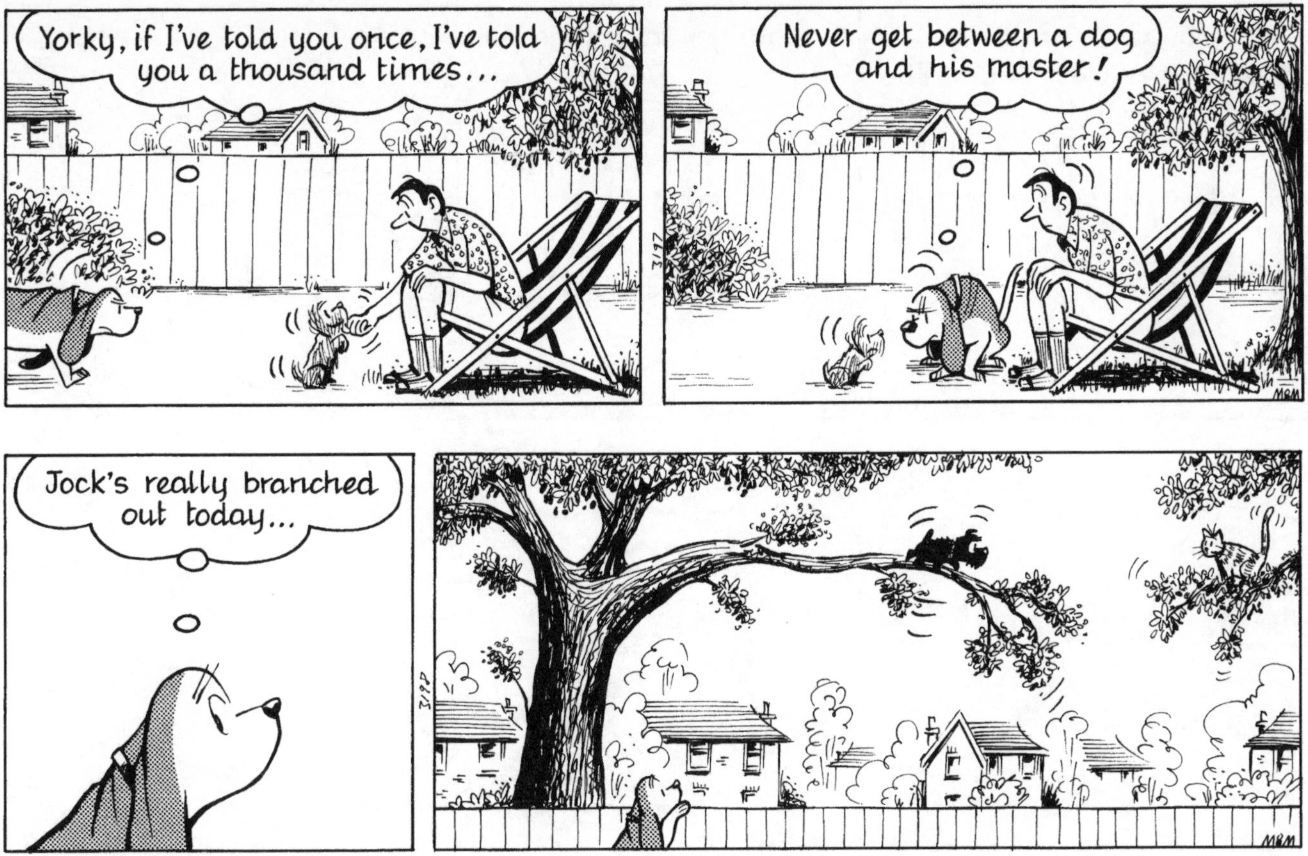
Yorky, if I've told you once, I've told you a thousand times...
Never get between a dog and his master!
Jock's really branched out today...

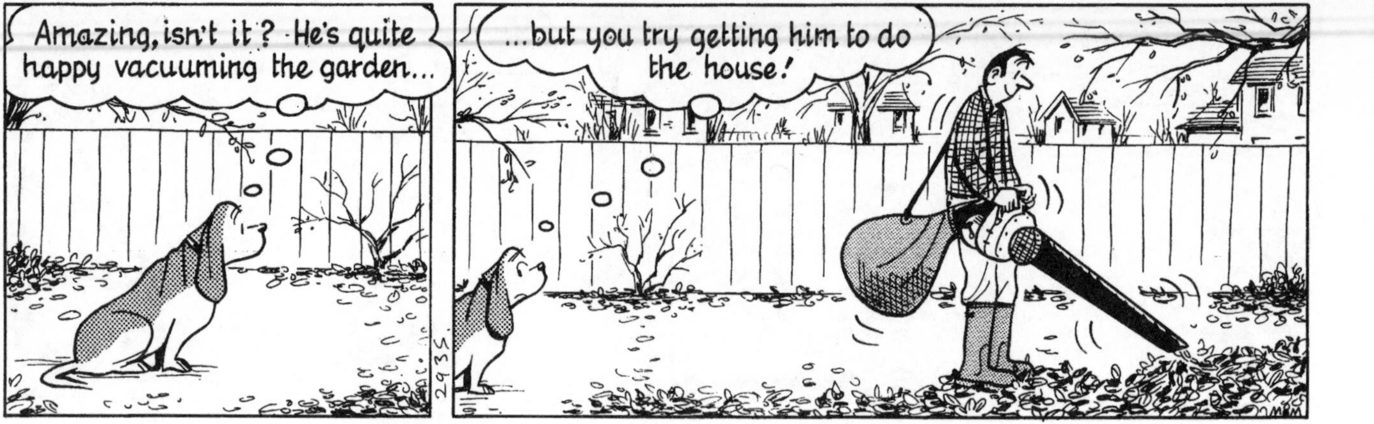

Amazing, isn't it? He's quite happy vacuuming the garden...
...but you try getting him to do the house!

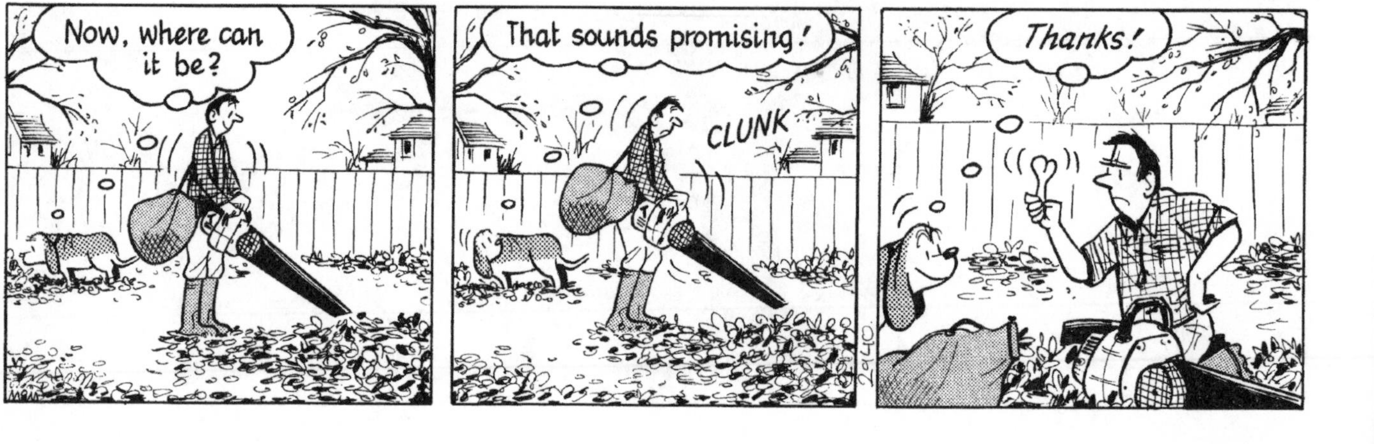

Now, where can it be?
That sounds promising!
CLUNK
Thanks!

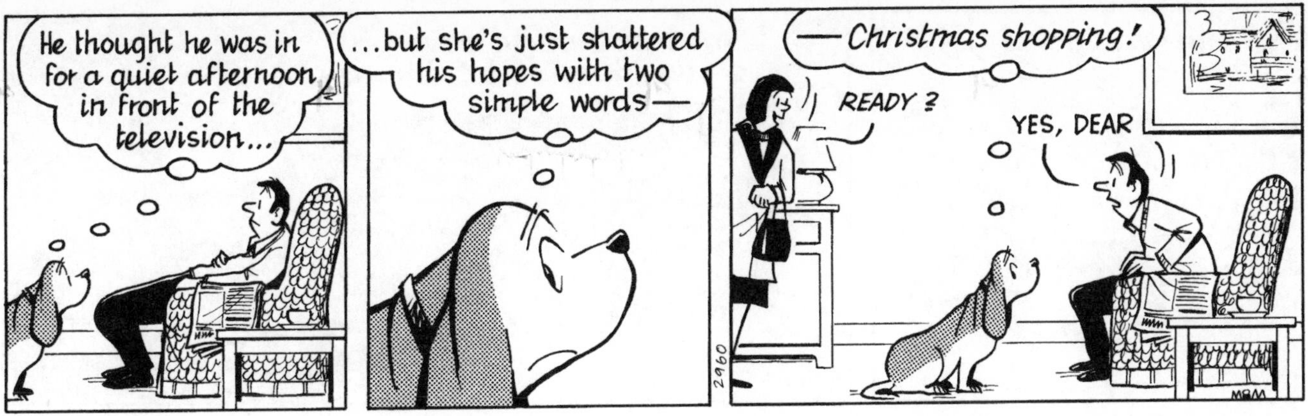
He thought he was in for a quiet afternoon in front of the television...
...but she's just shattered his hopes with two simple words—
2960
—Christmas shopping!
READY ?
YES, DEAR
MBM

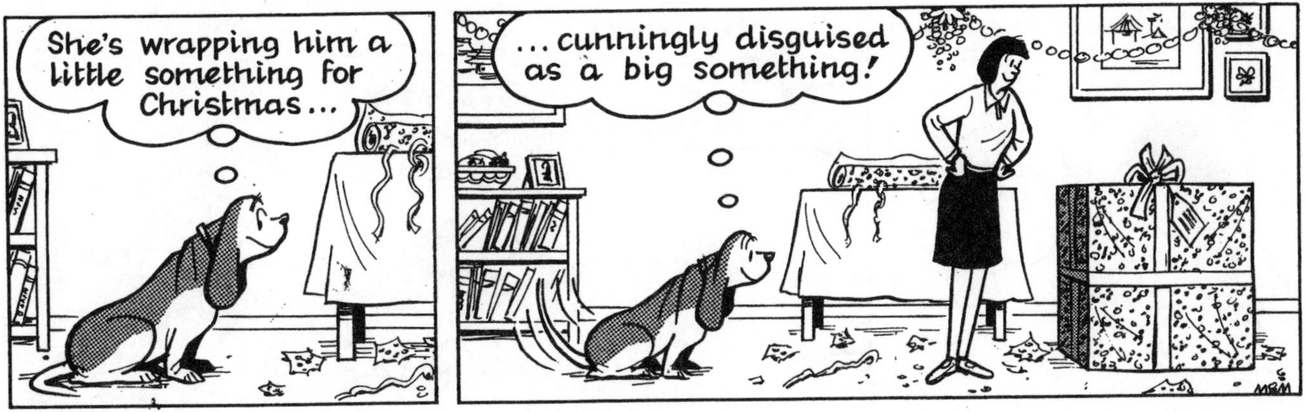
She's wrapping him a little something for Christmas...
...cunningly disguised as a big something!
MBM

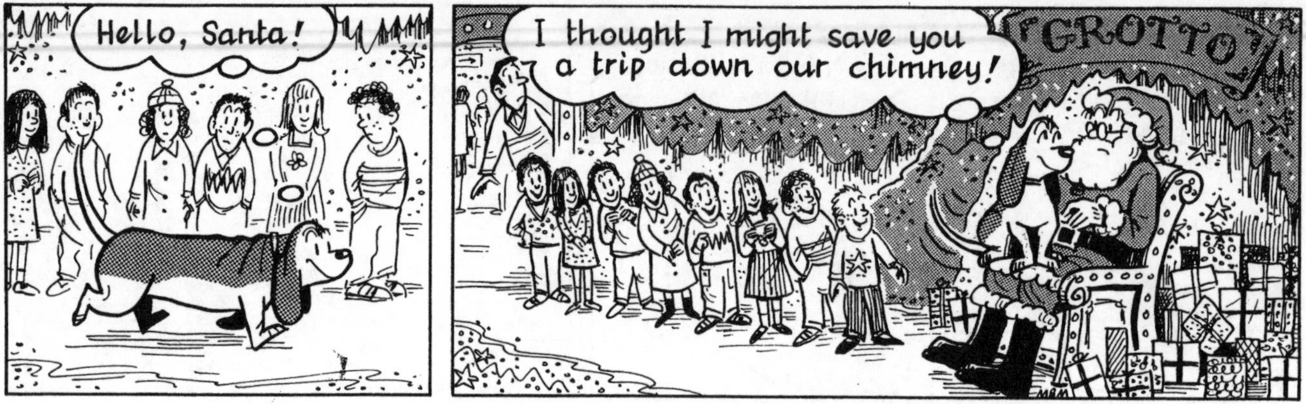
Hello, Santa!
I thought I might save you a trip down our chimney!
GROTTO
MBM

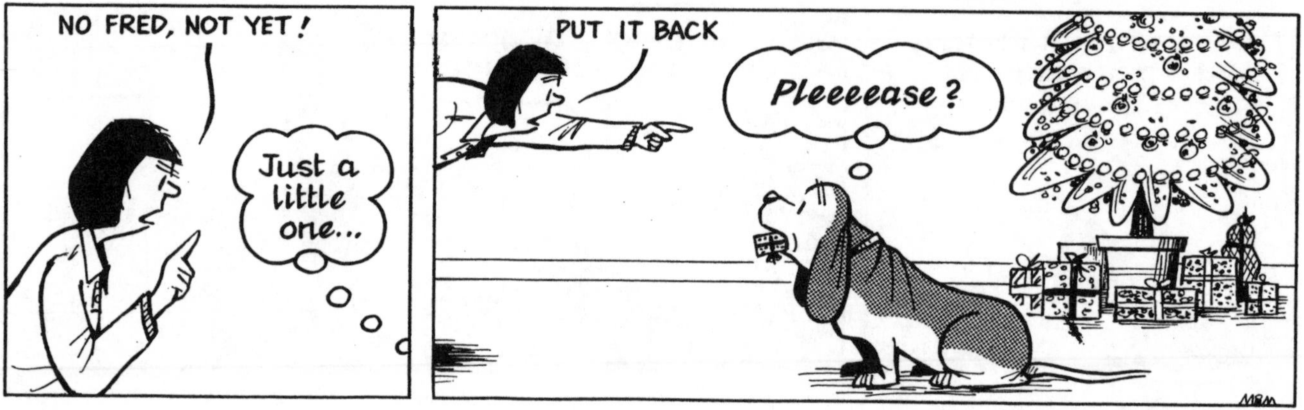
NO FRED, NOT YET!
Just a little one...
PUT IT BACK
Pleeeease?
MBM

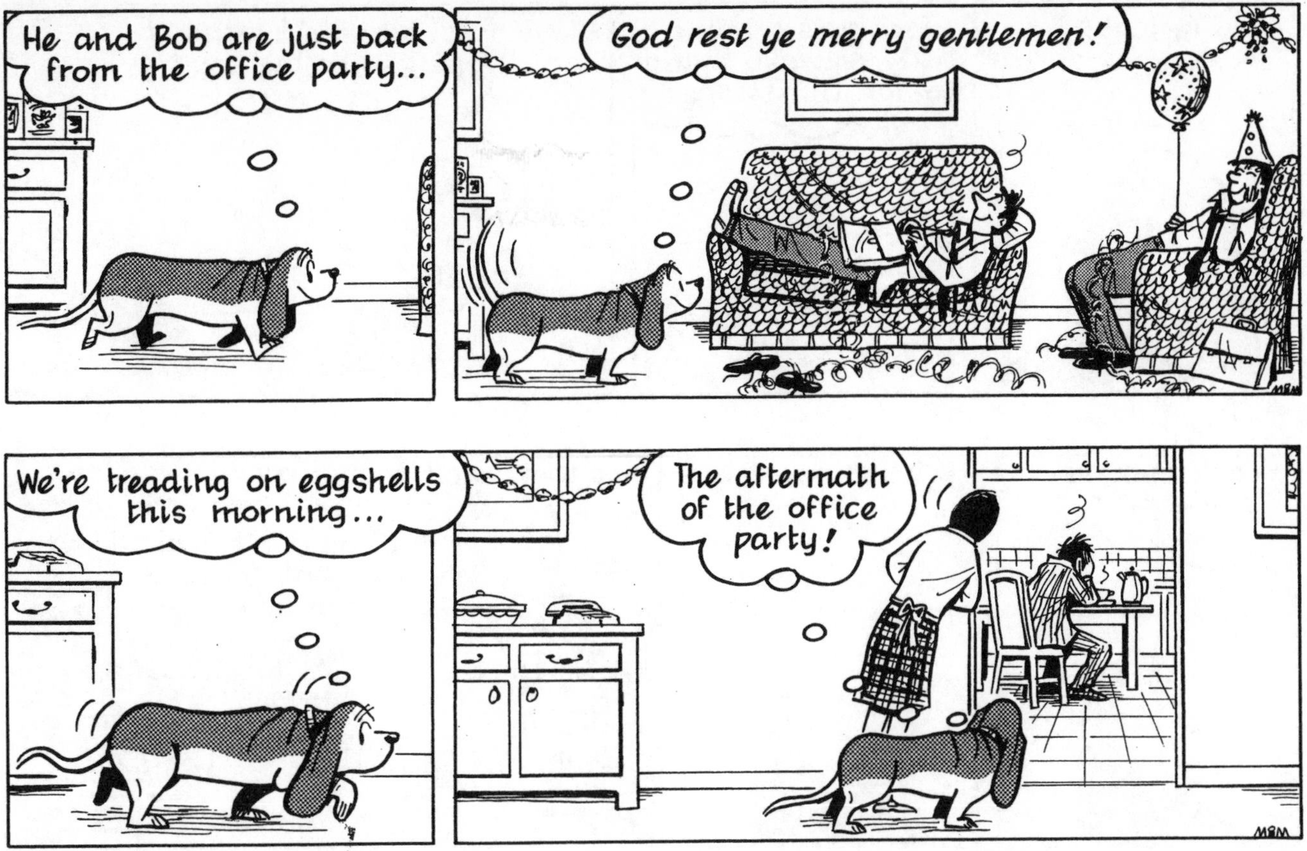
He and Bob are just back from the office party...
God rest ye merry gentlemen!
We're treading on eggshells this morning...
The aftermath of the office party!
MSM
MSM

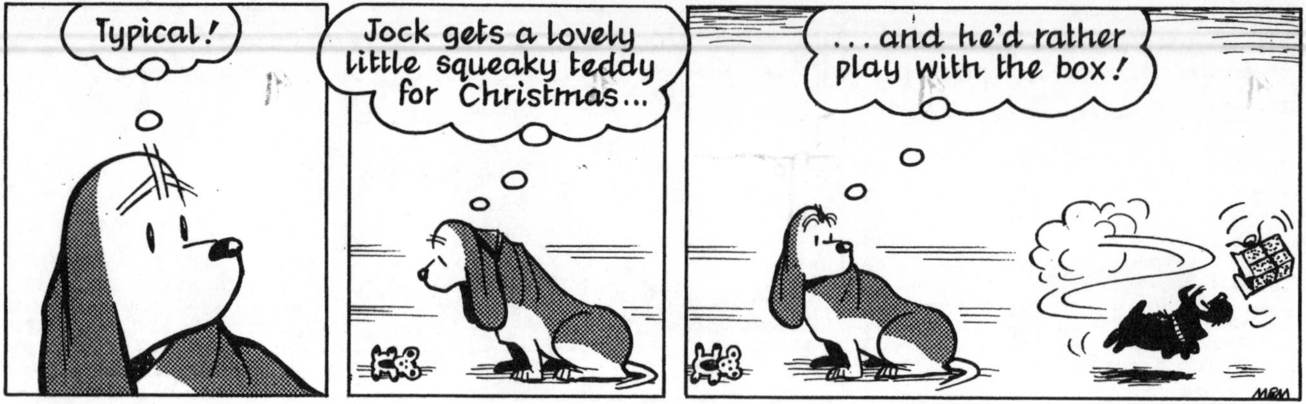
Typical!
Jock gets a lovely little squeaky teddy for Christmas...
... and he'd rather play with the box!

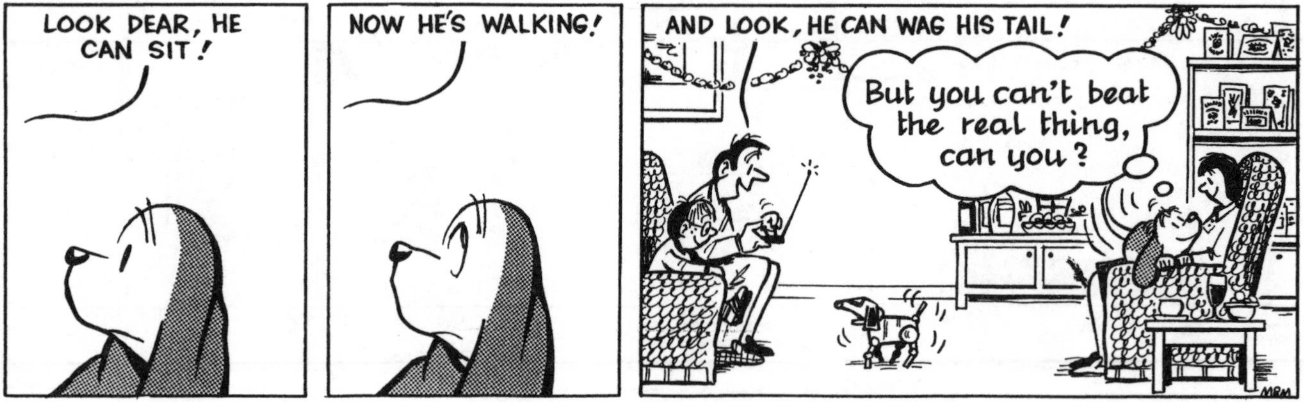
LOOK DEAR, HE CAN SIT!
NOW HE'S WALKING!
AND LOOK, HE CAN WAG HIS TAIL!
But you can't beat the real thing, can you?

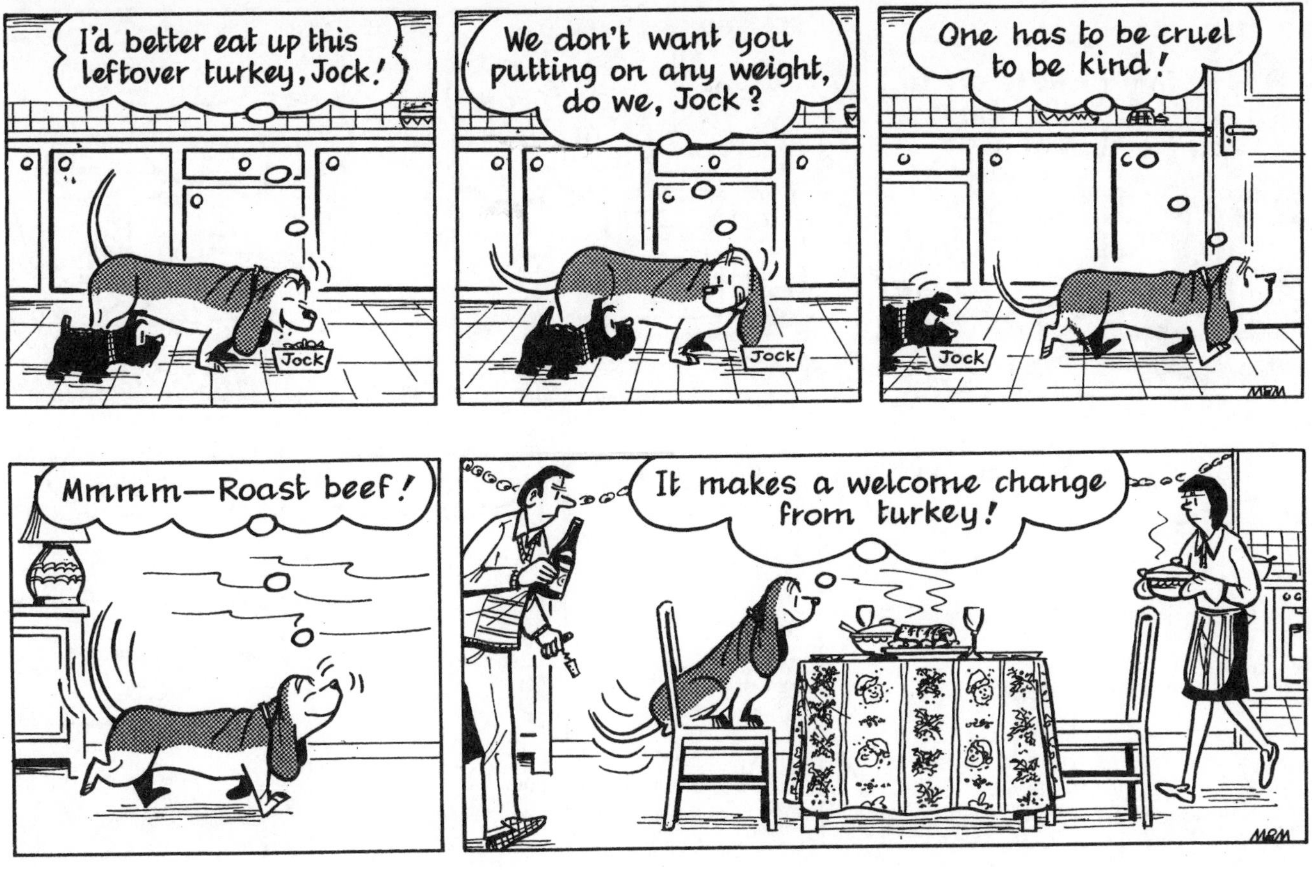
I'd better eat up this leftover turkey, Jock!
Jock
We don't want you putting on any weight, do we, Jock?
Jock
One has to be cruel to be kind!
Jock
Mmmm—Roast beef!
It makes a welcome change from turkey!

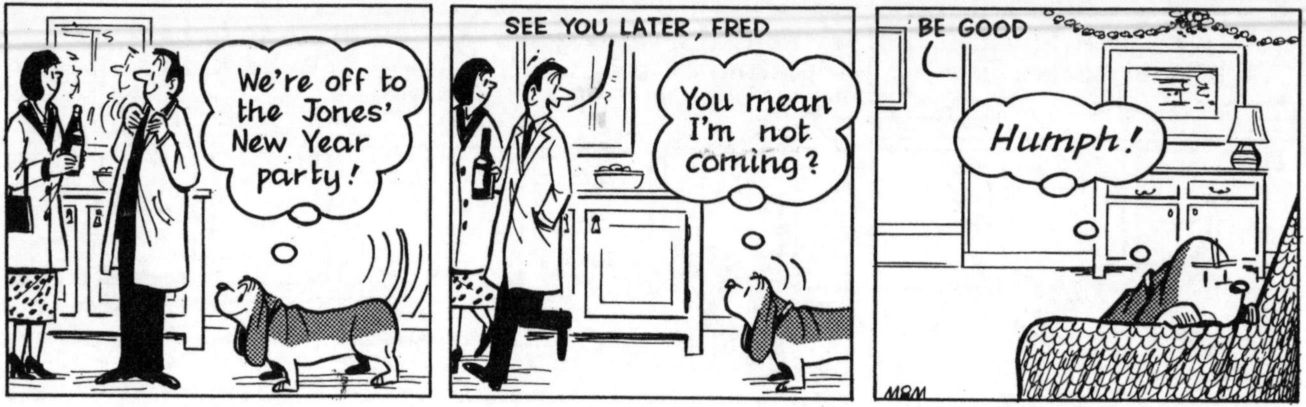
We're off to the Jones' New Year party!
SEE YOU LATER, FRED
You mean I'm not coming?
BE GOOD
Humph!
M&M

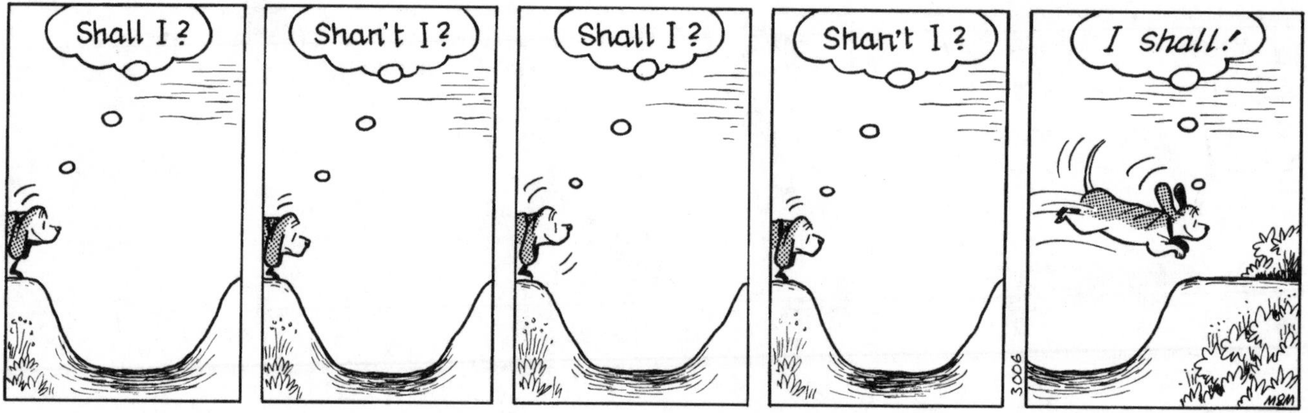
Shall I?
Shan't I?
Shall I?
Shan't I?
I shall!
3006
M&M